A Death in Malta

A Death in Malta

*An Assassination and a Family's
Quest for Justice*

PAUL CARUANA GALIZIA

HUTCHINSON
HEINEMANN

1 3 5 7 9 10 8 6 4 2

Hutchinson Heinemann
20 Vauxhall Bridge Road
London SW1V 2SA

Hutchinson Heinemann is part of the Penguin Random House group of companies
whose addresses can be found at global.penguinrandomhouse.com

Penguin
Random House
UK

First published by Hutchinson Heinemann in 2023

www.penguin.co.uk

A CIP catalogue record for this book is available from the British Library.

ISBN 9781529151558

Typeset in 13/15.5pt Garamond MT Std by Jouve (UK), Milton Keynes
Printed and bound in Great Britain by Clays Ltd, Elcograf S.p.A.

The authorised representative in the EEA is Penguin Random House Ireland,
Morrison Chambers, 32 Nassau Street, Dublin D02 YH68

www.greenpenguin.co.uk

MIX
Paper | Supporting
responsible forestry
FSC® C018179

Penguin Random House is committed to a
sustainable future for our business, our readers
and our planet. This book is made from Forest
Stewardship Council® certified paper.

To my mother

As I write, four men have admitted to my mother Daphne's assassination. Another four men, who deny wrongdoing and are presumed innocent, are awaiting trial. There will be more cases against more defendants, and, at some point, people will lose sight of my mother. This book is to introduce you to her before she is lost again.

I

My father, to keep himself going after the murder, began organising things around the house. He did our old bedrooms, then he turned to my mother's desk, and then to files full of her magazines and clippings.

He started putting them in file boxes and storing them on the shelves where she'd kept her shoes. The shelves, he told me, were now sagging under the weight of all her writing. He was flipping them over, using the boxes to flatten them out again.

'That's clever,' I said.

'An old trick. Don't you do anything at home?'

Every now and then, he would look into a box and rummage through the clippings. A glossy full-colour one caught his eye. It was a magazine interview my mother had given, titled 'My Favourite Photograph', and it must have been from the late 1990s.

The photo she chose shows my brothers and me as small children. Our father isn't in it. It was taken in a bay on another island, during one of the trips we'd gone on when she pulled us out of school for our safety. 'I just love the way the photo turned out,' our mother told the interviewer, 'the boys all lined up, and the way it shows their characters.'

I was biting my lip as I tried, unsuccessfully, to climb onto a wall to sit near my eldest brother Matthew. For some reason, I was holding a pink hairbrush – whose? – in my right hand. 'Paul,' she told the interviewer, 'is mischievous but not wild.'

'The other one' – Matthew had made it onto the wall and sat there with his head turned towards the camera, smiling – 'is very naughty and you can see it in his eyes.' Our middle brother, Andrew, 'a very calm person and I think it shows in the picture', was still blond, and was leaning against the wall, looking out to sea. We were 'small and portable', our mother continued, and 'really dependent on me'.

She once described the three of us, during one of our fights over who took whose jeans or whatever, as an *qaqoċċa* (pronounced a-ocha), an artichoke, which in Malta is small, with leaves tightly wound around the heart.

Looking at the photo, I thought about how the years that had passed since then had taken us – naughty, calm, mischievous – to different parts of the world, leading different lives. And how we had been brought back to Malta again, our hearts ripped clean out, when a bomb went off in our mother's car near the family home, landing the chassis in a field where artichokes normally grew.

Picture an island twenty-seven kilometres long and fifteen wide, roughly the shape of a fish. Indent its southern end to perfect its mouth, and pinch the northern end to make its tail. Hack at the coast around the tail to form sandy beaches, and all along the north for coves. Raise the southern coast to bare sheer cliffs, plunging the northern coast into the sea, where some of the coves form deep harbours.

Malta comes with the smaller Gozo and Comino islands, and many still smaller islets. The islands are dry and rocky, as though chipped from hot Africa and cast into the cool blue. They were in fact formed long after their southern neighbour, through the accumulation of marine creatures' skeletons. The archipelago has no mineral or metal deposits; those are the products of much older plant and animal matter. Its rich limestone crumbles into fertile soil, but the archipelago is so new that the layer of soil is thin and vulnerable to wind and rain, especially on such rugged terrain.

The hills, back when they were covered in oak, juniper, olive and pine trees, must have looked alluring from a distance to the settlers who sailed south from Sicily some seven thousand years ago. But when they began clearing the virgin country to plant barley, wheat and lentils, they quickly strained the arable land.

They cleared more virgin land, to allow the old to recover. In time, the farmers cleared most of the landscape, exposing its thin soil to erosion. Its yields grew unpredictable. Drought struck, the land reached its limit, and the farmers vanished. But the fragile country they left behind endured.

The next inhabitants formed cults. They threw their resources into building temples, which still stand, and into rocks they carved spirals said to represent eternity. They too overexploited the land, disappeared, and then ... nothing. The saltbushes and salt trees, sea lavender and sea chamomile were exposed to nothing but waves smashing blue to white, the Atlantic's grey mist and mild rains, the Sahara's vast skies and dry winds.

The winds brought passing tribes, heroes and saints. The Phoenicians found the country had few trees because shipwrecked Ulysses had felled so many for the boat he built to sail back home. They used the country as a trading post and, in all likelihood, gave it its name: Maleth, haven. The Romans called it Melita, raided it, and later settled it. One of their prisoners, the apostle Paul, was shipwrecked there. The Bible says the 'barbarous' but 'kind' Maltese kindled a fire for him. Then, a viper came 'out of the heat, and fastened on his hand'. It bit him, but he did not 'swell up or suddenly drop dead'. Snakes in Malta then lost their venom: a miracle. Malta converted and Paul became its patron saint. Effort has gone into showing that it has remained Christian ever since.

But the truth is that in 870, Arabs landed, sacked the capital Melite and massacred almost everyone. Muslims gradually repopulated the country and rebuilt the capital as Mdina, a walled city on a hill in the middle of Malta. The walls were not enough to withstand a small party of Norman knights who, some two centuries later, brought permanent Christian settlers with them from Sicily. Christians eventually outnumbered the local Muslims, who were expelled or forced to convert. The people were becoming homogenous. But the language, liquid of vowel and harsh on consonants, remained an Arabic dialect: Alla became God; Ramadan became Lent (Randan); Eid became Easter (Għid); and Mawlid, the birth of the prophet Muhammad, became Christmas (il-Mieled).

Wayside churches and statues of saints spread in the hundreds across this small territory, as the Maltese fastened themselves on to the Catholic Church. In a place whose natural environment had long ago been degraded, the Church provided a sense of permanence. But shepherds roaming the countryside still saw Muslim raiders land, enslave or kill their compatriots, and steal their sheep and goats, slaughtering the animals on board as they sailed away, leaving the witnesses to search for survivors. Even when the raids and sieges ended, the long memory of plunder remained.

It was as if the Maltese attitude had been cast in that memory. No amount of Christianity could undo the sense that, at any moment, land might be seized, lives cut short. If the future might be brief, why not ravage the country yourself, while you still had it? The plundered became plunderers. Already in ancient times, a law had restricted the hunting of the game birds that abounded in Malta's valleys. Within two decades of its passing, the law was obsolete: there were no more birds.

We spent much of our childhood in my mother's beige Citroën. I can still remember the burnt-rubber smell of the overused clutch and feel the polyester covering the back seat where I grazed elbows with my brothers. There were more crashes – one where the rear window shattered onto us – and more punctures than I care to remember. There were beach trips, errands, school runs, all life and death.

She was driving us fast to Buskett, an area in the south of Malta where bird hunting was meant to be prohibited, when one of the front wheels of her car got stuck in the gutter of a pigsty. It was 1990 and we were miles from the nearest telephone. We boys were all too young to walk that far with her, and too young for her to leave us in the car. So we sat there until some birdwatchers appeared in the late afternoon, lifted the car back onto the road, and guided us up a hill where we looked through their binoculars at an Eleonora's falcon, and watched as hunters shot it down.

Sometimes she drove us to her classes. At thirty, when we boys were seven, eight and nine, she decided to take an undergraduate degree in anthropology and archaeology. We would sit in the back row, so as not to distract the class. My brothers would listen to the lecturer, I would read comics, and my mother, 'already a star columnist', a fellow student remembers, would draft her columns in big round letters, using a felt-tip pen. But there was one anthropology lecture in particular where she stopped writing and listened.

The lecture touched on a book called *The Moral Basis of a Backward Society*, a 1950s study of a southern Italian village. The village had no newspaper, no charities, a single social club and decaying schools. The villagers only thought of 'the immediate, material interest of the nuclear family'.

They voted for politicians who gave them pasta, sugar and clothes. They did not report corruption because they feared retribution, and because they didn't trust the state. In this village, there was no civic feeling and only one rule: maximise your family's short-run advantage and assume others will do the same.

My mother listened and thought that this 'amoral familism', as the study called it, explained so much of what she saw around her.

'What a sad island,' she once wrote, 'one giant freak

show of a retarded Sicilian mountain village circa 1950, with twenty-first-century exhibitionism plastered on top.'

My mother's speech was not as forceful as her writing.

I listen for her, and I can hear the lilt of her voice. It had something of the up-and-down Maltese cadence, but it was gentler than was typical, and it came with more pauses, some to think and others to let sources talk. There was a shyness about her that meant she always felt more comfortable expressing herself in writing than out loud. I have a trace of that shyness too, and it reminds me how driven she was to do her work. 'I love it,' she told an interviewer ten days before her murder. 'It's a compulsion to write.'

As she wrote, so she gazed: with intensity. When I lied to her about coming home late, or not at all, I felt myself wilt in her eyes as she listened.

Aside from her writing and her own indelible impression, she left her things, mostly books. There are the ones from when she began in journalism: edited collections of the New Journalism, *The Faber Book of Reportage*, the staples of narrative non-fiction. There are the phases of her taste in fiction: Edith Wharton, Virginia Woolf and Doris Lessing; Bret Easton Ellis and Jay McInerney; Rose Tremain, Jonathan Franzen and Alice Munro. There are books about food and architecture from when she launched her own magazines. There are the Maltese history books, including the ones about witch trials of women accused of having a 'nasty tongue' and sentenced to death by Catholic inquisitors. But the books show it wasn't only the Church that carried out the witch-hunts. Neighbours conspired with officials to erase women who were already marginal. It's all there in the books.

No one knows what to do with her clothes. They are all that remain of her human shape. They are a source of anxiety, especially for my father. 'Do your girlfriends want them?' he asked me and my brothers. 'There are just so many.' There are piles of clothes and shoes. All of them colourful, some quite loud. She loved purple and avoided black, which reminded her of lawyers like my father, and of the drab days of her youth, when she and her friends would buy white plimsolls, the only casual shoe available then in Malta, and dye them different colours.

She likened their lives to those of young people behind the Iron Curtain. The clothes they mocked up and the music they listened to were their 'salvation' and brought the 'civilised West' closer to them. 'We could pretend for the duration of an LP,' she wrote, 'that we didn't live some-place where we had to hitch a ride on an army lorry to get home from school.' She continued to play music – Bob Dylan, Neil Young, Tracy Chapman and, for reasons I would learn only after her murder, Bob Marley – loudly and repetitively for the rest of her life.

Looking back now, I can see that the music, like the reading, was an escape: the country had grown more pros-perous during her time, but the society she longed for never arrived. The old Malta lingered. Troublesome women were still branded as witches.

My mother taught me and my brothers to read widely, to think and speak freely, to care. To care for one another, our friends, family, all our dogs, our guinea pigs, our ham-sters: an *qaqoċċa*, a Maltese image of solidarity. Sometimes we managed. Sometimes we used the manners she taught us, and which she was rigid about: to show more of an interest in others than yourself, to be interesting and to hold doors open, to know when to say this and when to wear that. The rules were not novel. They were the rules of decorum of any middle-class household. In fact, they seem like a relic, a part of old Malta that she held on to. 'She always hated coarseness and people being frivolous,' her first love told me. 'Your mother could be aloof, haughty and proud.'

She didn't marry that first love. Instead, she married my father, had us three boys with him, and moved us to the countryside. Up to that point, her life seemed conventional. The rules and manners, marriage and children. But when early on in her domestic life she felt suffocated, she began to write. No longer only in the diaries she kept constantly by her side, or scraps for trade publications, but more professionally. She took a part-time job as an editorial assistant on a quarterly magazine shortly before I was born.

My father put down her profession on my birth certificate as 'Housewife and Editor', and his own as 'Advocate'. During our naps and stays with grandparents and aunts, she edited copy that she always told her boss was poorly written and boring, and needed rewriting. Soon she began writing herself, and her writing quickly got her noticed. In 1990, the *Sunday Times* of Malta offered her a column. She became the country's first female columnist, and the first journalist to write under their own name; all of the others wrote anonymously, out of fear of reprisals. Two years later, she helped launch a newspaper.

Almost immediately, she began to criticise Maltese society. The values she insisted on at home were no different from those she found lacking in her country. Why should there be, for example, a distinction between a prime minister's personal and public behaviour? 'You vote for the whole person,' she wrote. 'It's not an office job.' She criticised what politicians wore, their posture, the way they spoke. She reviled the Catholicism in everything, the misogyny, the pollution and overdevelopment. In time, as the country's problems changed, she would investigate drug traffickers, neo-Nazis, presidents, prime ministers and opposition leaders. She would pioneer financial journalism when Malta became an offshore haven, turning leaks like the Panama Papers into dramas that kept a population in suspense.

In a country of around half a million people, her personal blog received as many visits a day, and more than a million during election campaigns – a greater number than the combined circulation of Malta's daily newspapers.

Everyone read Daphne; our surname was redundant. Our first names were redundant. My father was known as Daphne's Husband; my brothers and I as Daphne's Sons. Interest in our lives began to overshadow her work. She resented it. She refused media appearances, saying that things in Malta were so depressing, so predictably rotten, that she was what passed for a celebrity there.

And the retaliation for her writing came. My brothers and I grew up thinking it normal to have our mother's name all over the newspapers and broadcast media, for politicians to sue and slander her, to have our house set on fire, to have police at the garden gate to guard or arrest her, to answer the home phone and hear obscenities about her, to find parcels of human excrement in the post, and to see her check the underside of her car for bombs before taking us to school.

As a boy, I used to wonder why my friends' mothers were so different to mine. As a young teenager, I resented the difference. I sometimes felt that our lives might be easier if she wasn't a journalist. It was only at the end of my adolescence that I began to see there was a problem in Malta, and that the problem was not my mother.

She wanted to write a book about that problem. She wanted to see how far amoral familism went towards explaining the culture of corruption that had come to dominate her reporting about Malta. The idea had become unfashionable among anthropologists, but towards the end of her life she began talking about it again. It was only when I prepared to write about her and listened to the interview she had given ten days before her murder, the one where she described writing as a compulsion, that I realised something else.

The book was really about her trying to understand her own place in the country. 'I never really felt I fitted in,' she told the interviewer. 'I always had this perspective of somebody on the outside looking in, which is what they say the classic thing is in anthropology, the outsider looking in.'

And so on the day when I sat down to write the book my mother never got to, I realised I did not understand her essential thing. I did not know how she had become the outsider looking in. She had produced me, and I did not even know where she had come from. I began to feel I was now her instrument, here to put her and her country on the record, and that this was why she had always wanted me to write.

2

One summer when I was seventeen years old and not going anywhere fast, always at the beach and out every night, my mother asked, 'Isn't there anything you're interested in?'

I was never into sports and would just lie down at the back of our little boat when our father took us sailing, watching time flap on the mast. I skipped the football lessons my mother sent me to. I never had a hobby. My parents had tried to interest me in painting, cooking, the recorder, but nothing stuck.

My mother hired me to help with the food and design magazines she had launched and edited alongside her journalism. I wrote a piece on sunflowers, which my friends teased me about. I filed my copy late, received a few Maltese pounds, and saw heavily edited versions in print. She was a tough and patient editor, and over that summer I finally got my interest: writing. Not yet doing it myself – that would take many more years, more practice – but learning how words locked into place.

I was still writing for my mother when a few months later she dedicated the entire autumn issue of her design magazine, *Flair*, to the history and architecture of Valletta. Set on a peninsula in the north of Malta, the capital city was built as a fortress, bordered by walls nine metres thick and stretching thirty metres high. It had won its United

Nations designation as a World Heritage Site early, protecting it from us. I found it utterly beautiful.

I always liked how the city's grid plan was imposed on rugged land, so that its order retained an underlying wildness. The wildness shows in its hills and drops. I liked how the contours play with your sense of place, making you feel you are far from the sea when it surrounds you. I liked its grand houses, with their windows cut high into their stone facades and their corner statues of saints. I liked how even along this thin strip of land there were three parish churches and a cathedral. I liked how, from the sea, the calculated lines and angles of its fortifications gave this ancient place an appearance of jagged modernity.

Maltese labourers had built Valletta for the Knights Hospitaller. An order of aristocrats from all over Europe that had been founded to care for pilgrims in Jerusalem, its mission expanded during the First Crusade to protect the Holy Land itself. When the knights lost the Holy Land to Muslims, they fled to Cyprus and then to Rhodes before washing up in Sicily, whose overlord, Charles V, offered them Malta as a home.

Eight knights sailed from Palermo to Malta in mid-July 1524 to have a look. By August, they had seen enough.

'The island of Malta,' they reported to their grand master, 'is merely a rock of soft sandstone . . . the surface of the rock is barely covered with more than three or four feet of earth, which is likewise stony, and very unfit to grow corn and other grain.' The climate was 'extremely disagreeable – indeed almost insupportable – particularly in summer . . . except for a few springs in the middle of the island there is no running water, nor even wells: the want of which the inhabitants supply by cisterns'. Most of the twelve thousand inhabitants lived in houses like 'African huts'.

At least the knights found that Malta 'produces an abundance of figs, melons, and different fruits; the principal trade of the island consisting of honey, cotton and cummin, which the inhabitants exchange for grain'. Although they thought the country was 'not worth the parchment . . . employ'd in writing the deed of gift', they had nowhere else to go and so took Malta in exchange for a falcon to the Viceroy of Sicily every All Saints' Day. The Maltese were assured that they'd retain the semi-autonomy and rights they'd enjoyed under the Viceroy.

But it was a ruse. Soon after the knights arrived in 1530, they overrode the country's governing bodies and denied positions of real power even to local noblemen. They denigrated the inhabitants as 'dark-skinned', 'very religious' and 'superstitious', citing their belief in the evil eye and – a legacy from their patron saint – in snakes' eyes as an antidote to poison. Soon the Maltese became powerless in their own country.

But they also became a bit richer. The knights' estates across France, Italy, Aragon, England, Germany and Castille funded the building of auberges, small palaces that served as their headquarters in the country. While most Maltese continued to survive on vegetables, bread, water and goat's milk, and to speak their Arabic dialect, an urban population sprang up around the auberges, speaking Italian and living in handsome houses. During bad harvests, the knights would initiate building projects to employ Maltese labourers. Their patronage allowed the population to grow beyond a point the country could otherwise support. So did the security they provided against marauders.

Most raids had been small until tens of thousands of Ottomans besieged Malta in 1565. Both sides fought ferociously. The Ottomans gashed crosses into the chests of slain Christians. The Christians fired the heads of Ottoman prisoners from their cannons. Many died in combat, but perhaps the Ottomans suffered heavier losses from 'the blood flux' (dysentery), 'putrid fevers' and 'tifo' (typhus) as they camped on the island. In the end, the knights prevailed. They won funding from overseas to build Valletta, named for Jean de la Valette, the French knight who founded the city.

Valletta was completed within five years and never attacked. The religious war had already faded away, and the knights began losing their purpose. Soon, they began losing their wealth too, as Napoleon confiscated their estates across Europe. The Maltese, who had tolerated the knights because they provided an external source of money, now saw them only as despotic.

When Maltese men grumbled that the knights, despite their vows of celibacy, were taking their wives and daughters as mistresses, the knights had the men exiled. After many years under their rule, a French consul would write, Malta had 'a great number of natural children, the result of adulterous intercourse and the licentious lives of the Knights'.

One such child, according to family lore, was a girl called Caterina, born to a knight's mistress. Only one description of her mother, by a Maltese historian, exists:

'adventurous'. Caterina took a different path. She married the descendant of a servant and their children took his surname of Vella. They had two sons who left a trail.

While working on the Valletta issue of her magazine, my mother took me to the Church of St Paul's Shipwreck. It was built in the middle of Valletta around the time the city was completed. Its facade was rebuilt in the nineteenth century in the baroque style, all Ionic columns and cornices.

Inside, it is much older. There's the relic of St Paul's right wrist bone, part of the column on which he was eventually beheaded in Rome, and a seventeenth-century gilded statue of him that's paraded through Valletta on his feast day. The floor is paved with large, rectangular tombstones depicting images of death, skeletons and scythes.

It was for a tombstone that my mother took me to the church. The one she wanted me to see was distinctive, made of marble inlay of different colours, featuring the image of a whale rising from the sea to spit out a man: Jonah, who was swallowed by a whale after disobeying God, then spat back onto land after praying for forgiveness.

The tombstone belonged to an ancestor of hers, one of Caterina's grandsons. Whatever had linked him to the biblical story has been lost. But I can now see what my mother read into the way it stood out from the other tombstones. It provided a foundation for her sense that she was from, but not of, Malta.

The Maltese had, at first, welcomed Napoleon. 'Why should we not take possession of Malta?' Napoleon wrote to the foreign minister Talleyrand in September 1797. 'The inhabitants, who number one hundred thousand, are friendly to us and greatly disgusted with the Knights. They are dying of starvation.' Talleyrand agreed and the plan to take Malta went ahead. On his way to Egypt in June 1798, Napoleon and his Army of the East anchored off Valletta and took the country in two days.

Most of the knights defected. 'How,' Napoleon asked those who remained, 'could you ever believe it possible to defend yourselves, with a few wretched peasants?' He gave the knights pensions and European estates. They left. To the Maltese, he promised they would 'continue to enjoy as in the past the free exercise of the Apostolic and Roman Catholic Religion'.

But it was another ruse. The French were quick to limit the Church's power. They abolished papal jurisdiction, restricted the consecration of new priests, and expelled foreign clerics. They began melting down and auctioning Church treasure to finance reforms in line with French revolutionary principles, including equality before the law and compulsory schooling.

Upset by the French garrison's desecration of holy relics, the Maltese went to Mdina, murdered the Frenchman in charge, then butchered the rest. A British agent reported to Admiral Nelson that the Maltese then decapitated the French corpses, put parsnips between their teeth, and paraded the heads around, in revenge for the French having said there were no provisions available in Malta but parsnips.

The remaining French troops barricaded themselves into Valletta. Many Maltese were locked in with them. Those outside asked for help from Britain, at this point the only major European power fighting against Napoleon's advances through Europe. It arrived in the form of muskets and a naval blockade that stopped supplies from reaching Valletta. The city began to starve. A market for rats developed.

An elderly Maltese priest gathered some men and plotted to infiltrate the capital. The men hid in a storeroom but were found by French troops, who opened fire on them. Some were killed, others injured and taken prisoner. Caterina's sons, Salvatore and Michele Vella, were among the prisoners. Held in a fort at the tip of Valletta, the brothers were sentenced to death by firing squad. Michele was executed. He was twenty-five years old. Salvatore managed to escape. Nursing a gunshot wound in his neck, he swam across the harbour on Valletta's western side to safety.

Sliema, on Malta's northern coast, was little more than fields and farmhouses. It supposedly got its name from a chapel dedicated to Our Lady of Good Voyage, the patron saint of seafarers. As legend had it, passing sailors would say the Hail Mary, which in Maltese begins with a corruption of the Arabic word for peace, *salaam*: *sliem*. Sliema would become home to Salvatore's descendants, including the son buried under that distinctive tombstone in that church, and my mother's father, Michael, named for Michele. It was he who told her this family history, about fighting and dying for your ideals, and it meant a lot to her.

When a Maltese writer once accused my mother of trading in her 'common Maltese surname' for my father's 'double foreign one', she pointed out that with 'immense regret' Maltese law did not allow married women to keep their own surnames. She told the story of the Vella brothers, adding: 'I myself may leave nothing behind, but I come from people who waved the Maltese flag when the price to be paid was a bullet in the neck.'

But it turns out the story was a lie. Salvatore had escaped, a historian documented, because he 'managed to corrupt the president of the French Military Commission which had condemned him to death'. This version, a story of corruption and self-interest rather than of idealism, might have made my mother feel more Maltese after all.

In any event, the revolutionary reforms promised by the French were never implemented in full. The Enlightenment passed Malta by.

About a year after Salvatore escaped, in August 1800, there was another escape. Two French ships managed to slip out of the Grand Harbour on Valletta's eastern side. One made it past the British blockade and back to France. The other was caught and escorted back to Valletta by HMS *Superb*. The British sailors found dispatches on board that warned France its Malta garrison was about to crack. A week later it did. The Royal Navy entered the Grand Harbour, and it would stay in Malta for the next 178 years.

The French marched out of Valletta, flying their flag, beating their drums. The Maltese militia celebrated. They had defeated France, with their young rebels, their old priest and the muskets they were given. As the Maltese celebrated, the British forces inspected Valletta's fortifications and found the militia had done little damage. They raised the Union Jack above the city. Malta was British.

The Maltese celebrated again: they had ushered in a new, modern ruler. 'To say the truth,' Nelson wrote to the second Earl Spencer, the First Lord of the Admiralty, 'the possession of Malta, by England, would be an useless and enormous expense.' The British decided to run the country as a naval base. The Maltese reconsidered their ideas about British rule and demanded a more democratic form of governance.

London sent a royal commission to Malta in 1812 to assess the demand. It concluded that the 'Maltese temperament was incompatible with an ordered system of representative government'. It gave complete authority to an experienced colonial governor. 'I have seen a good deal of corruption in the West Indies and in the East,' Thomas Maitland, the first governor, reported, 'but nothing like what I find in Malta.'

He reformed archaic institutions, reducing opportunities for bribery. He rooted out Maltese nepotism by bringing in English workers. And he put himself in charge of all branches of the state. He introduced jury trials, but there was no independent judiciary. There was no elected legislature. There was only Maitland, whom the Maltese called 'King Tom'. He established a chivalric order – a 'big Shewy Star' – to reward loyal Maltese. He punished others.

Maitland blocked Salvatore's request for a military pension from the secretary of state for war and the colonies, noting that Salvatore had retired early so as not to be discharged and sentenced for dishonourable behaviour. Salvatore pushed his son into the colonial administration instead. John Vella rose to oversee Malta's customs and ports, to sit on its unelected council of government, and to earn one of Maitland's showy stars. He made enough money to support the rest of the family and, in the end, to pay for his elaborate tombstone at the Church of St Paul's Shipwreck in Valletta.

In the generations who followed, my mother's family bound themselves to the colonial administration. It provided material security and social prestige. They anglicised their names and began speaking and writing in English.

At the turn of the nineteenth century, about a tenth of Malta's population was literate. Half of that minority could read English, and half Italian. Most of the population could speak Maltese; the working class spoke it exclusively. The Italianate class was made up of doctors, architects, professors and lawyers, like my father's family, who felt more patrician than the English.

Their use of Italian, which one foreign correspondent wrote they spoke with a 'limited vocabulary and peculiar intonation', was a hangover from the time of the Knights Hospitaller, when Italian had emerged as the language of the educated class. It remained the language of the Church, the law courts and the schools. Unlike the Vellas, who went from Francesco to Francis, Maltese to English, my father's forebears insisted on speaking Italian at home and using names like Giovanni Batista and Emanuele Luigi. Like everyone else, they were Catholic, and the Church, uneasy with the Protestant administration of the British, stayed closest to this Italianate class.

The 'Language Question' came to dominate politics at the end of the nineteenth century, by when the colonial administration allowed a legislative council to be elected. Never mind that the colonial governor could suspend the council on a whim, that the people had no true democratic power, that the economy depended on British military expenditure. Everything turned on the Language Question.

Attempts to answer it set Malta's partisan division. The Anti-Reform Party was established to retain Italian as an official language and worked with the Church to retain the power of the professional class. It argued that the use of Italian allowed Malta to be part of a bigger intellectual and political entity. At one point, its leaders wanted Malta to integrate with Italy. This faction would evolve into the Nationalist Party. The Reform Party wanted to limit the power of the professionals and of the Church. Its support was in the thousands of industrial workers at the Royal Navy dockyards around the Grand Harbour, who depended on British military expenditure, and clerks in the colonial administration, who worked in English. This faction would evolve into the Labour Party.

A pro-Empire party was established to call for full anglicisation. Its support was rooted in the small Anglophile middle class, of which the Vellas formed a part. They laid claim to what they saw as English ideas – of a country ruled by law, of voters as civic beings not clients, of politicians as public servants not patrons. They wanted a kind of imperial citizenship.

The parties campaigned, debated and fought, but, in the end, the Language Question was settled from outside. As tensions between Britain and Italy rose over the Abyssinia Crisis, and rose further when Mussolini allied his country with Nazi Germany, the colonial administration in Malta promoted Maltese as an official language alongside English to displace Italian. When Mussolini began bombing Malta from his airfields in Sicily alongside the Luftwaffe, anti-Italian sentiment became strong enough to settle the Question once and for all.

But new questions arose. In the decade after the Second World War, decolonisation movements spread across the world. Though they were often difficult and bloody, they were sometimes more straightforward. In Malta, Britain no longer saw the value in maintaining an expensive Mediterranean naval base. The region had ceased to be a geopolitical locus, and war, it seemed, would from now on be fought with long-range missiles, not naval destroyers.

The ideals of the pro-Empire party that the Vellas supported had become an anachronism, and it dissolved. In a country where party affiliation was practically genetic, the family became what the Maltese called 'party-less'.

Most Maltese gave their support to one of the two major parties. The Labour Party, which was in power after the war, wanted Malta to go from a colony to a constituency of the United Kingdom, meaning that Britain would continue spending money in the country, especially at the dockyards.

That the idea had little appeal to Britain itself didn't stop the Labour Party's leader, Dominic Mintoff, from calling a referendum on integration in 1956. The Archbishop of Malta, fearing that the country would be subsumed by Protestantism, claimed that Mintoff had declared war on the Church and urged people to vote against integration or to abstain. The referendum passed, but voter turnout was too low for it to hold. Relations between the government and the Church, both vying for control of Maltese society, collapsed. The archbishop told an official at the Colonial Office that he wanted to 'punch

Mr Mintoff's nose' and that he'd 'smash' the Labour Party if pushed too far.

There was partisan rioting and violence. The colonial governor suspended Malta's constitution and imposed direct rule. He worried that the Maltese would not be able to accept 'British standards of democracy'. His concerns: the police force was under 'party political control', the civil service 'gravely impaired by Ministerial interference', and radio broadcasts 'exploited for political purposes'. Yet no one really knew what to do with the place. Britain did not want to spend more resources on reforming Malta, but neither did it want the Labour Party, which had turned anti-West, to have it.

The Nationalist Party opposed integration with Britain. It argued for Malta to become a dominion, a kind of colony-plus status afforded to Canada and New Zealand. Someone at the Colonial Office summarised the party's position as resentment at being 'lumped in under the C.O. with a lot of African and Eastern territories, whilst they regard themselves as part of European society'.

The Colonial Office tried to resolve the problem of Malta by allowing a general election in 1962. The Church declared it a mortal sin to vote for Labour. Mintoff called his supporters who defied the Church 'Soldiers of Steel'. They were overpowered. The Nationalist Party won, but it didn't have any idea how Malta would survive without British expenditure. Its leader, Giorgio Borg Olivier, asked London for an end to Malta's colonial status but to continue its military expenditure in the country.

Borg Olivier lived in Sliema and was part of the Italian-ate upper class. He was always smartly dressed and always late. He believed in the evil eye and sought to dispel it with the *scionguro*, a gesture in which men pull their right hand into horns and grab their balls in the left. He had an aversion to change and dragged out negotiations with the British over Malta's independence for two years.

'You're asking for my jacket,' the secretary of state for the colonies, Duncan Sandys, told Borg Olivier during the independence negotiations.

'You're asking for my trousers,' the prime minister replied.

In the end, he appeared to keep his trousers. Malta lost its colonial governor but got a British governor general who was the monarch's unelected representative in the country. The monarch was still the head of state, and the country was still part of the Commonwealth. Its court of final appeal was the Privy Council in London. It was still dependent on British military expenditure and its currency was still British. So its international status was ambiguous and, domestically, its institutions remained colonial.

The prime minister's office absorbed the powers of the colonial governor, acquiring the authority to appoint and remove police commissioners and to appoint judges, magistrates and attorney generals. The legislature, which now contained fifty seats, was dominated by the two parties. Whichever one was in power would fill its seats with ministers or give its MPs government jobs, so there would be no backbench opposition to the executive.

The independence settlement didn't foresee what would happen when a powerful executive was given to a country where corruption was a way of life, with partisan division increasingly bitter. It was all lost in the optimism of independence, which arrived on 21 September 1964 at a gravelly space outside Valletta called Independence Arena. It is now a parking lot.

'It was hot,' my father, then a young schoolboy, told me. 'There was a lot of dust.'

Buckingham Palace had worried that the Queen's representative at the ceremony, the Duke of Edinburgh, might get caught in the crossfire of an assassination attempt on Borg Olivier. They sent him anyway. Mintoff boycotted the ceremony and stayed at home.

The Duke handed the prime minister the instruments of independence. The prime minister gave a rousing speech in Maltese. The crowd applauded.

'I have not understood a word except independence,' Sandys said.

At midnight, the Union Jack was lowered and Malta's flag – white and red with a George Cross for heroism during the siege of Malta in the Second World War, when the country sustained unrelenting air raids – was raised in its place. It all happened to the background accompaniment of 'Din L-Art Ħelwa', 'This Sweet Land', a hymn written by a priest and set to music by a doctor in 1922, now the national anthem.

'It was a glorious day,' Malta's attorney general recalled. 'One which anyone present could never forget.'

'Everyone forgot it by morning,' my grandfather Michael told me. 'I didn't even attend. I had other things on my mind.'

His first child, my mother, had been born a few weeks earlier, on 26 August 1964, at a hospital run by nuns. While my grandmother Rose rested after the birth, the nuns took the baby into a nearby room, placed her in a cot, and named her Jennifer.

When Rose woke, she found Michael sitting in her room with the stack of novels they had brought to the hospital. She picked out Daphne du Maurier's *Rebecca*, published in 1938, the year both she and my grandfather were born, then in its 21st or 22nd printing, and lay back to read. Michael told her that the nuns had decided on a name.

'I haven't,' Rose replied.

A doctor came to check on her, saw the book she was reading, and asked, 'So then, are you going to call her Daphne, so that she'll be a writer?'

My grandparents laughed. But when the doctor left, they fell silent, thought a little, and then agreed Daphne was a good name.

The nuns were not pleased. There is no Daphne in the Bible, no St Daphne, no Daphne in the family line. And in any case, women did not become writers in Malta. The registry office, they warned, would not accept the name because it was not Christian. Daphne was a Greek nymph, a figure of myth and fantasy.

A compromise was reached: the girl's name would be Daphne Anne, Maltese and not Maltese.

3

My father offered to take my brothers and me for a drive. He thought that to go and look at places that reminded us of my mother in a different way would help. I was not ready to think of her like that: as a memory.

But I went anyway. The house had begun to feel oppressive, and I wanted some kind of movement. We did the short drive to Sliema where we first lived.

The pink of its concrete promenade, which had always seemed absurd to me, looked more so in the hard afternoon light. The gnarled tamarisks running along the seafront were still, but I could hear the wind and the sea. Everything felt strange, as if it was both in motion and not.

Wind and beating sea had left behind a smooth limestone coast, in this light the colour of ivory. Steps from the promenade led down to it. Even in October, it was still hot enough to swim. Some of the people who were lowering themselves into the water recognised us and stared. There was a horrid calm. We walked back to the promenade. As we climbed the steps, I saw how the over-development of the past few decades had disfigured the landscape.

In the nineteenth century, Sliema became a popular summer resort for people looking to escape the busyness of Valletta. The first houses were in the British style, with bay windows and columned porticos. When art nouveau came into vogue, the Maltese copied the style, building grand houses along coast-hugging Tower Road. My father grew up in one of those. My mother was raised in one of the three-storey town houses that stood behind, on Milner Street, named after the colonial official who had drafted Malta's first constitution.

Little of that remained. Now apartment buildings rose and fell along Tower Road, some narrow and some wide, some with open balconies, others without, a jumble of badly planned buildings in all manner of colours and styles and materials. Nothing came together. Everything was covered in a grey film of dust.

My maternal grandparents still lived on Milner Street, surrounded by flats. I walked to their limestone house: a wooden balcony with shutters, a large window with yet more shutters below, and a double front door, painted red. It had belonged to my grandfather's uncle, the most senior Maltese official in the colonial administration. He sold the house to my grandparents after they got married. Michael fixed it up, did the plumbing, and made this eternal-seeming thing a base for our family. I stood in front of their red wooden door, thinking about how many times our mother had dropped my brothers and me there, and we had rushed through it. I tried to retrieve an image of her from before the three of us existed. It was as if I'd reached for the door handle to open up her past.

The door, it turned out, was a good place to start.

Newspapers fell through it every morning. At about fifteen pages, the *Times of Malta*, the country's newspaper of record, did not make much of a thump. It featured international news on its front page, and 'the rest was just chit-chat', Michael told me. 'It just didn't challenge anything. So we subscribed to foreign magazines.'

'*Newsweek*, *Punch*, the *Spectator*,' Rose added. 'We used to get everything.'

Magazines piled up all over the house. Rose would have her four daughters cut them into confetti for the parish feast of St Paul's Shipwreck each year. After Mass was celebrated, people would pour onto the narrow street, and others would throw confetti from the balconies and windows above. Children would dance in the blizzard, kicking a year's worth of journalism into great piles.

Or almost a year's worth. My mother would cut around the articles she liked and take them up to her bedroom. She read and reread them, collected them in a scrapbook, and wondered why there was no writing like it – wideranging and irreverent, colourful and personal – in Malta.

'And that's where it all started,' Rose told me. 'Obsessed with reading from then. And when she was reading, the walls could have fallen down all around her and she would not have noticed.'

A girl reading is the way my mother's friends remember her.

They all lived within walking distance of one another in Sliema. They formed a book club. 'We pooled our books,' a former member told me, 'and, as club president, your mother kept them in her bedroom. We started with Enid Blyton. But, you know, we moved on to things like Alcott's *Little Women*.'

The book club soon branched out to magazines like *Cosmopolitan* and *Pink*. 'They kept us in touch with the world,' her friend said. 'It was a time in Malta when each year less and less became available. No products in shops, no variety in clothes. At the airport, customs used to check people's bags to make sure they weren't bringing in foreign chocolates.'

I had heard the history lesson many times from my mother: Malta changed, you do not know how lucky you are. She always began with a memory.

It was 1971, and my mother was six years old. She was reading alongside Rose on the balcony overlooking Milner Street when she heard shouting and grunting from below. My mother looked out and saw men, jubilant but seeming lost, driving around lorries full of bulls.

'Why are there bulls everywhere?' she asked Rose.

'They're farmers on their way to market.'

When you're six, anything is possible. The men were Labour supporters. They were looking, in this alien territory of Sliema, for the house of Prime Minister Borg Olivier, who had lost a general election to Dominic Mintoff that day. The men were chanting Mintoff's name.

'Oh,' my mother said. 'And what's Mintoff?'

Rose, wanting to cut the conversation short, told her Mintoff was 'a kind of vegetable'.

Mintoff was a compact man with a quick temper from a working-class town on the Grand Harbour. He made it to university, won a Rhodes scholarship, and married a British woman, whom he allowed little money and the car only on Saturdays. He rose through the ranks to lead the Labour Party. After he lost the integration referendum, his tweed jackets and smoking pipe gave way to open-neck shirts and large belt buckles. He delivered fiery speeches on the stump, in Maltese. He roared, the crowds roared. He became a champion of the non-aligned movement, but preferred socialist and communist states as allies. The Church thought him an 'extreme Left Wing Socialist'. He was, in short, a contrast to Borg Olivier.

In the prime minister's last term, people began to mutter, 'Don't shout or you'll wake the government.' Borg Olivier spent Sundays drinking with lawyer friends at a restaurant in St Paul's Bay in the north of Malta, where the saint is said to have been shipwrecked, and Saturdays at his country house in Mosta in the centre of the island, with a retired English actress named Dawn Addams. His wife had begun an affair of her own – with a Catholic priest. The affair produced a son just as the country went to the polls.

The bulls Mintoff's supporters were pulling around were a reference to Borg Olivier being a cuckold – a *kornut* – which in literal Maltese means horned. 'In their primitive southern Mediterranean mindset,' my mother would later write, 'his male honour had been impugned because his woman had gone with another man, and therefore he had lost face irreparably.' They took the bulls onwards to Valletta in their lorries and pickup trucks. On the way there, one man pulled his bull into a bar and poured whisky down its throat. It began frothing at the mouth, then collapsed.

Borg Olivier gradually left public life after losing to Mintoff. His wife moved alone to Mellieħa, a village at the northernmost tip of Malta, to raise her new son. The Church sent the priest to Australia, where, according to Rose, 'he was hit by a car and died'. In Sliema, they still say

Borg Olivier lost the election because he was 'very distracted'.

But there were other issues. The post-independence economic model – some manufacturing, low taxes to attract wealthy foreigners like Dawn Addams, and grants of public land for hotels – benefited Borg Olivier's base in the import and distribution trades and the professional class. But while he broadened the availability of national insurance and pensions, the welfare state remained threadbare. The working class struggled. Industrial labourers made £10 a week. Maids and gardeners made £2 a week. The country was poor and inequitable.

'My only exposure to the villages,' my grandfather told me, meaning any place outside Sliema and Valletta, 'was through the maids and my father's employees.' He added, 'We had one girl in 1963 who had never been to the beach.'

Mintoff was elected on a mandate to address inequality and welfare, a task made harder as British military expenditure was in decline and, with Britain's retreat from the Mediterranean, would soon end. In this, he saw an opportunity. He wrote his non-alignment politics into the constitution. Malta now had to be, he said, 'equidistant' from the Cold War superpowers. He said this provision would guarantee Malta's national security more than hosting a garrison had. But in truth it was a ploy that allowed him to pit Britain and its fellow NATO members against the Soviet Union and its allies for a hold on Malta.

A few months into his premiership, he secured £14 million a year in rent for five years for Britain's use of Malta as a military base. Other NATO members could use the country as a base only if they paid additional rent. But

Britain and NATO did win Mintoff's guarantee that he wouldn't provide military facilities to Soviet states. He called the deal a 'great victory'. His supporters began calling him 'is-Salvatur ta' Malta', the Saviour of Malta. He made some noises about British 'settlers' in his country, then flew to Beijing to discuss 'diplomatic and economic matters', that is, foreign aid.

Money remained tight despite the deal. Mintoff instituted high tariffs and rigid quotas on imports, sometimes prohibitions, to grow domestic industry. Import licences were distributed to his supporters. Bribes were traded for restricted goods, including telephones and colour televisions. But even without the corruption, Malta's domestic market, consisting of some three hundred thousand people with small incomes, could not support Mintoff's policy. Products were unvaried and of low quality. There was only one brand of chocolate, Desserta, which tasted like wax.

My mother never forgot that, and later she would buy her own children excessive amounts of chocolate and other sweets. I liked to think it was how memories were passed on, changing inexorably for the sweeter from one generation to the next. But I was to learn that the process was not always so smooth.

My mother's paternal grandfather had been the president of the National Bank of Malta, a large private bank. One day in 1973, Mintoff summoned him to an emergency meeting.

The prime minister had moved his office to the Auberge de Castille, where his father had worked as a naval cook. A grand palace built in the baroque style in the early eighteenth century for the knights from Castille, the auberge had served as headquarters for the British, becoming a symbol of power. It still is. Sitting at Valletta's highest point, the auberge overlooks the Grand Harbour, its imposing facade of eleven bays divided by pilasters and panelling, with ornate windows, split into two levels by a cornice. A flight of deep stairs leads up to its big wooden door – topped by the Knights' Grand Master's bust, coats of arms and trophy of arms, and flanked by columns – through which my great-grandfather passed for his emergency meeting with Mintoff.

The prime minister demanded all the shares in the bank that belonged to its board. As the government deposited its own funds there, he threatened to start a run on the bank unless they complied. He also threatened to repeal the board members' limited liability, exposing them to personal losses. He said he would raid their houses 'down to the last candelabra'. My great-grandfather, white as a sheet, took the message back to the board. They told Mintoff, who had suspended the constitutional court, that his demand for their shares was a breach of their human rights.

'I don't give a damn about the constitution,' the prime minister replied. 'I didn't write it. I don't give a damn about the judges and everyone else.'

After the meeting, Mintoff gave an interview to the government-controlled television station, warning people about trouble at the bank but telling them not to 'behave like a stampede of cows'. Of course, that was just what they did. To finish off the bank, Mintoff sent police officers to shareholders' houses to harass them into signing over their holdings. The bank was wiped out in three weeks. Mintoff then nationalised it and renamed it the Bank of Valletta.

Similar efforts at nationalisation were happening around the world. In Britain, a Conservative government had nationalised one of the country's largest companies, Rolls-Royce, and its Labour successor went on to nationalise shipbuilders and aircraft makers. But in Malta the rule of law was weak, and nationalisation came at a high and lasting cost.

Mintoff nationalised everything – banks, shipping, energy, dockyards, hotels. He'd then load them with supporters, using their payrolls to win votes. The bloated corporations struggled and drained public resources for decades. In all this, the previous owners got little or no compensation. And his war wasn't only on them.

Industrial relations in general collapsed under his rule. Doctors went on strike against a law Mintoff passed that required newly graduated doctors to serve two years in the public health service before receiving their licence. The dispute began in 1977 and would last a decade. Mintoff locked striking doctors out of the health service and replaced them with foreign doctors. One doctor, a Mintoff supporter, was accused of being a strike breaker. A letter bomb addressed to him was sent to his house. The bomb was covered in wrapping paper and his fifteen-year-old daughter, thinking it a present, opened it. The bomb exploded in her hands. She was rushed to the hospital, where she was seen by a foreign doctor. On the operating table before him: a mass of organs, floating in blood. The only sign of life were her eyes, which, he'd recall, were full of excruciating, unbearable pain, set in a head no longer recognisable as such. She died. At her funeral mass, the archbishop called her death the 'first terrorist act in the country'. The case would never be solved. It would take more than three decades for a court to rule that the murder of Karin Grech was political, and her family owed compensation.

It would take longer – forty-one years – for the court to rule that the rights of the National Bank's shareholders had indeed been breached, and that they were due compensation from the government. And in the interim there would be more bombs, shootings, deaths in police custody, bodies found in fields and wells.

The episode became known as the National Bank Scandal, and it scarred my mother's family. Her grandfather retired from public life, rarely emerging from his home. For the first time, my mother overheard politics being discussed in the house on Milner Street. When, twenty years after Mintoff nationalised the bank, a Nationalist government re-privatised it – but kept for the government a majority stake and the power to appoint its chair – she would devote a column to how both political parties were 'disguising its gory origins'. She wrote, 'The ranks have closed against those who once owned the bank because nobody wants to remember, less still redress, the terrible wrongs done.'

Years later, she would dig up clippings about the bank scandal and send them to me and my brothers. At the time, I wondered why she wanted to perpetuate it. After her death, rereading what she'd written alongside the clippings, I began to understand what she'd been trying to tell us.

She refused to forget because she did not want to return to a time when human rights could be suspended and power could be wielded autocratically. She passed on the story to her sons because she did not want us to live in that kind of country.

One October day in 1979, my mother and her sisters were sitting on the balcony of their grandfather's house in Valletta. The view was onto the *Times* of Malta's building, where Mintoff's supporters were booing and hurling objects at the facade.

The newspaper, one of the few not controlled by a party, a labour union or the Church, had been questioning Mintoff's increasingly autocratic rule and his anti-Western stance. It criticised him for isolating Malta and for stoking partisan division, albeit in anonymous columns. Even that much scrutiny was too much for Mintoff and his supporters, whose booing at the *Times* was a familiar sight.

But on this particular day, the protesters went further. They stormed the *Times* building. Inside, the mob ordered an editor to show them to the printing machines. He led them to a storage room in which the *Times* kept old presses. They hit him on the head, then went at the defunct machines.

In another room, where the functioning machines were, the *Times* staff kept the newspaper running. They continued working until the mob set fire to the building. 'As the flames roared and raged out of control,' the assistant editor would write years later, 'journalists and printers ran for their lives.' My mother and her sisters watched as the mob outside laughed and jeered.

Mintoff's office at Castille was only a few metres away. He wrote to the newspaper's owner to express his 'regret at the unfortunate incident'. He explained that 'police vigilance failed because the excitement of the crowds was unprecedented', an analysis with which his attorney general agreed. 'I hope you believe me,' Mintoff concluded.

He needed that last sentence. It was difficult to believe that no one at Castille had heard the noise or smelt the smoke. It had been plain to see that the police force was under the control of the party in power. Many of its officers acted as Mintoff's paramilitary, working alongside thugs to suppress dissent. Police officers stood by as the opposition leader's home was ransacked that same day, his wife's earrings ripped from her earlobes.

No one faced justice for the arson attack on the *Times*. But the police did prosecute its company secretary for failing to make the gutted building safe within two months. In later statements, Mintoff justified 'the unfortunate incident', saying that the newspaper 'never served the interest of the people'. As the prime minister sanctioned an attack on the free press, the idea that dissent and scrutiny weren't publicly permissible became a fact. And, without them, corruption continued to flourish.

4

In the Sliema neighbourhood where my mother grew up, the children all knew one another. They played on quiet streets and walked down to the seafront to buy magazines from the stationers, Morris or Manché, or bottles of Coke and *pastizzi* – savoury pastries filled with ricotta or mushy peas – from Allies Bar. On weekends, no plans were made other than to walk out of their houses and wander around until they bumped into one another. On weekday evenings, they ran in and out of one another's homes, which were mostly alike.

At the Milner Street house, the bedrooms of my mother and her sisters were piled high with books and comics and toys. They were like those of other children with more 'Westernized, sixties-style' parents. Other friends, whose parents remained more conservative and religious, had 'absolutely perfect' bedrooms without the trappings of childhood. Although many were from privileged backgrounds, they'd have little more than a single teddy bear or doll placed on a stretched-out bedspread.

'Then,' my mother would recall, 'there were the bedrooms of the children I hardly knew, classmates I visited on strange, rare occasions, who lived in towns that seemed completely alien, as tended to be the case in the socially and geographically divided Malta of the early 1970s.' These bedrooms were a revelation to her – no toys, no children's books – some children didn't even know what comics were. It felt like an unbridgeable cultural divide to her, one that, at that age, she didn't even know how to express. She gave one girl a comic book only for her to return it, repeating what her parents told her – that comics were a waste of time and money.

St Dorothy's, their convent school, which was a short walk from Milner Street, sponsored pupils from the villages. My mother and her friends once noticed a girl eating a sandwich filled with broad beans, something they had never seen before. The girl snapped at them: 'I know you think I'm a *ħamalla*.' The word is Maltese for a brash working-class woman and derives from the Arabic for 'to load' and its words for 'porter' or 'stevedore'. It was another early lesson in class and the humiliations of privation.

So close in age, my mother, who went by Daph, and her sister Corinne – Cora – remained close. They drew their own comic books on the sly with their friends at school. One featured a priest who taught them about religion. Cora did the jacket design and my mother wrote the story, in which the priest became Tarzan, jumping from tree to tree in pursuit of the school's nuns.

The nuns may have missed the comics, but they noticed my mother reading novels during their lessons, hiding them behind her propped-up textbooks. The maths teacher once caught her and told the class that if they wanted the lesson to continue, Daphne Vella had to leave. My mother grabbed her novel and walked out. Her classmates remembered her 'quiet subversion' against the school's authority and its petty rules.

And the teachers forgave her. My mother's reading

shaped her writing, and her writing won her praise. At the age of ten, she was given an English exam paper by the nuns intended for students finishing secondary school, without being told what it was. She got an A equivalent. St Dorothy's own secondary school was in Mdina, the old capital. The nuns steered my mother towards the sciences; the arts were regarded as the avenue for girls with poor grades. It made no difference to my mother – she continued reading her novels. The school building in Mdina was cold and damp in winter. There were iron bars outside the windows. The girls called it St Dot's Prison. Their uniforms were made of crimplene. They were served 'dishwater soup' and so much beetroot that they grew to hate it for life.

A lifelong distrust of religion and clerics set in, although my mother would become close to some priests and would rationalise certain rituals. Praying to St Anthony, patron of things lost, 'focused the mind'. The evil eye was about 'forces of good and evil'. The nuns talked in class about what the 'cruel Jews' did to Jesus. 'If the nuns told you that,' Rose told my mother at home, 'then they are cruel.'

With four daughters – my mother, Cora, Amanda and Helene – Rose, like her own mother and most women of her background, stayed home to care for them. Michael had a pharmaceutical import and distribution business he'd inherited from his father. On summer weekends, my grandparents packed their girls into their red-and-white Volkswagen van and drove to a sandy beach at Għajn Tuffieħa, the 'spring of apples', on the north-west coast. The family spent winter weekends at Michael's family's country house in San Pawl tat-Targa, in the northern part of the island, then nothing but a brief street of one-storey houses leading off from a chapel and surrounded by fields. The house had a large garden full of plants wild and tame, where my mother and her sisters played until the gardener chased them back inside, accusing them of trampling on his plants. Inside, an old bookcase held children's novels from the Edwardian era, including an original edition of *The Secret Garden*. The book, along with the garden itself, shaped my mother's love for 'mysterious, magical gardens full of nooks and crannies' and made her feel at odds with the general Maltese hostility to nature.

At home on Milner Street, Michael could be strict with them. When my mother spent a good bit of her pocket money on jeans that she immediately tie-dyed, he cut them up. When she played her records too loudly, he switched off the electricity supply or burnt the records. My mother even tried her mother's patience. When Rose found her gardening the morning before her final English exam and asked whether she had read her Shakespeare, my mother replied, 'Leave me alone. I read half of it.' Daph passed her exam anyway.

On graduation day, in the summer of 1980, the Mother Superior approached Rose.

'Mrs Vella,' the nun said, 'this girl should study journalism. She has an enquiring mind. She is always asking questions, and she writes well.'

But where could a girl study journalism in Malta? The Mother Superior had ideas. She herself was Maltese, but she had studied in America. The experience had transformed her outlook. American colleges enrolled almost as many women as men, and offered a wide choice of study programmes. The press was robust and free. Women aspired to careers.

My grandmother never told my mother about the exchange. My mother, as it happened, had dreamt of working as a journalist outside Malta. But it was too difficult to go away back then. There were restrictions on foreign exchange, travel was expensive, and scholarships few and far between. 'Daphne would only have been disappointed,' Rose thought.

My mother found her way into journalism in the end, though she had to build it from scratch. There were no role models or career paths to follow. There were no satirists to emulate. There was little robust investigation into or critique of the powers that were. But because she had to invent her own way, she developed a singular journalistic persona and capability. Although she could not see it at the time, it was Malta's very limitations – the ones she longed to escape – that would make her, what one obituary called, a leading light of journalism.

Mintoff was still in power in the early 1980s. His version of socialism continued to wrestle with the country's enduring Catholic conservatism. Government clinics began to advise on family planning, for example, but they provided only diaphragms and information on natural methods of birth control. Abortion was, and still is, illegal in Malta. Girls were kept in the dark about sex, and to a great degree so were men. Girls learnt to walk in ways that protected their bodies from harassment.

When women married, they had to give up their public sector jobs. Few worked in the private sector. They had to surrender any property they possessed to their husbands. Divorce wasn't available. And yet the best thing girls could hope for was marriage, their only route to security, wealth and status. They had anxious conversations about being left on the shelf. My mother didn't like what lay beyond school.

But she liked what existed outside Malta. In the British Sunday newspapers that my grandparents sent her to fetch from the local newsagent, she was exposed to a country governed by a woman, one who seemed to be stripping back the state's control over people's lives. She read about its promise of openness, excess and luxury. She developed a sense that what was happening in Malta always had to be questioned and compared to what was happening outside the country. At the time, the British papers were reporting on Valium's harmful side effects on the brain. The tranquilliser was widely prescribed in Malta to women, whose lives were so constrained and monotonous. Did they know about the side effects? Did the doctors care? Did the men? My mother would return to this topic years later when arguing against drug liberalisation with me and my brothers. She saw the prescription of Valium as 'just another way of silencing women'.

Her friends, at least, provided solace. Some were original book club members and others she'd picked up over her time at St Dorothy's. They listened to the Rolling Stones, Jethro Tull and the Beatles. They expressed themselves through their clothes, and poured beer onto one another's hair to lighten it. In private, they talked politics all the time. My mother's opinions were 'very strong', her friends told me, and she always wondered about a life beyond the rocks. She began feeling the real world was outside, beyond, overseas.

Some of that world was accessible through the young foreigners they met in the evenings at bars along the coast. They were mostly boarding-school boys from St Edward's College whose fathers worked in the oilfields in Libya, 350 kilometres south across the sea. They enjoyed hearing about the boys' lives and felt that they could be their true selves with them.

Among them was a boy called Steve, who was half-Jamaican and half-British. When school let out for the summer, he did not go home to Britain. He and my mother were drawn to each other over that summer. He introduced her to the music of Bob Marley, and they spent days at the beaches along Malta's north coast. Steve had brought a white ankle-length djellaba back from a visit to his father in Libya. They took turns wearing it, catching the wind, 'like Peter O'Toole in *Lawrence of Arabia*, laughing and joking all the time', Steve told me.

Seeing him, some Maltese assumed he was Libyan. They swore at him and remonstrated with my mother for consorting with a Muslim, a grudge the country continued to bear. Steve was embarrassed and ashamed, but my mother stood her ground and let rip. My grandparents, too, didn't approve of her hanging out with a foreign boy who seemed unconventional to them, especially as there were rumours of rife marijuana smoking at St Edward's. But the disapproval could only have strengthened these teenagers' feelings for each other. They began to choose beaches further away. One day they trekked to an area called il-Blata l-Bajda, White Rocks, where there was not another soul in sight and the water was full of sea urchins.

When Steve returned to St Edward's in the autumn,

though, the headmaster confronted him about his poor grades and about drug abuse at the school. Most of the drugs came from a Maltese boy, but Steve, as a foreigner, was an easier target for expulsion and he went back to Britain. Michael drove my mother to the airport so that she could see him off, which Steve thought was good of him. 'It was a hard parting,' he told me. 'A very difficult farewell.' They kissed and hugged, as Michael stood a respectful distance away. The love affair came to an end.

My mother never talked about it, although Steve would surface many years later, in one of the stories she wrote about Malta. At the time, their abrupt separation only added to my mother's sense that there was nothing for her in the country.

She went up to sixth form at St Aloysius for her last two years of schooling before university. For her three main subjects, she took English because she loved it and accounting and economics because she thought she'd end up working for her father. St Aloysius was run by Jesuits and was, according to a former book club member who joined my mother there, 'rigid and unimaginative'.

My mother and her friends spent most of their time at a nearby bar called the Stagecoach. The bar owner gave them a set of keys to open up in the morning and asked them to help make coffee for customers, replace beer kegs and switch on the jukebox. 'And when we heard Bob Marley playing full blast,' a friend remembered, 'we knew your mother was already there.'

Only her English literature lessons absorbed her. Now Shakespeare had a hold on her. Chaucer brought her under a spell. Literature began to move her forward again; it reminded her what writing could do.

She began editing a college magazine, a duty she took very seriously. 'She wasn't like the other girls at college,' her friend, who worked on the magazine, remembered. 'You know, they could be a bit frivolous.' Another friend remembers talking to her for hours at their bus stop. There was 'something almost dark hanging over her. We used to talk a lot. She listened. I mean, *really* listened. She once told me that she felt out of context in Malta. She told me she felt she was in the wrong place.'

They were waiting so long at their stop because drivers were on strike against Mintoff's attempts to reform the bus service. He ordered the armed forces to use their lorries to pick up passengers instead. Sometimes no lorry would turn up and they would walk the six kilometres home to Sliema, where they would drop their school bags and kick off their shoes at one house or another. 'Then we got dolled up in our Adam Ant gear,' my mother wrote years later, 'played Duran Duran and Depeche Mode, and pretended that we didn't live in a sad black hole.'

Malta had only one university, and Mintoff had closed its arts, humanities and social sciences programmes. He believed these subjects belonged to a colonial past he wanted to 'reshape'. He wanted practical, useful courses that would produce teachers, architects, doctors and lawyers. He said it was a way to 'assert ourselves as Maltese'.

But there was no past for him to reshape. There was only a myth he had constructed, expressed in one of his slogans, 'Malta for the Maltese'. He declared the country a republic and ruled it like a king. He changed the country's currency from the British pound to the Maltese pound, also known as the Maltese lira, which he pegged to the British. His only assertion was of his ministers' power. Some became rich; a CIA report described the minister of public works as 'venal'. Most Maltese remained poor.

Mintoff reserved almost all places at the university for applicants with a public sector sponsor. 'Unless you knew someone in the government,' one of my mother's Stagecoach friends told me, 'you had to find fake private sponsors to get in. But there was nothing your mother wanted to study there anyway.'

She went to work for her father. His business importing pharmaceuticals was coming under strain. Maintaining import licences was an increasingly onerous process, an occasion for government officials to extract bribes and kickbacks. He needed help dealing with the government's licensing office.

My mother became his gofer. Blue, green, pink, white and yellow copies of the licences fluttering, she drove from office to office to get one stamp or another, before taking them to the licensing office for processing.

One day in the queue there, she noticed that all the other gofers had Lm10 – equivalent to £10 – banknotes paper-clipped to their licence forms. No processing fee was officially required, and the clerks had no formal power to speed licence applications; only ministers did.

'The rank corruption at the top seeped all the way to the bottom,' my mother later wrote. The clerks could not speed up applications, but they could slow them down. They could forget about them or lose them. 'The bribes ensured that the bribers got *what was theirs by right*. That was the extent of the rottenness.'

She left that job soon after, but she kept using my grandfather's office because there was a Smith Corona typewriter in it, with a cream upper deck and yellowish-green lower deck. She eventually took it home and began using it to write, 'just as a hobby'.

Two worlds, corruption and writing about it, collided.

5

The house on Tower Road in Sliema where my father grew up was once his family's summer house. It had twenty-four rooms over three floors, with high ceilings and a garden where they kept chickens. The sun rose over the sea in front of the house, and sunlight and warmth would flood through the bay windows and across its wooden balconies on its art nouveau facade. The family had multiple properties, but its main residence was originally a town house in Valletta where they had a wet nurse and a cook who'd join them in Sliema over the summer.

My great-great-grandfather Antonio Annetto Caruana bought the town house in the late nineteenth century. He had trained to become a priest, but walking to church with his fellow seminarians one day, he heard a young woman playing the piano. He and Maria Metropoli fell in love, and he forgot about the priesthood. He became an archaeologist, uncovering crypts and catacombs, and was eventually appointed rector of the university. He oversaw the appointment of his and Maria's only son, Giovanni Caruana, to the chair of constitutional and international law at twenty-three years old.

At that same age, the young professor married Giovanna Galizia, daughter of Malta's principal architect, Emanuele Luigi Galizia, known for his 'exotic and flamboyant arabesque' style. The couple took over the Valletta town house and had ten children. They gave their first-born daughter over to a convent. They expected their other girls to marry well. The boys had to join one of the professions. Giovanni wrote about the decadence of English liberalism, made money in private practice and acquired property. At the house on Tower Road, a blood clot lodged in his brain killed him at the age of fifty-seven.

His eldest son, Anton Caruana, became the patriarch. He too was a lawyer. He added Galizia to his surname so that, he used to say, people didn't confuse him with another lawyer of the same name who was 'an idiot from one of the villages'. His siblings also adopted the new surname because, my mother once told me and my father, 'being so unusually short, they felt they needed a long surname to make an impact'. Anton chose to speak Italian and Maltese, and although he was a successful lawyer, he spent a lot of time womanising around Valletta and drinking at his club, the Casino Maltese, which was established because the country's only other club – the Union Club – did not accept Maltese people as members. The Casino Maltese's other members used to say Anton could make love to a woman atop the club's flagpole.

One day in February 1942, Anton walked out of the Casino Maltese and was killed in a Luftwaffe bombing raid. The rest of the family left Valletta for the summer house; they never lived in the capital again. They now spoke English and Maltese, and they survived off their properties until the children made their own ways. The youngest boy, my grandfather John Baptist, never quite did. He developed what the family referred to as 'occasional mental distress' – we would say clinical depression – that ended a brief engagement in his twenties and affected his ability to work. He remained in the house on Tower Road and shared a Valletta office with his industrious brother Victor, a law professor. He took siestas on a chaise longue he kept in his room, drank whisky, often with Giorgio Borg Olivier, and became an executive committee member of Borg Olivier's Nationalist Party. He played tennis and bridge, and married my grandmother Marcelle, also from Sliema and seventeen years his junior, whom a niece described on their wedding day as 'extremely striking in a sultry Spanish style'.

Marcelle's patience with John Baptist was rewarded with a son, my father, nine years into their marriage, in 1956, and a daughter, Antonia, ten years later. So, my father grew up mostly alone and developed some of the habits of a lonely child, lost in his thoughts. When I once asked him why he knew how to do wiring and plumbing, he said it was because he used to follow workmen around the house.

When his 'mental distress' allowed, John Baptist taught my father bridge and took him to the Casino Maltese for lunch. He took him to the beaches around Sliema in summer, days that he'd get through with a flask of Pernod, and on walks in the countryside in winter. When there was no break in the clouds, he sent my father for carpentry lessons at a government-run youth club close to the Sliema seafront. My father noticed that the other boys there wore cheaper clothes and could speak only Maltese. None of them came from the houses along the seafront or the town houses right behind them. 'I realised after a while that all the other boys walked up from the coast,' my father told me. 'I was the only one who walked down.'

He attended St Aloysius for all his schooling. As with

the nuns at St Dot's, the Jesuits saw it as their mission to take in pupils from the villages. But they didn't put them in classes with the sons of lawyers, doctors and architects where my father met his friends. These boys were placed in a single classroom with pastel-pink walls. 'They used to say we wouldn't pass exams in Maltese,' my father told me, 'and called us "snobs".'

Even for these snobs, life was bare. As teenagers they rode around Malta on their single-speed bicycles. There were few cars then, so the roads and lanes were open to them. Each weekend they would explore a new part of the countryside or a new village. It was either that or house parties, which my father threw at his family's properties.

Mintoff, now the prime minister, was quick to requisition unoccupied private property, so the family sent my father from one house to another to show signs of occupancy. He'd invite his friends, and a couple dozen of them would show up, bringing bottles of wine and spirits. He was, one frequent guest told me, 'always droll and often in a velvet jacket'. They danced to the Beatles, the Rolling Stones, Black Sabbath, and Emerson, Lake & Palmer. The parties continued as he started university where, inevitably, he read law. The law course took a hundred students every two years. Fifty of them graduated with my father. Many would become judges who'd preside over his cases. One was a classmate who used to become so nervous before his university exams he'd get diarrhoea.

My father joined the family's law office. The pace was slow. Victor had died years earlier. As John Baptist had never learnt how to drive, my father would take him to Valletta on his orange Vespa. But John Baptist didn't have many clients, so he'd find a way home for lunch and wouldn't return for the rest of the day.

My father struggled to build a practice. But as one case led to another, his sense of independence grew, and the conservative views he had inherited from his family gave way to something more pragmatic. He took Malta as he found it, and focused on his work. He was eventually able to rent his own flat on Tower Road. And it was in his flat that in March 1984, as he played bridge with friends, he heard the noise of a student protest coming from the road.

Had he looked, he would have seen my mother.

She was nineteen years old by then. Walking home after work at Michael's office, she bumped into an old school friend. Continuing on together, they came across the protest.

Mintoff's long-running war with the Church had by this point extended to its schools. Mintoff held that they should be free – 'Free or nothing' was his slogan. The Church resisted, so Mintoff was heading for 'nothing'. His supporters turned their focus where he directed. They began to bomb Church property, using TNT scavenged from unexploded shells fired by Royal Navy vessels during training exercises around the islands. They placed explosives near churches, outside priests' houses, at the papal embassy. Then they said they would target school buses. Mintoff's education minister said parents should stop 'sacrificing their children for the archbishop'.

The archbishop, as a safety measure, closed the Church schools, which enrolled a third of the country's pupils. The parents – including my maternal grandparents, whose two youngest daughters were still at convent school – began hosting secret lessons in their homes. Freed from the rigid routine of a Church school, the pupils began staging protests. 'There were protests against the school closures every single week,' Rose remembered. 'The one at Tower Road was probably the biggest.'

The protest had drawn thousands of people. My mother and her friend stopped and sat alongside a cordon that the police force had put up. They joined in the chanting. 'Then, all these policemen just charged at us,' the friend recalled. 'One picked up your mother and threw her to the ground. He yelled at her and then punched her chest with his right hand. He had leather gloves on and God knows what was underneath them. He was ferocious. Five other police officers had to drag him off her.' Some of their friends appeared and began shouting at the policemen. When my mother was finally free, she and her friend fled home.

'Two days later, they found me,' my mother's friend said. 'I had forty plaits in my hair, beads and a bandana. I stood out.' The police arrested her and took her to headquarters. Her parents were not allowed to see her. She had been given no time to get warm clothes or food. They held her in a cell that measured two metres square for twenty-six hours without access to anyone. There was excrement on the walls, and the toilet was filthy.

She was interrogated by a lumbering, moustachioed police inspector named Anġlu Farrugia who would later become deputy leader of the Labour Party. He asked her and the other half-dozen young people already in custody to name their companions, and drove each of them around Sliema so that they could point out where their friends lived.

Farrugia came to visit the following day. Rose opened the door. 'Is this about the policeman who punched my daughter?' she asked him.

He pushed past her and made his way into their living room. He sat down on the sofa and asked where Daphne Vella was.

'At work with her father,' said Rose.

So Farrugia went to my grandfather's office, arrested my mother and took her to headquarters for questioning. Like her friend, she was without warm clothes or access to anyone, and the holding cell was disgusting. A female police officer conducted a cavity search before passing her back to Farrugia.

He refused my mother's repeated requests to see her parents, who unbeknown to her were waiting outside with a jacket and food. He refused her requests to see a lawyer and said he had photographs of her hitting a police officer. She told him that the photographs must be of someone else; she had not hit anyone. She was returned to her cell.

Later that night, he dragged her out again and presented her with a confession he had prepared. It was, she later wrote, 'full of lies, a confession to crimes so absurd that, if I hadn't been so frightened and worried, I would have laughed out loud in his face'.

She could only go home if she signed the statement, he said. Thinking of all the bruised and dead bodies to have emerged from police custody under Mintoff, she felt undone and humiliated by fear. She signed.

The police offered her cold eggs, cold coffee and mouldy bread. She was released on bail against a personal guarantee of Lm100 – then equivalent to £160, as Mintoff had unpegged the Maltese lira from the pound, and what many people earned in a month. She found her father waiting outside. He put a jacket over her and took her home. They received notice that my mother was to be charged with eleven crimes, from blocking a public path to vandalism and assaulting a police officer.

The experience showed her how fear demoralises people and breaks them down; how it keeps doing so until most of them can no longer even imagine a different way of living. It was a feeling she never wanted to experience again.

'It was a real turning point for your mother,' her friend told me. 'She was ready. On full attack. I wasn't. I wanted out.'

Their paths diverged. My mother wanted to write and began pitching around. She found her first job on a magazine called the *Exporter*, which was owned by the government's investment promotion agency but edited by a former *Financial Times* correspondent. She turned up at his office with writing samples that were overwritten and, he recalled, 'had a ring of Enid Blyton about them'. But he recognised her drive to make it as a writer and took her on. She filed piece after piece – for a relatively generous Lm25 (£40) each – and her writing sharpened. But the topics – electronics, furniture exports to China – bored her, and her editor was usually running around outside the office, leaving her and the secretary to answer calls from his wife. When the university launched its first journalism diploma, my mother took the opportunity to leave the *Exporter* and enrol on this new evening course. One of her lecturers had edited a Labour Party newspaper called *Is-Sebħ* ('The Sunrise') in the 1950s before he was imprisoned for libel. 'She was very eager and diligent,' he told me, adding that 'I taught my students to leave private family matters alone.'

My mother's friend, meanwhile, took up windsurfing. By then my father too had become a keen windsurfer. He would sail out from Exiles, a rocky beach on the Sliema coast. One day as he was rigging his sail, he noticed my mother's friend next to him. She had the same Sailboard Vario, white with green and yellow stripes.

As they talked, he noticed something else: a tall slim woman in a yellow bikini in the background. It was my mother. She was lying on the rocks, reading. My father began angling for an introduction. He got one, finally, at a bar further west along the coast called Saddles.

'Daph,' her friend said, 'this is Peter.'

She yawned. Playfully, he thought, he put his index finger into her open mouth.

'I know – what a bloody *creep*,' she once told me.

The criminal case against my mother was the first time she entered the Maltese public's mind, somewhere she'd live for the rest of her life. The proceedings against her and the eight other defendants played out over nine months. A protest in support of the defendants was ongoing outside.

Inside the courtroom, one of the small ones that magistrates preside over, there were three rows of dark wooden benches. The defendants occupied the first row and their friends and family filled the rows behind. Their lawyers lined up in front of the bench, and on the opposite side of the room to the prosecution. Journalists stood on either side of the courtroom. Present were reporters from the *Times*, which by now had dropped 'Malta' from its title, and the Nationalist newspaper *in-Taghna* ('Our'), which had dropped 'Nation' from its title after Mintoff prohibited non-government publications from using those words.

The magistrate was visibly appalled as my mother described the way the police had treated her. He was otherwise inscrutable. When one of her friends was preparing to testify, he raised his right hand, unaware that in a Maltese court a witness must kiss a cross to be sworn in. 'What do you think this is?' the magistrate barked. '*Perry Mason?*'

My mother's lawyer was nervous. She had just turned twenty, and he felt her future was on his shoulders. The charges carried prison terms ranging from one month to three years. In the prison, drug abuse and violence were rife.

On the day of the judgment, in December 1984, the courtroom was packed. The magistrate read out the charges, then paused before announcing his ruling.

Not guilty of all charges, he said.

The judgment was damning. It was the police who were aggressive and out of control, the magistrate held. They'd given false evidence. They'd failed to produce a key witness: the police officer they'd claimed was assaulted had in fact done the assaulting himself. The police's behaviour must be 'condemned and severely censured'.

'With regards to Daphne Vella,' the magistrate continued, 'some observations must be made.' She did not hit anyone: she raised her arms to protect herself. Her confession was coerced. In custody, she was 'forced to undergo a bitter experience, which need not be explained in detail'.

My mother's friends were similarly acquitted, and they felt vindicated by the court's censure of the police, which was already a rare occurrence.

My father was present in the courtroom. 'I was so relieved for your mother,' he told me. 'She was still so young, you know.'

My father was almost nine years older than my mother, and perhaps it was the age difference that moved their relationship forward so quickly. In arguments, she would often call him 'Edwardian'. He did not mind. He felt the age difference said something about his manliness.

Their first serious date was a wedding. Another young lawyer had asked my mother to go with him, but she took my father instead. 'She told me it was because she could wear six-inch heels with me and he was too short,' my father told me. 'Quite shallow.'

More dates followed. There were drives around Malta on my father's Vespa and weekends in Gozo. There were long days at the beach, with her sitting on the back of his Windsurfer as they sailed out from the coast. 'Maybe not so shallow – fun-loving. Your mother was more colourful than my previous girlfriends. And I used to make her laugh, you know.'

He gave her a set of keys to his flat. She would move his few pieces of furniture around, which upset him. 'She was always there, even when I was at work. Your grandparents were a bit strict with her at home. I suppose they could sense she had no brakes.'

Their sense was correct. One early-summer day in 1985,

she was sitting out at sea on the back of my father's wind-surfer. The winds were slow, the sea smooth as oil.

'I'm feeling sick,' she told him.

'But it's so calm. Seasick?'

'I don't know.'

He sailed them back to shore and they talked. Three positive pregnancy tests later, my father said, 'We had better get married.'

'Really fucking romantic,' she replied.

My mother had just turned twenty-one. In pictures of the wedding, she is not yet showing. She looks happy, with a wry smile. My father, slim and sharp in tails, looks pleased with himself.

He did not have enough money for a honeymoon, so her uncle gave them one as a gift. One week in Vienna and another in Budapest, which was then behind the Iron Curtain. My father remembered that she packed ten books for the trip. They took a Russian hovercraft down the Danube, and she was nauseated the whole time. When they returned to Malta, they moved into my father's Tower Road flat. He thought they might settle down, but my mother had other ideas.

A march was called one Saturday in November. It was organised by a group called Youth for the Environment, protesting against the construction boom across Malta's countryside. The march made its way down Merchants Street in Valletta. When it passed by the foreign affairs ministry, my parents and their friends noticed the minister speaking to a group of thugs. They understood immediately what was going to happen. Within seconds, the men were running at them. The minister turned his back and walked into his building. The protesters scattered. My parents got separated.

One of my mother's friends tried to pull her away from the crowd. One thug, whom my mother would describe as a 'compact mad, dangerous beetle', chased them in a 'wild rage' with what looked like a garden hose. It was a length of heavy chain threaded through a rubber pipe. He was going after the women, swinging it at the protesters' legs. My mother and her friend took shelter in the doorway of a post office, as the thug and his associates ran towards them. The postmen managed to pull my heavily pregnant mother inside. Her friend, left outside, was beaten so badly she had to be hospitalised.

Other marchers were injured, but they were too frightened to go to hospital, where their injuries would have outed them as anti-Mintoff. But my mother's friend's injuries were too severe to let go. Her boyfriend reported the incident to the police, naming the thug. The police did nothing but hold him, my father and some other protesters until late that night.

Matthew was born a few months after. Our parents stopped going to the protests, but the country remained violent.

In a small village called Gudja, in December 1986, the Nationalist Party was celebrating the opening of a social club where party supporters could meet and drink.

Raymond Caruana, a carpenter, was standing just inside the club's open front door, talking to friends. He was twenty-six years old and engaged to be married. It was night-time and the village was quiet, until a Labour cabinet minister's chauffeur drove by, spraying bullets at the club's facade. One bullet went through the open door and into Caruana's jugular vein. He fell face down, into a pool of his own blood.

That was how the Nationalist Party's leader found Caruana when he arrived at the crime scene. Angry and confused, he walked out onto the village's main street and yelled into the dark, at the closed shutters and wooden doors.

'Did anyone see what happened?'

No one came forward.

The police investigated a nearby farm and found a gun. They charged the farmer with Caruana's murder, but witnesses had spotted the police visiting the farm with a Labour cabinet minister a few days earlier to plant the weapon. Some individuals took out full-page advertisements in the newspapers, declaring their belief that the farmer was innocent.

'They did so because the newspapers were not functioning as they should have been,' my mother would write. 'That was the Malta we knew then: a Malta without newspaper columnists who put their name and face to what they write, and who express the fears, concerns and views of the people who read them.'

The farmer was eventually freed. 'It was a nightmare,' he said. But no one was charged with the attempt to frame him or with Caruana's murder. He was now the Nationalists' martyr, a counterpart to Labour's Karin Grech, the fifteen-year-old girl killed by letter bomb in 1977. One side's call for justice was countered by the other's, and neither ever answered.

*

A general election was held the following year, 1987, by coincidence on the day that should have been Raymond Caruana's twenty-seventh birthday. It provided an opportunity for change. For my father, whose family had long voted for the Nationalist Party, the choice was obvious.

For my mother, it was less clear. Some months before, her own father had founded something called the Malta Democratic Party with a friend from Sliema, a former Labour Party official, to contest the election and to put an end to the factionalism of the Nationalist and Labour parties. My grandfather Michael was its president, his friend the general secretary. They were the new party's only candidates. They ran on a platform of decentralisation, environmentalism and pluralism. Their slogan was 'The citizen first'.

Malta was not interested. The party received 380 votes. My mother cast one.

The Nationalists won, by a whisker, on a platform of unity and modernisation. The new prime minister was Eddie Fenech Adami, whom my mother would describe as a 'village lawyer', a nickname he'd later use as the title of a chapter in his autobiography. When it came to the police force, Fenech Adami avoided sacking even its most corrupt officers, because 'doing so would have created turmoil'. He said reconciliation needed to be managed over time.

Time would tell that the reconciliation promise was a sham. There would not be a single successful prosecution of corrupt officials, MPs or former ministers, let alone of the thuggish police. There was no progress on Caruana's murder, and nothing to discourage another of its kind.

The 1987 election was meant to be Malta's end-of-history moment: liberal democracy achieved, not just as the country's next phase, but its final phase. The Nationalists had presented it as an inevitability, campaigning on the biblical-sounding slogan of '*Is-sewwa jirbaħ żgur*', 'The right-eous will always win'. 'I've never thought so,' my mother would write years later. She thought that 'the triumph of the undeserving' was inevitable, unless you actively campaigned against it.

But, at the time, she was distracted. The new government quickly made plans for Malta's accession to the European Union. 'Europe,' my father told me, 'meant everything to your mother.'

They had argued about the election in a way that laid bare their political differences. In my father's pragmatic conservatism, joining the European Union was about Malta liberalising its economy. The accession requirements demanded it. So state intervention, a large public sector, high tariffs on imports and a dependence on foreign aid were reversed. It was now all about privatisation, foreign investment and market liberalisation. Brussels placed little emphasis on the kind of institutional reforms Malta really needed, and the Nationalist government had already decided it would just be easier – for almost everyone, especially itself – to leave the 'undeserving' alone.

My mother had had much higher hopes for what European Union membership would mean. She had assumed that a democratic culture, with its attendant accountability, would follow a modern economy. She took issue with my father's view that the country was unlikely to change in any deep way, and that a modern economy was the best they could hope for. After one of their blazing rows, he put his childhood carpentry lessons to work and gave my mother a wooden plate with a raised rim that he had made for her on his lathe. After another of their fights, she threw it away.

In the period of liberalisation that followed, more products appeared in shops. And more advertising supported more publications.

One, the *Circle*, was a quarterly magazine posted directly to affluent households. Its founder hired my mother as an editor in 1987. 'But she was always pregnant,' he told me. 'It became difficult.'

At the time she was pregnant with Andrew, who was born a year and a half after Matthew. She developed a routine of leaving Matthew and Andrew at her parents' house, an eight-minute walk from my parents' flat, and returning home to work on the magazine.

One November day in 1988, while heavily pregnant with me, my mother set out to drop Matthew and Andrew at my grandparents'. The walk took longer than usual. Debris blocked the pavement. Cranes and trucks jammed the roads. The air was thick with dust. More and more, Sliema's old seafront houses and town houses behind were being demolished to make way for blocks of flats. My mother could see that the town of her childhood was drowning in concrete.

'She was angry when she arrived,' Rose told me. 'She said she was going to write about it.'

The next day, instead of leaving Matthew and Andrew at my grandparents', she pushed them in their double pram up and down Tower Road. She noted the door numbers of each and every building site, and found most of the road was under construction, much of it in breach of planning rules. She wrote up her findings for the *Circle*, headlining her report 'Sliema Scandal'.

'Sliema, where dust grows on shrivelled trees and on the bedroom floor,' her introduction ran. 'Where the rivers of concrete flow freely across the road. Where it's not the willows that weep but the women left at home to withstand the dirt and noise between 7am and 4pm. If there is no peace for the wicked, then Sliema is Gomorrah.' She wrote about the building contractors and their machines, each one like the 'screaming-pitch noise of a stone-breaking, earth-moving, baby-waking monster'.

A few days after her report was published, the day after my birth, one of the *Times* of Malta's still anonymous columnists praised her work, saying that it 'encapsulates the craft of journalism in terms of language, style, content, and message' and that it deserved a 'prize for the best contribution to journalism in Malta'. But there was no response from the government, and the construction continued. My mother tried another approach.

Some months later, she was elected to the inaugural eleven-person committee of the Sliema Residents Association. Its aim was to encourage residents' civic pride. It was the only association she ever joined, apart from the Cactus and Succulent Society of Malta, for which she would take out a lifetime membership. She was the association's public relations officer. In this capacity, she wrote a letter to the *Times* about Sliema's sewage problem, stemming from an outlet on a bay where she used to take us swimming. The government responded by banning swimming there.

Anthony Montanaro, the venerable editor of the *Sunday Times* of Malta, asked my mother to interview the minister responsible for development. It was her first newspaper assignment. The interview appeared under her byline and was headlined 'AN ERA OF ARROGANT CITIZENS'. In it, she asked the minister about his links to the private companies under his regulatory oversight ('I know them, many of them, because I used to be a practising architect'); corruption in land use ('as old as the hills'); and his failed attempts to control it ('we have written on more than one occasion to the Commissioner of Police'). 'What do you have to say about your rumoured arrogance?' she asked for her last question.

'Arrogant? Me? Who says I'm arrogant?' he replied. 'You should read some of the letters I receive to know what arrogance means. I replied to one only recently remarking that it seemed the era of arrogant ministers has been ushered out by the era of arrogant citizens.'

The exchange revealed the way Maltese politicians viewed the Maltese people: as levers to power, or as obstacles to power. The attitude was so deeply ingrained that most voters hoped not for a politician who represented them but one who didn't forget them once in power. Some of them saw my mother's interview as a personal attack on the minister rather than as an accountability exercise. They said she was seeking attention and causing problems. The minister, wounded, would spend the rest of his long career sniping at my mother.

He was part of a crop of new Nationalist MPs who were meant to herald Malta's era of openness. But in his interview with my mother, he displayed no concept of himself as a public servant. The people were in his way; the era of arrogant ministers continued. The country opened up but remained the same.

6

My parents lost hope that Sliema would improve and moved us to Bidnija, a lonely hamlet in the less arid north-west. It was only a twenty-minute drive from Sliema, yet people always asked why we lived so far away, and taxis often refused to go there. I once got one home by telling the driver I needed to go to Mosta, a large town five minutes away. When we arrived at the edge of Mosta, I asked the driver to please keep going, just a little bit, down the hill to our house. He said, 'You fucked me, friend, this isn't Mosta,' and demanded an extra half-fare. Broke, I got out halfway down the hill and walked the rest of the way home.

The simple geography of southern Malta breaks into small then larger hills as it moves north, rising and falling into ridges and valleys as it reaches the north-west part of the island. The crooked little fields that terrace the narrow slopes become wider as the valleys expand on either side of Bidnija. The smell at the start of summer is of wild thyme, which cracks under your feet, and later, in September, it was of manure put down by farmers. In winter, torrential rains bring a warm, earthy smell. Most of the year, the land looks burnt brown and dusty. Dusty from the dry cracking soil, dusty from the limestone quarries nearby, dusty from the southerly winds that bring Saharan sand across the sea. But the area is lucky in water: a fresh-water spring rises from the bedrock, which the farmers draw on through the cool green winter and into midsummer, when it finally runs dry. The spring takes its name from the myrtle – *riħana* – that dots the area: Għajn Riħana.

It's the Bidni olive, though, which has grown in this valley since Roman times, that gives its name and purpose to the area. Farmers built their farmhouses around the spring and the olives, which turn a shining purple at maturity. Most of the farmers have been in the area for generations. One who left to join the Royal Navy at the lowest rank returned with his pension and the same rank as 'il-Ġeneral'.

The chapel the farmers built in 1920 at the top of the Bidnija Hill and dedicated to the Holy Family still stands. Its bell rings out on the third Sunday of July, Bidnija's feast day. Some cram into the tiny church to hear Mass, others stand in the square outside where a brass band borrowed from St Paul's Bay – Bidnija is too small to staff its own – plays to a dull beat. A priest swings his silver thurible from side to side, releasing frankincense, and leads the farmers, faces of creased leather above white robes, out of the chapel with a statue of the Holy Family on their shoulders. They proceed down the hill, around an empty field, and back into the chapel where they leave the statue for another year. Fireworks are set off, cold lager is passed around to most of the hamlet's two hundred or so residents. When my brothers and I were growing up there, they'd give us shandies.

Halfway up the hill is our family home: Dar Riħana, Myrtle House. A gravel lane connects it to the Bidnija road. The farmer who works the fields that run alongside the lane used to say an old Maltese rhyme when I walked past: *Pawlu Pasparawlu, taħt is-sodda jisparawlu / ommu tibkih u missieru jidħak bih*, which translates to *Paul Pasparawlu* – a nonsense name – *they shoot him under the bed / his mother cries for him and his father laughs at him.* The house was built at the end of a ridge separating two valleys. Its east-facing side is visible from the valley opposite, Wied tal-Ħżejjen, and the back of the house is visible from a smaller valley to the north, Wied tal-Arkata. North of tal-Arkata is the sea at St Paul's Bay.

The house was made of the island's limestone, a layer of rock called globigerina, formed through the compression of plankton. Paper-white when first cut, it turns amber after sun and rain and more sun. There were seven rooms with wooden shutters and single-pane glass windows. When we moved in, the furniture was tired and the plaster chipped. The wooden shutters had been eroded. Black-whip and leopard snakes slithered in through the gaps, looking for cool floor tiles. Sparrows came down the chimney in spring, robins in autumn, fleeing hunters roaming the valley.

Hunters' shotguns fired day and night in a double-barrelled rhythm: load, snap, one shot then another. It was this, the steady buzz of cicadas and the noise of two-stroke diesel tractors, whose engines echoed around the valley, that made up the soundscape of Bidnija.

There were no neighbours and no objections to the music my mother played loudly and on repeat: Bob Dylan, Neil Young and, still, Bob Marley. The garden, with its citrus trees, its giant reeds, and the white mulberry tree whose fruit she picked for her gin and tonics, became her haven.

And ours. Matthew got his own bedroom and I would eventually be separated from Andrew, with difficulty, taking a room with a window onto a young mock orange tree.

We liked the white-gravel hill that ran along the east side of the garden and ended at a flagstone path, marked black and yellow by lichen, which went right to the garden's northern edge. Beyond the edge was a three-metre drop to the valley below. As the tal-Arkata valley is open and wide, the previous owners had planted a row of giant reeds for privacy. The reeds flourished, growing tall and dense, swaying in the cool breeze that lifted off the valley bed in summer. We discovered that the reeds were so thick they would not break when we jumped into them off the garden edge. They bent under our weight and then buoyed us back up. They made a kind of trampoline.

Bored with the jumping, we built a ramp out of chipboard planks we took from my father's workroom. We put the ramp at the end of the flagstone path, facing out to the valley. Then we took our BMX bikes to the top of the gravel hill, raced down along the path and up the ramp, and hurled ourselves, bikes and all, into the air. A crimson bougainvillea flashed by, looking like a smudged watercolour. In mid-air, we let go of the bikes and twisted ourselves around to land backwards on the reeds.

On one such run, Andrew lost control of his pedals by the time he hit the ramp. His BMX went straight into the reeds and he flew, really flew, into the air. He managed his twist, but he landed out of sight. Matthew and I rushed to the edge to see what had happened to him.

We found him laughing among the reeds. He wanted to know whether we had seen the height of his jump. But our eyes were fixed on the single reed stem that had pierced the back of his jeans, cutting its way clean through to the front and missing his crotch by centimetres.

We climbed down and extracted Andrew. We quietly dismantled the ramp, putting the chipboard planks back in the workroom. We put away our BMXs and hid Andrew's pierced jeans in the valley. Let's go inside, we said. Let's keep this quiet. No one needs to know.

As soon as we walked into the house, my mother saw us. 'Andrew,' she said. 'Why aren't you wearing trousers?'

My parents had the reeds cut back and burnt, and so, for a time, nothing interrupted our views onto the open country. There was a tall Aleppo pine my brothers and I used to climb. From there, I would look out over the valley and think: Where else could we have lived but here?

My parents planted more citrus trees, a bay laurel and cacti. They had work done on the house. The builders always seemed to be covered in fine white dust, like limestone moving. In the heat, they moved with economy: lifting blocks onto their shoulders, swinging pickaxes. They built a room of my mother's own.

She was still working on the *Circle* when its owner and Anthony Montanaro, editor of the *Sunday Times* of Malta, asked her to set up a monthly *Sunday Times Magazine*. She worked part-time there, editing and writing, while she continued to produce the *Circle*, which was now distributed with the newspaper.

In April 1990, she interviewed an anonymous government medical consultant for the magazine. The consultant talked about the hospital's staffing problems, its lack of organisation and the poor quality of its general care. The government's director of information responded over a two-page spread in the *Sunday Times*. More government medical consultants got in touch with my mother, revealing additional information. She protected her sources but lamented that people would only speak anonymously. She described the problem in the magazine's next issue.

'Fear, unfortunately, is the greatest enemy of freedom of expression – and of dialogue,' she wrote. 'Fear leads to the dangerous situation where individuals are gagged, forced to retract what they have said through some form of intimidation, or by some other means discredited ... Individuals should never be nailed for exercising the legitimate right to speak their mind. We can truly call ourselves a democratic people – as opposed to a democratic government – when more of us do the same, without fearing the consequences.'

Her principles were tested a few weeks later when a yacht called the *Esmeralda*, carrying the uncle who had paid for her honeymoon, sank in a storm some thirty kilometres south-east of Sardinia.

Her uncle died, but the *Esmeralda*'s owner and another man mysteriously survived. When the owner was brought back to Malta, he gave an interview to the public broadcaster Xandir Malta. He said that my mother's uncle, a former water polo player, didn't make it because he swam away from their dinghy, back to the *Esmeralda*, to save the yacht's engineer, who could not swim. Then, he said, a 'huge wave' separated the dinghy from the yacht. A badly decomposed body, probably belonging to the engineer, washed up on a small Italian island. But my mother's uncle was still missing.

Like the rest of the country, my mother's family watched the interview and, thinking the uncle might still be alive, pushed for the search and rescue missions to continue. My mother, though, found the owner's account implausible, and the interview hopeless.

In a letter to the *Sunday Times*, she wrote: 'If I could have snatched the microphone from the ill-prepared journalist, I would have asked the following.' Among the sixteen questions she listed were these: Why did the distress signal come so late? Was it true the dinghy had room for just three people? How was the owner able to see her uncle swim away in the pre-dawn darkness?

She offered her own explanation of what had happened. Her uncle, 'horrified' that the other two men were ready to abandon the engineer, swam back for him, then got stuck on the yacht with him. At that moment, the huge wave must have separated their 'souls from their bodies'. She concluded, 'I apologise to my family for causing them further suffering by writing this letter, but it had to be written.' If not, the dead men's families would 'spend the rest of their lives besieged by doubt as to whether they searched enough'.

If her letter wasn't sufficient to get the attention of Malta's newspaper readers, the next edition of the paper carried a statement from her about the accompanying *Circle* magazine. She had devoted that issue to Valletta, with a specially commissioned cover picture. But the *Circle*'s owner, who was responsible for its production, had made changes to the issue just before it went to print. A sponsored feature titled 'Gozo's Potential for Development' had been added, its import directly counter to my mother's editorial position on construction and the environment. And her political one: after her father's Malta Democratic

Party failed, my mother had switched her support to a new Green Party, founded by former Labour officials and environmental activists with the slogan 'Not on the right, not on the left, but forward'.

So my mother had insisted that the paper carry a statement in which she disassociated herself from that issue of the *Circle* and announced her resignation. She was only twenty-five years old, and she had just quit her first big journalism job. But she had a plan.

On a hot August day, too hot to go outside, my mother was stuck at home with the three of us. As we chucked toys around, she flicked through the newspapers.

Malta had been experiencing drastic change since 1987, but the papers were like her sons: overtly male and with nothing interesting to say. There were still no bylines, no probing interviews.

Why were no writers looking to annoy their readers, she wanted to know, 'because getting annoyed is crucial intellectual and emotional stimulation'? She knew that the culture of silence was a product of the fear of reprisal, the conservatism of Maltese culture, in which the expression of an unconventional opinion could be grounds for ostracism, and the country's smallness. Even her own friends reacted to her writing with an uneasiness that came from 'growing up, living from cradle to grave, surrounded by the exact same people' and 'so nobody does anything to upset anybody else'. But for her, the silence had grown intolerably suffocating, and to write felt more important to her than to be 'invited to a party'.

When she'd told a friend earlier that year that she wanted

to write about politicians, to criticise and expose them, her friend said that it would be too shocking for Malta. My mother countered that it was 'a perfectly normal thing to write, outside this little rock'.

'But you're living on this little rock,' her friend replied.

'Yes,' my mother said. 'It doesn't mean that this little rock is a special place and we have to be weird and we have to be different. We're calling ourselves European . . . so you can't say, "Ah, you can write that in England, you can write it in Rome, but you can't write it in Valletta."'

So, while we continued to chuck our toys around on that hot August day, she brought out my grandfather's old Smith Corona and hit one key after another. Never good with correction fluid, she had to retype and retype until she had finished three sample columns: on the desperate need for real news; on Freemasons, who were common in Maltese politics and the judiciary; and a mishmash on minor celebrities and construction in Sliema.

We had no fax machine, so she bundled us into her battered old Citroën and drove to the offices of the *Times*. There she left an envelope containing the columns, with a short note for Montanaro.

Then she took us to my father's office, hoping he'd provide her with some reassurance. She was nervous, he was busy, and we were fidgeting, so she took us back home. She picked up the newspapers again and told herself, nothing ventured, nothing gained. At least she had tried. We returned to our toys.

The next day, she decided she wanted an answer. She called Montanaro, 'my heart colliding with my stomach, preparing for outright rejection'.

'Of course I'm going to use them,' Montanaro said. 'They're exactly what I've been looking for.'

She told Montanaro that, aside from writing a regular column, she wanted to interview politicians. An ambitious young journalist: I know the type. She wanted to ask the questions that were never asked, but which people wanted answered. There was nothing in the newspaper, she said, that let people rate 'the things their politicians said and did, their hopes, their fears, their views. There was, in other words, no voice.'

'Very well,' Montanaro said.

'I was so thrilled,' she wrote, 'I almost began chucking toys around the room with the rest of them.'

On 12 August 1990, my mother's first column appeared in the *Sunday Times* of Malta. The newspaper, still not using bylines, headlined it 'THE GOOD, THE BAD, AND THE UGLY', a name my father, a spaghetti western fan, had suggested.

That column looks different to me now. In her optimism that Malta could change for the better, my mother criticised a *Newsweek* piece titled 'Lost in the Mediterranean – Malta seeks a place in the new Europe'. The piece had said that Malta was turning away from tourism and light manufacturing towards soft-touch finance. The piece was wrong, my mother wrote, when it argued that 'if one makes lots of money by unacceptable means, and one wishes to launder it, then Malta will open its arms'. It said that Libyans still commanded an important presence in the country and might work or buy property without visas, which my mother wrote was untrue. But her biggest issue with the piece was that it seemed to suggest that Malta wasn't ready for European Union membership. It put at risk what she had seen, since 1987, as a silver bullet for the country's failings.

Yet the *Newsweek* piece saw more than my mother. The problem wasn't just wealthy and corrupt Libyans. Many small, poor countries were learning they could scrape fees and create banking and legal work from people who wanted to hide their money. Money was already pouring in from former Soviet states. It was not yet clear to my mother how eagerly Malta would embrace the offshore model and what would happen when our colonial institutions met large, dirty financial inflows – not just to us, but to Europe too.

Still, she was a hit with readers from the start. They wrote in, asking who was behind the new column, egged on by clues she'd write into it, such as being born the year Malta became independent. Four Sundays later, she persuaded Montanaro to carry her byline. 'I say that anonymity is not to my liking,' she wrote, 'and I disapprove of people who hide behind a pen-name to attack the world.'

And there it was: Malta's first named independent columnist. And its first woman columnist: Daphne on Sunday. 'And this thing was a double shock,' my mother recalled. 'I used to have people actually telling me, "But does your husband write them for you? Does your father?"'

My mother would describe the situation as 'really crazy': their first named columnist was a woman, but there were no women on staff in the newsroom because the *Times* – the country's newspaper of record – didn't employ women, as a matter of policy. When my mother first asked Montanaro for a staff position rather than a freelance one, so that she could write more often, he said it wouldn't be safe to send a woman out to cover political rallies and crimes. She kept writing her column as a freelancer.

The letters pages would soon fill with comments. Many readers still wrote in anonymously, sheltering under 'Concerned Citizen'. 'Daphne represents the view of many Maltese who feel that Malta should, could, and deserves to be a better place to live in if only we could stop our individual spineless daily murmurings expecting others to do something about it and for once to do something about it themselves,' one wrote. 'May Daphne keep maturing through her writing and others through its impetus.'

Montanaro was privately harassed: Why do you let her write? Who is she, at the end of the day? Does she know what she's saying? He was too discreet to pass these comments on. My mother kept writing, while my brothers and I continued chucking our toys around outside her writing room.

Within eight months, for her interview slot that ran alongside her column, she landed the prime minister.

'In 1987, cynics said that a change in government did not necessarily mean an end to corruption, that it merely meant a change in the cast of characters who may be corruption-prone,' she prefaced her first question. 'Can you really say, with your hand on your heart, that there is no corruption within your government?'

'I think one can say that one can never eliminate corruption completely,' Fenech Adami replied.

The interview ran across three pages. It was the first time a named journalist in Malta had tried to hold a prime minister to account. She asked the questions no one had ever posed before: Why won't you declare donations to the party? Why are people given permits to develop green areas? Why are party officials allowed to dispense 'favours'? And finally: Why can't you control drug trafficking?

As an independent, English-language newspaper, the *Sunday Times* of Malta had no real competition, and it made good revenue: Lm1 million (£1.8 million) a year. But although it had come a long way, it was still far from what Malta's increasingly open-minded population was seeking.

In 1992, a group of wealthy Maltese businessmen saw an investment opportunity. They started planning a new English-language newspaper, the *Malta Independent on Sunday*, which would prioritise Maltese stories. They went to London to interview potential editors, but were disappointed.

They agreed that one of them, who owned a furniture company, would run the newspaper as its general manager and editor until the right person could be found. He began headhunting journalists in Malta. My mother was the first name on his list. He offered her a better salary than the one she received at the *Sunday Times* and said she could have the editorship in due course. My mother accepted and joined an editorial staff, along with four other people.

From the start, she had definite ideas about where the newspaper should go: more investigative work and personal scandal stories. This made the general manager anxious. 'Our relationship wasn't easy,' he told me. 'She was always with you three and used to work from home a lot. And then she'd come in, like a whirlwind, and change everything.'

There were missteps. She reported on staff disputes at

the state television broadcaster, Xandir Malta. One unnamed man, she wrote, had suffered a nervous break-down. A complaint against her was filed with the Malta Press Club, claiming that the unnamed man could be iden-tified by what she had written. The press club appointed a committee of three men, none of them journalists, to consider the complaint, and found my mother had breached its code of ethics. It asked my mother to respond in person and said she could bring a lawyer. 'I thought this particularly hilarious,' she wrote. 'I had no intention of justifying myself to the Press Club nor of appearing before its council, because I was not a member.'

The club said it claimed jurisdiction over 'all journalists' and warned as it published its finding against her that 'it could not allow its work to be obstructed'. My mother wrote that 'clubs may only assault their own members' and that she had 'absolutely no respect for a Press Club that operates in this way'.

She was right that there wasn't really anything the club could do about it and, in fact, nothing came of it. But the episode may have coloured the general manager's impres-sion of her. By this point, he was looking to step away from his editor role, as planned. My mother, who had joined as an associate editor, began pushing to replace him.

But the editorship went, in 1993, to a rising star from the *Times* of Malta. Before taking the job, he met my mother in a public garden to talk it through. Their mutual respect was, he told me, 'outstanding'. She said she'd back him up. But before their meeting, my mother had written a letter to the management of the *Independent* to support her own application to be the new editor, saying she'd back him 'completely' – and could work alongside him, perhaps as a co-editor, as 'the icing on the cake'. She had left her computer on, and someone found the letter. At the office, they started calling my mother 'the icing on the cake'.

Disappointed, and perhaps a little embarrassed, my mother returned to the *Sunday Times*. Her readers and sources followed.

Steve, my mother's first love, had joined the HM Customs & Excise Investigation Division team at Heathrow airport in London. He was investigating a Brazilian cocaine trafficking ring when, one day, a Maltese name jumped out at him. It was his old classmate, who'd evidently graduated from bringing drugs into school to bringing them into the country. And that boy's father, then a senior soldier, was now brigadier of the army – and so responsible for controlling trafficking at ports and the airport.

The Maltese was a peripheral player in the trafficking ring, which used a Brazilian coffee company as cover to bring cocaine from Rio de Janeiro through Heathrow and into Malta. The Maltese police had been following him. They noted how when he landed at Malta's airport he would either be collected from the runway in an official car or breeze through security, then staffed by soldiers.

In his interview with my mother, Fenech Adami had said that the country's drug problem was 'much larger than most people would like to admit' and linked it to 'the problem of a decline in moral values'. His solution was to 'upgrade moral values' and have a 'more efficient policing system'.

He made some progress on the second point. In 1993,

the year my mother moved back to the *Sunday Times* and took on some reporting duties, the police caught the trafficker's sister with a kilogram of cocaine. She told them the package belonged to her brother and he had given it to her at their brigadier father's house in Sliema, which the police raided. They arrested her brother, and he was later convicted of drug trafficking. The incident embarrassed the brigadier of the army, but not enough for him to resign.

This time, my mother used the prime minister's head of secretariat as a 'government source', who said the brigadier was embarrassing the government, that his family loyalties and official duties were in conflict, and that he should resign or be forced out.

At twenty-nine, my mother had her first major exposé. It ran on the front page of the *Sunday Times*, with her byline as a staff reporter. 'She had already cultivated a lot of sources,' her editor Laurence Grech, who had succeeded Montanaro, told me. 'I trusted her.'

The brigadier cited my mother's report in his resignation letter. 'I was deeply hurt and offended by that article,' he said. It was 'un-Christian-like and malicious'.

From his prison cell, his son, the drug trafficker, wrote letters to the *Malta Independent* advising my mother to seek 'professional counselling' for her 'mad cow disease' and plotted revenge on behalf of his father. His brother, once a close friend of my mother's, soon cut her off completely. My mother then overheard the trafficker's wife say at a bar, 'That bitch is gonna get it.' It was the first serious threat she had received. From then on, she said, she 'felt very terrorised. I felt as if somebody was coming for me.'

*

In a small country, you are never far from your enemies.

My brothers and I, aged eight, seven and six, attended the same school as the trafficker's nephews, sons of the sister who had been caught with the cocaine. My mother asked the headmaster to keep us under supervision on the playground, though she said nothing about it to us. We stopped using the school bus and she started doing the school run herself, and it was then that I first noticed her checking the underside of her car every morning. Still feeling uneasy, she took us out of school altogether and to a safe house in Gozo for a few days, telling us it was a holiday. 'I did not want to stay home,' she said of that time.

On the first anniversary of my mother's report, in December 1994, the prime minister's head of secretariat, my mother's source, survived a stabbing that missed an artery leading to his heart by millimetres. Arsonists looking for Dar Riħana ended up at a nearby house with a similar name, and set fire to a car parked outside. 'This was for you, Daphne,' our neighbour said.

Then someone slit the throat of our border collie, Messalina. We found the dog lying dead across our doorstep when my mother brought us home from school. She convinced us that Messalina had accidentally eaten snail poison, something that had happened with another dog.

Then, one night, our wooden front door went up in flames. My mother told us she had accidentally dropped a lit candle against it. My parents had a wall built around the front of the garden and put in a gate. They told us it was to stop our new dog from running out.

Our world began to close in just as Malta was opening up. And it was opening up not to what my mother had

imagined – public integrity and a sense of civic identity –
but to drugs and dirty money. The trees we used to climb,
the white-gravel hill we used to ride down, slowly took on
a new meaning. They were our borders and turrets, providing a view from our fort onto hostile country.

7

In 1994, seven years after the government restored the university's arts and humanities courses, my mother enrolled as a full-time student, as she continued to write and report.

Sometimes she left us boys in a theatre class for children on campus. Once she left us with a chemistry professor who sat the three of us in a row at a lab bench, froze a tomato with liquid nitrogen, and then smashed it to pieces with the single blow of a hammer. 'You see?' he told us. 'That's what happens.' But when we weren't in school ourselves, we were mostly in class with her.

Her fellow students were bemused by the sight of us in the lecture room. As one said, it 'only added to your mother's mystique'. She was already widely read, and her writing was loud, so the other students expected a know-it-all. They were surprised to discover that she was reserved and soft-spoken. Instead, it was her style that jumped out at them: the large earrings, the colourful clothes on her skinny frame, deeply tanned in summer. 'It just said,' another student told me, '"This is who I am."'

My mother wasn't keen on archaeological digs, but she used them as childcare. We dusted rocks, moved stones, sieved soil. I never found anything. Matthew once found a piece of Bronze Age pottery that was sent to the archaeological museum in Valletta. My mother struggled with

Latin, passing with the lowest possible mark, but otherwise she did well. She began a dissertation on the archaeologist Antonio Annetto Caruana, my father's great-grandfather, arguing he was a pioneer who made 'mistaken assumptions' and 'erroneous conclusions', an outsider whose methods of enquiry were unorthodox, but who was above all someone who cared about the country and who had 'drive, initiative, and will-power'. In 1996, she made the dean's list. That same year, her journalism almost came to a halt.

'One Saturday in 1996, your mother filed her piece very late,' Laurence Grech told me. 'We had a slight disagreement over it.'

The piece was about the deputy prime minister's daughter. A lawyer, she was defending the drug trafficker my mother had reported on two years earlier against the charge of attempted murder of my mother's source, the prime minister's head of secretariat. My mother wrote that the deputy prime minister's daughter taking the brief was 'appallingly insensitive' and that the case was a 'Pandora's Box of stinking sleaze'.

When her editor read the piece, he worried. The deputy prime minister was also a board member of the company that owned the *Times*. Grech called Anthony Montanaro, who advised him not to publish.

'It's libellous from beginning to end,' Grech told my mother. 'Let's just say you're away.'

My mother put down the phone and sent her column to the *Independent*. It agreed to carry the piece under the headline 'THIS IS NO NORMAL DEMOCRACY'. 'Our reading at the time was that the *Times* just didn't want to write about one of its board members,' the *Independent* newspaper's then acting editor told me.

When Grech found out what my mother had done, he sacked her. 'My pride was hurt, you know. I said to her, "Daphne, once you went to the *Independent* you can now stay there."' And so she did, for the rest of her life, despite the deputy prime minister's attempts to stop the newspaper from hiring her.

I walked into the living room to find my mother watching television. The broadcast was in Maltese. Before she could change the channel, I glimpsed the photograph of her that the *Sunday Times* used for her column. If her reporting on the drug trafficker and her columns had made her name, this episode made her a national story.

'What was that?' I asked.

'Nothing, Paul,' she replied. 'What do you want?'

The deputy prime minister, a small proud man, had convened a press conference to announce that my mother had been sacked from the *Sunday Times*, and to condemn her for what he described as multiple transgressions against his family. He had another concern: an upcoming general election that Labour looked set to win. The Nationalists had begun to feel my mother was on their side, although she hadn't yet voted for the party and was from a family that never did, and it was their sense of betrayal that drove the wider controversy surrounding this piece.

The deputy prime minister didn't pursue the matter any further, but his daughter did. She sued the *Independent* and, separately, my mother. She argued that as a lawyer she couldn't turn down a client, even a drug trafficker charged with the attempted murder of a senior official in her father's government, and that my mother's opinion of her work as sleazy was libellous. The judge ruled in the lawyer's favour. My mother was advised to appeal. But the application to appeal was delivered to the *Independent*'s office and wasn't passed on to her in time for her to lodge one. The judge's ruling stood.

It was the sacking, not the ruling, that marked my mother. 'It left her,' a colleague whose shoulder she cried on remembered, 'completely heartbroken.' The *Sunday Times* was the journalistic home she had fought so hard for, carving out a new role for herself there, a new kind of journalism. She was devastated.

'And because of this issue, I always felt vulnerable and I didn't like it at all, because, I said, "I'm supposed to be an opinion columnist, but at the same time, I can't write what I really think because I'm always conditioned by my employers,"' my mother said years later. 'And I was also aware of the fact that if ever they got angry for any reason or decided they needed to sack me or whatever, I would be left without anywhere to write.'

She aspired to true freedom of expression in a place that never allowed or even wanted it. When a Maltese patriot went to London in 1835 to campaign for a free press, he acknowledged that the country wanted only a partly free one. He felt absolute press freedom would degenerate into immorality and upset the Church, which had one of the two licenced presses in Malta. The other belonged to the colonial administration.

The secretary of state for the colonies supported the patriot more than he wanted, arguing Malta should be governed in 'the free, open, and confiding spirit' that Britain was, and so 'the censorship of the press should be abolished and without delay'. A royal commission visited the country and, while it privately thought the patriot just wanted to be bought by the government 'body and soul for two hundred pounds a year', it recommended abolishing its press censorship. The aged Duke of Wellington told Parliament that 'we might as well think of planting a free press in the foredeck of the Admiral's flagship'. He was ignored.

Malta's colonial governor ended press censorship in March 1839. It was earlier than many other countries, but it was hampered from the start. The colonial governor proclaimed a law of libel that was particularly sensitive to issues around Catholicism. Offenders would be tried by a court of three judges, without a jury, and face fines and imprisonment.

The first case arrived within six days of the law coming into force. The editor of a Protestant newspaper in Malta wrote that Catholicism was 'a system of religion the most detestable the world ever saw!' He was prosecuted, found guilty, and ordered to pay a big fine or spend six months in prison. He was imprisoned. In time, cases would be tried by a judge and a jury, then a single judge, and finally a magistrate. The magistrates would invoke the same conservative interpretations of libel during my mother's life, and the country would retain criminal penalties for libel until after her death.

So, Malta introduced weak press freedom when other countries had none and continued with it when those countries truly liberated journalism, falling further and further behind. At a time when my mother couldn't express a well-founded opinion on the deputy prime minister's place in a high-profile criminal case, the British press was reporting the intimate details of Prince Charles and Diana's divorce.

Looking back, it was never only about the law. The Maltese had been skittish about a truly free press, and they'd remain so. Malta still didn't really have a culture of free expression. And the press everywhere is always dependent on something: on law, money, its owners and, above all, on the surrounding culture.

The initial reason my mother lost her job at the *Sunday Times* was a conflict with its owners. But the real reason, she began to feel, was that Maltese culture placed no value on free expression. It was then that she developed the sharp edge that really made her controversial – and more widely read. She began expressing an impatience not just with the politicians but with the people too.

A new Labour leader, Alfred Sant, had taken over the party four years earlier and cleaned out its corrupt and violent Mintoffian elements without apologising for them. He modernised it, establishing its television and radio stations, but kept some of the old politics. Labour's anti-Westernism became his Euroscepticism.

He told his supporters that the EU restricted countries' progress by imposing the same rules on all member states.

He gave the example of value-added tax, which Malta had implemented as part of its accession to the EU that the Nationalists had formally begun in 1990. Six years on, in the lead-up to general elections, Sant told the electorate he would repeal VAT and, instead of making Malta an EU member state, would make the country a 'partner' to the EU and a 'Switzerland in the Mediterranean'. The EU's enlargement commissioner said no form of relationship other than membership was possible. The Labour leader said the commissioner should 'bite his tongue or I'll bite it for him'.

The electorate was splitting, as usual, almost perfectly. Labour supporters, under their new leader, were against EU membership. Nationalist supporters continued to be in favour of it. 'For heaven's sake,' my mother wrote, 'are we one nation or two tribes?' Her writing, though increasingly acerbic and popular, was in an English-language news-paper that most Labour supporters didn't read. It was also drowned out by the party's newspapers and its new radio and television stations. Through this media empire, the new leader kept pushing the line that a 'partnership' with the EU was possible and, in fact, better than membership.

My mother described Labour's campaign as a 'waking nightmare'. In one column, she asked: 'Has the Labour Party even bothered to apologise for screwing up much of our lives?' She warned the young: 'My generation of 18- and 19-year-olds was reduced to straggling around and begging, pulling strings or getting our parents to do so.' It was during this election campaign that she began support-ing the Nationalist Party, seeing it as the only force capable of keeping Labour out of power.

But Labour won a wafer-thin parliamentary majority. One of its MPs was Anġlu Farrugia, the police officer who had arrested my mother in 1984. Sant, now the prime minister, replaced VAT with a levy that would prove unworkable, but not before shopkeepers drove around smashing their VAT receipt-printing cash registers.

He then called for a study on the possibility of introducing divorce. Sant had ended his own marriage through an annulment about a decade earlier. My mother's editor at the *Independent*, the man who had beaten her to the job, received a tip that a court expert in the annulment proceedings found that Sant 'does not believe in marriage'. He used the quote as a headline for his report on the expert's finding. He wrote a leader to go along with it called 'Personal Agenda', arguing that Sant's views of marriage were in the public interest because of his plans to legalise divorce. It was a turning point in the Maltese media's treatment of public figures, in its focus on the personal, but it was not universally welcomed. The *Independent*'s board called it an invasion of privacy and warned the editor not to carry another story like it again.

A week later, he carried my mother's column on the issue. She wrote that she agreed with her editor's report 'fully' but felt readers were 'shortchanged'. The rest of the annulment proceedings revealed Sant's 'coldness and absolute absence of human feelings', showing up his claims that he was a 'modern and caring 1990s man who feels for women and the plight of wives'. Not for the first time, but for his last, the *Independent*'s board summoned the editor and asked him why he had 'let her write what she did'. He told them that 'with Daphne, you either carry the whole thing or nothing at all'. They kept my mother's weekly column, reasoning perhaps that she moved too many copies to dismiss, but replaced her editor with a Catholic priest who edited the Church's newspaper *Il-Ħajja* ('Life'). The new editor wrote that my mother's use of the annulment filings was 'sleaze', 'sick', and 'like peeping through keyholes, delving in wastepaper baskets'.

Sant's annulled marriage was to my father's first cousin, a left-wing academic. Once, after my father had been severely beaten by ten policemen while he tried to help his mother, this cousin's aunt, get away from a protest, she told him: 'If they come to arrest you tonight, call me and I'll make sure Alfred' – who was at the time president of the governing Labour Party – 'does something about it.' Her comment upset my father as much as my mother, but it wasn't until my mother wrote about the annulment that family relations broke down – or some of them, anyway. My father's extended family cut off my mother, but they remained friendly to him. My father found the situation amusing because, as he revealed to me, he had been her source for the annulment filings. And, he added, she always protected her sources.

My mother had bigger issues to write about. In his promise of a 'partnership' with the EU, Sant froze Malta's accession to the bloc. She felt the Labour Party was about to take Malta back to the isolated, anti-West days of her youth, and that the country was slipping further away from the democratic values she held so dear. She could only explain the move as the outcome of 'a vast army of ignorance, as always'.

The ignorance was encouraged by a young Labour

propagandist named Joseph Muscat. He followed Sant everywhere, so my mother called him the Poodle. He would become the prime minister himself. But back then, he was a young man living in an annexe to his parents' house in Burmarrad, about a kilometre away from us in Bidnija.

His mother was from one of the area's tenant-farming families. The Muscats were religious, and as a boy, Muscat had delivered the Sermon of the Child, a Maltese tradition in which a child preaches at midnight Mass on Christmas Eve. The farming families were usually politically conservative and voted for the Nationalist Party, but Muscat's father was a follower of Mintoff, and had raised his only child in that tradition. He also had a monopoly on the import and distribution of fireworks in Malta. In a country where each village and town has a patron saint, sometimes two, and each saint has an annual feast celebrated with fireworks, the business did well. It was successful enough to support Muscat's time at St Aloysius where donations, after Mintoff's policies had done away with school fees, were expected. As a schoolboy, Muscat was stout with a ginger mullet, so the other boys teased him. In the opinion of a former classmate, one of his bullies, 'it fed a latent, bubbling anger'.

But the Jesuits who ran the school liked him. Sent home to Burmarrad with a bus fare to pick up the vest he'd neglected to wear under his school shirt, and to return for detention, the punishment for the infringement, Muscat went to a friend's house two blocks away and asked his friend's mother for a vest. Back at school, the Brother who'd sent him home asked how he'd made it back so fast.

'When I told him the story, he told me, "Good for you, you used your head," and cancelled the detention,' Muscat would tell an interviewer.

He made a friend when a new boy joined the school for sixth form. Keith Schembri, from a poor harbour town near Valletta, was the only other known Labour supporter at the school. They started following each other around.

'We don't know why,' the former classmate said. 'Keith was a very, very nice, sweet guy. Very fat, but very funny.'

After sixth form, Muscat went to the university to study public policy. He wrote a dissertation about how anonymous donations enabled private interests to take hold of a political party and, if that party was elected, the country. He framed it as an argument for state funding of political parties, but in a few years he and Schembri would use it as a game plan.

Schembri postponed his plans to study law at the university and went to work for the Labour Party's television station instead. While he was there, he convinced his station manager to hire his old sixth-form friend. Muscat began appearing on Labour television shows, becoming a face – with glaring eyes like marbles pressed into the flesh – and working his way up in the party. As a politician, he characterised his family's business as 'an artisan micro-enterprise'.

At a big Labour meeting in March 1995, a young woman named Michelle Tanti spotted him. They had met before, but Muscat had cut her off because he thought she was involved with someone and he didn't want to waste time on her. Now, however, Tanti was Sant's personal assistant and public relations officer, a job she performed loyally.

And this time when she encountered Muscat again, they chatted for hours. A relationship blossomed. Muscat became Sant's main public relations man, and Tanti became his wife. They were on their way, a power couple.

The Labour Party commissioned Muscat to write a book for its publishing arm about a piece of public land in Gozo that had been given to a man linked to the Italian Mafia. Using metaphors of octopuses, spiders and cobwebs, with colour illustrations, the Poodle connected the mafioso to many different people. One was my mother.

She sued him and the party for libel. My father argued her case. 'Let me tell you,' he said to me, 'it is not easy representing your wife. As a client she was a nightmare and had to be dragged to court to give evidence – *in her own case.*' But she was over the moon when they won.

The judge found that Muscat had attached my mother to his octopus because of his 'animus' towards her. 'She has every right to criticise the Labour Party,' he ruled. 'This is the basis of democracy.' He awarded damages. Muscat paid promptly, and my mother spent some of the award on an expensive pen for my father, but the party did not. The court had to send bailiffs to its headquarters. It wasn't in good shape.

In 1998, the year Labour published Muscat's book, Mintoff, now a backbencher, expressed his intention to go against the government on a crucial vote because he did not like its plans to develop a marina near his home town. The Nationalists caught wind of this and wanted to trigger a loss-of-confidence vote and call a snap election. They were one MP short, though. The MP they needed – whose nickname was 'Johnny Cash' – was in Libya on unexplained business. So the Nationalist leader, still Eddie Fenech Adami, organised a private jet to bring him back in time for the vote. The Nationalists went on to win the snap election.

The private jet had been provided by Tumas Fenech, a man from a different Malta to my family's but whose legacy would bleed into ours.

Born in 1930 to a working-class family, Tumas left school early and began wheeling and dealing in property. He would send men to intimidate farmers into selling their plots. He acquired permits to develop the plots, selling them at a premium. And then, as there was no land registry, an oversight in the country's post-independence nation-building, he redrew the plot boundaries, selling the same land to different people. 'His brain,' a former Labour finance minister said, 'was a computer.'

Tumas acquired a 150-year lease on thirty-one acres of public land to rebuild the Hilton hotel that had been there since the 1960s. The lease agreement restricted the coastal land's use to tourism. Tumas immediately sought alterations – a marina with a concrete breakwater, a business tower, apartments – and got them from the government, thanks to a series of manipulations. There were dozens of meetings with planning officials, and minutes for none of them. There was a public hearing Tumas packed with his employees, where residents who'd turned out to speak and listen were treated, one remembered, like 'shit' and 'idiots'. There was the fax Tumas's son and chief executive, George Fenech, sent to the official in charge of major projects – 'I gladly enclose a donation of Lm2000 for the Hospice

Movement which is so close to your heart' – that had pre-
ceded an approval decision by a few weeks in 1998.

Construction started immediately, but Tumas died a
year later. In his obituary he was remembered as a 'self-
made millionaire' and 'a leading personality in the business
scene'. His family founded the Tumas Fenech Foundation
for Education in Journalism as one memorial, and named
the development after him – Portomaso, meaning 'port of
Tumas' – as another.

His son took over his enterprises. George was, one
planning official remembers, 'someone you would not
want to cross'. He chaired the horse racing club at Marsa,
a working-class town on the Grand Harbour, and his roulette number was 17 black – something everyone seemed
to know. When George in turn developed end-stage renal
failure, it was the elder of his two sons, Franco, who was
the candidate kidney donor. But Franco, a cocaine and
gambling addict and amateur boxer known as Tornado,
vaporised. The donated kidney came instead from the
spare brother, Yorgen. 'He was a very low-key operator,' a
schoolmate told me. 'You never felt his presence.' One of
their teachers described him as 'just a facade'.

At a school drama evening, this Fenech had given a
speech about his idol, Silvio Berlusconi, whom he found
fascinating not only for his wealth and popularity but for
his political power. 'Being what he is,' Yorgen Fenech said,
'one expected him to be involved in the political scandals
and corruption, but Berlusconi's business dealings were
always clean.'

The lesson that corruption and political scandal must

come with an appearance of clean business dealings was learnt. Now, with his father weakened and his brother missing, he could put it into practice. He had already made friends with Keith Schembri – 'There was chemistry,' Labour's budding power broker remembered – and, while still a university student, he began climbing his way up the Tumas Group, trying to prove himself to his father.

He worked in the Portomaso tower, which opened in 2001. With twenty-three floors, reaching ninety-eight metres high, it was Malta's first high-rise building. Many liked the idea of a glassy tower. It seemed to say the country was modernising. My mother, wanting to believe that it was, agreed.

'The Portomaso tower turned out to be stunning, with graceful and elegant lines,' she wrote. 'Way back when the Hilton project was at the planning permission stage, I seemed to be the only person on the beach who wasn't ranting on against it.'

The Fenechs' next major alteration to Malta's coastline wouldn't beguile her in the same way. She would come to see it for what it really was – a monument to corruption – and she would then be one of the few people ranting against it.

The beach my mother mentioned was part of a club in St Julian's. It made a change from the quiet beaches we used to go to along the north-west coast, where the sea had eaten through the softer limestone and clays, exposing headlands that separated three beaches of golden sand. My favourite one was the beach at Għajn Tuffieħa where my grandparents used to take my mother and her sisters. I felt drawn to it as if by some need.

There is a hillside behind the beach covered in golden samphire, tamarisk and wild thyme. Rain bleeds clay out of the hillside and cuts smooth grey veins into the sand. The sun sets directly ahead and the currents pull out. Waves rise in crest after ascending crest, breaking then crumbling as they flood the bay with blue.

My mother would stay on her towel and read while my father swam out to an orange buoy, turned onto his back, and like a hairy whale blew water out of his mouth.

The beach had been empty when we'd started going there, back in the early 1990s. The clay hills, the hundreds of subsiding concrete steps, and the irregular bus service kept people away. But not for long. First came the hippies with their bongos and moon crystals. Later, tourists and students who came to Malta to learn English started arriving on coaches. Concrete was put down and a kiosk went up. Parasols and sunbeds were offered. By then, we had started going to the beach club in St Julian's.

There, my mother would claim a sunbed and read through a stack of newspapers and magazines or a novel. Meanwhile, my brothers and I, now aged about eleven to thirteen, would swim out, heading east along the coast. Just before the coast turned to make Sliema visible lay the Portomaso construction site. Each time we swam out we saw it closer to completion.

On one outing, we saw that the concrete breakwater, to protect the expensive yachts that would moor there, had been finished. We swam out and climbed onto it, short of breath and with throbbing muscles. As we rested in the sun, the seawater evaporated, leaving salt crystals you could lick off your shoulders. The sea ahead of us could have been the same fabric as the sky, but for the ripples on the water catching the sunlight. It swayed this way and that, each shining crest fading, emerging like things that were going to happen to us.

8

School was close enough to our house in Bidnija that at this age my brothers and I could skive off and walk home through the tal-Ħżejjen valley. Our uniforms came with black leather shoes that grew heavy trudging through the valley mud in winter and, as summer approached, added to the heat under our black blazers. For years, our world was limited to this patch.

There was something about our life there that removed us from all the usual games and everyday detail – the grocers, butchers, churches and restaurants where everyone we knew went. We had different reference points, and that weakened the pressure, so strong in a small country, to assimilate.

The school was liberal by Maltese standards. My friends there were the children of my parents' friends, part of a group of families linked back over generations. A plump curly-haired boy in my class would one day be my best man. A freckled dark-eyed girl two years below me would become my wife. It was our world, and a closed one: pupils who did not join at the start, aged four, never properly integrated. There were few foreign students – none at all in most grades – and only a handful of pupils spoke Maltese. And liberal as it was, it was still Catholic. We had Mass, religion lessons, and a big day at age eight when children, considered to have reached the age of reason, received their First Communion and for the first time were given the Host by a priest.

My mother did not want to send me to school that day. Like my father, she believed in 'a God' but her convent school had put her off the Church. She rejected the blind devotion of many Maltese, 'moving as they do from home to church like hamster from feeding-bowl to treadmill'. A growing number of people had stopped attending Mass by this point, a trend my mother found 'alarming because the moral code of us Maltese has so far been embedded in our religion'. The Catholic rituals that did persist were to her evidence that 'our religious beliefs are often not beliefs at all, but heathen superstition rooted in cultish practices'. Holy Communion day at school felt that way to me and, while my mother didn't want me to go, she didn't want me to feel left out either.

All my friends, who unlike me were sent to weekly catechism lessons, were going. I wanted to spend the day at home on the PlayStation with my brothers, but that was not on offer. My mother sent me in a T-shirt, shorts and flip-flops.

Everyone else in my grade showed up that day dressed in traditional lacy white dresses or suits.

'Why did your mother send you in flip-flops?' a friend asked.

'I don't know,' I answered. 'Why did yours put you in a white tuxedo?'

All along, school had felt like a formality to me. What people did after school seemed to be independent of how they did at school. If their fathers were lawyers, they became lawyers. If their fathers ran a family business, they joined it. Few of my friends' mothers worked.

My report cards reflected my attitude. One described me, at age nine or so, as a 'class clown' who was 'always distracting others'. Another criticised me for swearing, something my headmaster thought I had learnt from my brothers until I told him that I picked it up from my parents.

'I'm fed up with everyone telling me how terrible Paul is,' I overheard my mother tell my father after one parents' day. 'You can start going, if you want.'

He did not. Instead, in my final year of secondary school in 2004, my mother came into my room for a pep talk. 'Paul, look, don't worry about your marks. When you leave, you can find a job with my friend – he set up a company that tracks delivery trucks.' I was fifteen, and for the first time I resolved to take control of my life. My mother later claimed it was a piece of reverse psychology. Either way, I passed my O levels that summer.

My parents lit a bonfire in the garden when my results came in. My mother asked me to bring out all my textbooks, so that we could throw them onto the flames. There was something pagan and wonderful about watching the embers rise and dance. My grades were not even that good – though good enough for my next stop, St Aloysius sixth form – but it was my mother who was really celebrating.

In a 2003 referendum, Malta had finally voted to join the EU. The result – 53.6 per cent in favour of membership – was confirmed when the Nationalists, still in government, won a general election five weeks later.

The Labour leader, still the Eurosceptic Alfred Sant, had fought bitterly against membership in the referendum and the general elections. His young propagandist Joseph Muscat – the Poodle – had presented a television show on the Labour Party's station called *Made in Brussels*, in which he told people to vote against membership, abstain or scribble over their ballot papers. In his columns for the party's newspaper, he used diagrams to show people how this could be done. When speaking to foreign journalists, Muscat attempted something more sophisticated. He told them that a small country like Malta 'really doesn't have any type of voice' in the EU, and that membership 'would lead to an erosion of competitiveness'.

For my mother, the Labour Party's campaign against EU membership during the referendum was the final straw. The party hadn't only failed to redeem itself for the violence and corruption it incited in her youth; it hadn't only frozen the country's accession in her adulthood; it was now, at the final hurdle, trying to stop Malta from leaving that ugliness behind forever.

EU membership, she thought, would draw a line under Malta's embarrassing international relations. It would end talk of becoming 'Switzerland in the Mediterranean' or episodes like the Maltese passport being coloured green in homage to Gaddafi, who for years gave financial aid and military support to Mintoff's government to weaken Malta's ties to the West. It would limit the control of Maltese politicians. It would offer her children the opportunities that had been denied to her.

She joined a referendum campaign group called Iva, which in Maltese means yes, with the mission of advising its members to focus on what membership would mean for the nation's children. In jingles and on billboards, Iva urged people to vote 'yes, for our children'. When the referendum passed, she told her readers, 'We're free at last, and free forever.'

'Boys,' she told us, 'you don't know how lucky you are.'

I remember the months that followed with a clarity that I do not have for other years. There was more colour. Import tariffs kept coming down, more products appeared on shelves, more clothes on racks. As a stamp of good housekeeping, EU membership attracted more foreign money. Travel became easier and cheaper.

But the deeper change – a transition to a true liberal democracy based on secular rather than Catholic ethics, on a civic identity rather than a partisan one – never arrived. The EU opened up the opportunity for this, but something else happened. It showed us that we didn't need to change; that we could be the same Malta, divided and corrupt, without any real consequences from Brussels, yet now with access to a global market.

The *Newsweek* piece my mother had criticised in her first *Sunday Times* column for being too pessimistic – that post-1987 Malta wasn't really reforming but only opening up to dirty money – had undercooked its own argument. EU membership turned the country from an isolated offshore haven into a back door to a much bigger, more respectable market. And as more money washed through Malta, the EU's smallest member state, it would slowly undermine the entire bloc's integrity.

In Europe, we saw little more than a moneymaking opportunity. The young politicians like Muscat and the new oligarchs like Yorgen Fenech saw the opportunity more clearly than most. And my mother saw that 'the way we look at life, or do not look at it' was a growing problem. 'We are becoming more and more shallow, more and more frivolous, less and less concerned with permanence, more and more self-involved.'

It was a grasping materialism I recognised when in 2005, halfway through sixth form, I took a summer job with some friends to earn money to go to more raves on beaches and in abandoned British barracks. The job paid Lm1.95 (£3.10) an hour and was close to my mother's delivery-truck prediction for me: delivering a Yellow Pages directory containing the contact details of every business to every household in Malta. It showed me the country as I had not seen it before.

We would meet every morning at the Yellow Pages warehouse in Marsa. Its limestone walls were stained black by exhaust fumes coming off the road into Valletta. My father would drop me there on his way into the city, early enough for him to miss the morning traffic, too early for my shift.

I would find myself sitting outside the warehouse, waiting for the others to turn up, feeling the sun heating up, and thinking: What a way to spend my summer. For the first time since school, I was back in uniform, a yellow, paper-thin cotton T-shirt with a Yellow Pages logo on the front, khaki shorts and running shoes. Alongside other teams of workers, we ran with books – 192,912 in all – from the warehouse to our vans, loading and stacking. The van's refrigerator box in the back was our cargo space. Too young to drive, two of us would sit alongside a driver, with another two in the cargo box. The books slid and slammed against one side then the other as the van turned, and those in the back would make a game of dodging them.

At van stops we would jump down onto the street, grab a stack of books and go out into the dust and heat and blaring car horns, knocking on doors, asking whether people wanted a copy. It was mostly women who answered, some old, some young. Some washing their front doors and their patch of pavement outside, some just waiting, holding their old directory. Around a third of women worked outside the home in Malta – by far the lowest rate in the EU.

We took their old copies – 60,482 in all – for recycling at the warehouse, so our arms were never empty. I can still feel the weight of those books. The crisp spines bruised our forearms; the plastic strapping around every four new copies cut our hands.

We grew unruly, and so did our deliveries. People called the Yellow Pages office to complain that we were flinging directories out of the back of the van as we drove past their front doors. 'That's not nice,' our manager said. 'Not nice.'

We took greater care. The books contained the familiar Maltese names, the hundred or so different surnames that cover three-quarters of the population. They contained the double-barrelled variations where a wife's surname is tacked on to her husband's to introduce some degree of difference, or to signal something more special, the introduction of a foreign-sounding surname, for example, as Anton Caruana had done with Galizia. And the books contained all those addresses and places we thought we knew, but each day discovered we did not.

The villages and towns we visited in our daily delivery schedules had until then been abstractions. No friends or family lived here. None of the bars or restaurants we went to were here. To teenagers from Malta's anglicised community centred on Sliema, a fraction of a fractured population who lived in relative comfort, this was a different Malta, a new country altogether.

We found unmapped alleys of one-storey buildings. I remember one in Żejtun, a southern town whose name means olive. It was a simple windowless building meant to house a car. Inside was an iron-frame bed and worn mattress, a wooden chest of drawers and a broken full-length mirror, a man washing himself with a piece of cloth he dipped in a tin bathtub, and a horse tied to the galvanised door. I asked, like an idiot, if he wanted a directory.

'*Ma naqrax*,' he mumbled. I do not read.

But he took a copy anyway. One man said he could not read and did not have a phone, and he still took four copies from my arms. He winked at me and told me he would find something to do with them.

It had taken me sixteen years in Malta to see it: the squalor, the desperation to leave. It had taken a delivery job one summer to get me a bit further along the coast, to see that you could go from a harbour area as deprived as Marsa, with its decaying shipyards and criminal gangs, to one as affluent as Portomaso, with its yacht marina and oligarchs, almost before you could finish a cigarette.

Apart from their clothes, the people looked the same – were the same – but they were unknown to one another. The people who lived in squalor, who had no phone or who could not read, were living alongside the Malta that aspired to be liberal and modern. But the first test of the country's values had revealed that, even among the second group, becoming European was only about becoming richer, faster. The country's aspirations were only territorial.

Malta became one of the EU's closest points to North Africa and, for some, a mirage of hope.

Asylum seekers began arriving in greater numbers, in rubber dinghies or old wooden fishing boats. Most were from Somalia and Eritrea, having worked their way through the Sahara in order to leave from Libya. Sometimes their boats capsized, drowning their passengers. Sometimes Italy and Malta argued over whose waters the boats were in until they sank.

The response to the refugees sparked conflicts within Malta. The country kept them in a detention centre in Marsa, but people lived uneasily with the arrangement. Many felt the centre degraded the surrounding town. One idea was to deport them. It had been done with some Eritreans, who were tortured after their return home, but, my mother observed, to most Maltese, 'Black people don't count. They count even less than Arabs. So here in Malta we have a shocked minority, in which I count myself, and a complacent majority.'

Another option, which became popular, was to tow the asylum seekers out of Maltese waters and leave them there. Then Malta would not need the Marsa detention centre. Next was the idea to shoot them before they entered Maltese waters. It was promoted by a new party called Imperium Europa, whose logo was a lightning bolt on a shield.

It was fascist pantomime, playing out in Malta in 2006. My mother described the party's leader as 'evil' and the party itself as a 'hideous Nazi group that advocates violence, murder and racism', saying that it was 'promoting a culture of violence in a country that has been peaceful for almost 20 years'.

Its supporters disagreed. They painted, in thick black brushstrokes, *DAPHNE SUCKS* on the left side of a wall split by the Bidnija road and *BLACK COCK* on the right. My mother saw the graffiti when she was bringing me home one day from sixth form. We looked at each other momentarily – me revolted, she humiliated – as she kept driving to the house. Inside, she made me lunch, picked up a bucket of paint and a brush, and drove back down the road to paint over it before my brothers, then both at university, saw it. I can still see her brushstrokes every time I drive up the road.

A week or so later our dog, a fox terrier we called Emilio, disappeared. Soon after, a group of people crawled up the valley behind our house one night, walked along the flagstone path through the garden, and stacked five car tyres and plastic bottles filled with petrol against a door that opened into our living room. They set the tyres alight and slipped back into the valley.

It was a Saturday night. I had been out late with friends and came home at 2.30 a.m. to see a large fire burning at the back of the house. Strange time for a bonfire, I thought. But the smoke looked heavy and smelt like rubber and I could hear windowpanes cracking in the heat as I came closer.

The house was on fire, and my parents were asleep inside. I ran in and woke them up. While my father rushed for the garden hose, I grabbed a shovel from his work-room and began throwing soil onto the fire. Inside, my mother moved the rugs and furniture far from the door, and phoned the police.

By the time they arrived, Matthew had woken – in our panic, we had forgotten he was asleep in his bedroom. The fire was out and we saw that it had not yet burnt through another stack of tyres, filled with more bottles of petrol, placed closer to my bedroom.

Some of the petrol seeped that night into the soil around the mock orange tree that grew right outside my bedroom. In the coming months and years, the tree began forcing a hard, black bulbous matter out of its pores, through the bark that had burnt in the fire. I used to chip it off with a rock and watched how, over time, the tree produced a new bark that wrapped itself like armour around the old until the whole tree had renewed itself. The mock orange grew tall enough to block our best view of the valley from a living room upstairs. My parents refused to cut it down or prune it. It was a kind of talisman, but not one they relied on to protect us. They had a wall built along the northern edge of the garden, joining it to the wall and gate at the southern edge they had built over a decade earlier. The house and surrounding garden were now enclosed. We lived in a compound.

At St Aloysius, my sixth-form college, people told me that it was irresponsible of my mother to have let me stay out so late. This was when I recognised that she was not the problem.

9

There were other attempts to stop my mother from writing that ran alongside the arson attacks, lawsuits and dog poisonings.

The *Independent*'s directors were sometimes offered increased advertising revenue from government agencies and businessmen in exchange for sacking or taming her. She knew the newspaper's owners 'always have to walk a tightrope' and must have asked themselves, 'How much are we getting in because of her, and how much are we losing because of her?'

They were difficult calculations, because she was the kind of journalist people bought the paper for and already a household name. But it was this very power and influence she'd amassed that brought the newspaper under pressure. And so once again the fear of being 'left without anywhere to write', as she had said after her sacking from the *Times*, reared its head.

'And then this miracle called the Internet happened,' she remembered, 'and I said, "Okay, I'll use that as a fallback." And this is how my blog, in a way, started.'

By 2008, the miracle of the Internet was more than a decade old. The Nationalists were still in power but had an unstable majority when the prime minister called a general election for that year. He promoted his record of strong economic growth. The Labour leader Alfred Sant campaigned on a platform of greater independence from the EU and cleaning up petty corruption.

My mother was sceptical on both points. She looked at Sant's stance on the EU with 'dire trepidation' and remembered how accommodating of corruption he had been in the mid-1980s, when he had been president of the Labour Party. Her writing had become increasingly focused on him, from his political hypocrisy to his 'wigs of fluctuating colour intensity and design'.

I was halfway through my undergraduate degree at the university in January that year when a group of students organised a debate on campus between the leaders of the Labour, Nationalist and Green parties, and a fringe right-wing group. It was the first debate of its kind in Malta, and I went along with my mother. The theatre was packed. The university's student body was still mainly middle class and Nationalist, young and pro-EU, so there was booing and jeering at the Labour leader. One of his television crews was there, and they began shoving their cameras in my mother's face. She ignored them, but I did not. I turned to one of the cameramen and said, 'Fuck off.' They retreated, and I felt successful.

By the time we got home, Labour's television station was broadcasting rolling footage of me. The clip was on their evening news, on their television chat shows, on their radio programmes. When my father came home from work, he asked me why my vocabulary was so limited. My mother received a call the following morning from the police, telling her they had information of a bomb threat against us.

The best defence is offence, my mother thought, but

her now twice-weekly columns for the *Independent* were not enough firepower. So she began posting article-length comments under other people's blog posts and under newspaper articles online. Still not enough.

So one day that March, a week before the election, she asked Matthew to set up a blog of her own which she would write alongside her *Independent* columns.

From a young age, Matthew had developed an interest in software engineering. He would write games with characters made of punctuation marks, save them onto floppy disks and sell them at school fairs. In time, his coding had developed to a level where he felt he did not need to keep studying. His computer skills seemed to sit strangely with the rest of him. He was always the wildest brother, always pushing Andrew and me to ride our bicycles faster, to sail further out, to climb cliffs higher and higher, and then jump off them into the sea. At school, he was in trouble often: for not doing his work, for graffiti, for talking back to teachers and for smoking. His grades oscillated between very poor and very good. One of his school report cards described him as an 'enigma' – 'like the code-breaking machine', our father told him. My mother worried and felt that she had to keep him on the straight and narrow. Matthew had attended university in Malta reluctantly and, at my mother's insistence, to study international relations and anthropology. When he was about to drop out, she pushed him back in, telling him that people were now applying the software engineering skills he had to journalism.

When my mother asked him to set up her blog, he cancelled his plans for the day and installed WordPress on a server in her office.

'You need an easy name for it,' he told her. 'Maybe DCG.com.'

'No,' she replied. 'Make it DaphneCaruanaGalizia.com.'

She called the blog 'Running Commentary: Daphne Caruana Galizia's Notebook'. Matthew showed her how to use the interface, how to upload a blog post and comments. That same night she sat down to write her first post. She uploaded it on Sunday 2 March 2008, at 2.02 a.m. Malta time. It was a stinging diatribe more than 3,700 words long, headlined 'ZERO TOLERANCE FOR CORRUPTION'. It took aim at Sant's claim to be a force against corruption, but above all, it framed the upcoming election as a contest of personalities. Drawing inspiration from the novelists she treasured, my mother thought a study in character would yield results.

She described the Greens and their leader as 'a cult', made fun of the 'golden-grey streaks and highlights' in the Labour leader's wig, and observed that the 'awful' far-right leader with his 'yellow fleeces and pink shirts' added to the 'carnivalesque' atmosphere. 'Next to this lot of rival party leaders,' she wrote, the leader of the Nationalists 'looks reassuringly sane. I think I'll vote for him.' In her second blog post, 'Amorality', she described Sant as a 'snake', 'sneak', 'coward', and 'not much of a man'.

By the time voting day came around six days later, her blog had received 120,000 visits, equivalent to 40 per cent of the votes cast. On polling day itself, her blog received more than a thousand comments. It was a greater share than any one newspaper website or blog. It was a greater share than most of them combined. The blog became a vital news source that day. The mainstream news sites were publishing only official announcements, as the vote count progressed. My mother's sources, meanwhile, told her that the widely expected Labour victory was slipping away. She called it.

Sant lost his third and final general election. The Greens did not get a seat and the Nationalists won, for the first time in recent history, a relative majority – less than half of all the votes cast, but still 1,580 more votes than Labour. It governed with thirty-five seats to Labour's thirty-four. Malta's first Internet election had at least one clear winner.

The Poodle had been using the Internet for a few years by the time my mother launched her blog. Maltastar was the Labour Party's first English-language news site. It targeted young, university students and white-collar workers. Muscat had told an interviewer that these were people who did not 'accept a statement just because Labour said it'.

It was a part of society that the Poodle was discovering through his 'real job' at an investment firm. 'I have this theory that you can always tell what a person's line of work is by the way he dresses over the weekend,' he said. 'If he's all dressed up for a simple meal at a restaurant it must mean that he doesn't have to put up with suits and ties during the week. On the other hand, I've seen a very rich man wearing a tracksuit in a smart restaurant. That incident must prove my theory right. I take every opportunity I can to dress casual.' The investment firm was owned by a financial adviser to the Labour Party, and after Muscat had spent his afternoons working there, the evenings brought 'party time. Party as in political party, I mean.'

Labour had asked him to stand as a candidate before, but more theorising got in the way. 'I have another theory, that to stand for the general elections you must be either a robber, a missionary or just plain crazy,' he said. 'I don't think I'm any of these.'

He wasn't a missionary or plain crazy when in 2004 he put himself forward as one of Malta's first candidates for election to the European Parliament, a legislative body comprised of members from each EU state. Campaigning on his close ties to the Labour Party leader and as someone who knew the EU, thanks to his 'Made in Brussels' television episodes, the Poodle was elected.

He joined the committee of MEPs that regulates financial services and drafted a response to the EU's proposed anti-money laundering law. 'The fight against money laundering and terrorist financing,' he wrote, 'should remain a top political priority.' His written response shows what he learnt. Financial crime flourishes when anti-money laundering authorities don't have 'adequate resources', when the uneven implementation of laws across member states creates 'loopholes', and when public officials, 'particularly those coming from countries where corruption is widespread', aren't subjected to greater due diligence.

He was called to present his response in the European Parliament. Half a minute into his speech, he realised there were no Maltese interpreters present. He pulled back from the microphone, raised his right hand in disbelief, and switched from Maltese to English to say: 'We get not even to speak our language in plenary! What the hell!' Some MEPs giggled. The president tried to apologise for the lack of interpreters. Muscat's tone became angrier and his lower lip quivered, as he called on the president to take 'necessary action'. Other MEPs, from the conservative and right-wing groups in Parliament, clapped as Muscat said, 'You either give us really our language or thank you and goodbye.' It was just the kind of populism that appealed to the Labour Party's predominantly Maltese-speaking, Eurosceptic base.

The chamber was finally rid of Muscat when Labour anointed him leader after the 2008 election. Unfortunately, this brought him back home, where he would put his newly acquired knowledge of financial crime to use.

Andrew had gone to university in Malta, but the desire to leave ran as strong in him as it had in our mother. He'd studied the same subjects as Matthew with a view to using them as preparation for a career in diplomacy. The way countries dealt with one another interested him, and the tact it required suited him.

His sometimes infuriating calmness made him a more patient and attentive listener than Matthew or me. It made him a bigger believer in meetings and discussion. Perhaps it came from his having to broker peace between us so many times, from having always to see it both this way and that way. Unlike Matthew and me, Andrew had rarely been in trouble in school. His shirt was always tucked in, his shoes and blazer clean, his tie in a good, simple knot. In this respect, in the rules around formality and convention, he was most like our father who, having failed to convince his sons to become lawyers, could adjust to the idea of having one diplomat.

Our mother was less keen. She knew that working as a

civil servant would put Andrew at the mercy of the governments she criticised. But she held her tongue, not
wanting her own work to interfere with his plans.

Both of my brothers left Malta around the same time.
Andrew took a position at the European Parliament, and
Matthew had heeded our mother's advice and gone to
study journalism in London. I could not imagine living in
the country without them, but I did not have a clear idea
of where to go or what to do. Writing was the only work I
enjoyed. But I did not want to fall in my mother's shadow,
and besides, Matthew was already on that path. So when I
left to join him in London a couple of years later, I wanted
to find something else.

It was 2009, and I was twenty years old. As a boy from
the Maltese countryside, I was fascinated by London. I liked
everything about it that was not like Malta. It was a haven: I
liked that the air was cooler, the parks greener. I liked that
I did not bump into everyone and their cousin when I went
out. I liked that I could follow the news with detachment,
that I wasn't grouped into one tribe or another, that the columnists were more outspoken and yet less abused than my
mother. I liked that the politics seemed boring.

Perhaps I liked it too much. I developed a sense that
many of these qualities weren't appreciated by Britons
themselves. Back then they seemed to have no experience
of life in a country where the politics was visceral and
everything was personal. They seemed to take their democracy for granted. Nor did they pay much attention to the
money from crooked regimes all over the world that was
swirling around. And it's perhaps for these reasons that its
politics would soon change dramatically.

The friends I made there couldn't understand why I found London so liberating. But then, I never talked about Malta. When my mother called me, we spoke only briefly about her work. I remember her gasping in disbelief when Muscat gave a public lecture on media ethics at the Tumas Fenech Foundation for Education in Journalism – 'like a talk on human rights by Robert Mugabe'. She devoted many columns to the Poodle's attempts, as the new head of Labour, to rebrand himself as a moderniser. I remember her feeling exasperated by the Nationalist government's infighting.

She was more interested in what was happening in London, somewhere she had always wanted to live. She lived vicariously through my stories of the simplest things: the restaurants and concerts I went to; the work I did, briefly as an analyst for Facebook and then as an economist at an investment fund; the people I met. When she visited, we went out: to eat, for drinks, and to public lectures. She would spend hours at markets and shops, soaking it all in.

I sometimes found her visits tiresome. I was young and in a hurry. It felt like the world was on offer and my time in Malta had been wasted. I could now do all the things I wanted to. My mother, I would discover later, felt similarly. 'One of the wonders for me when leaving Malta is knowing what normal life is like,' she said in the interview ten days before her murder, 'because I can be invisible, I can go where I like, without people staring or nudging, or whatever.'

She emphasised: 'I've been at it since I was twenty-five and experience hardens you and it just becomes your way of life. I *literally* know no other way of life.'

*

Things worsened for my mother in Malta after she started her blog. She was posting more frequently about what she called 'the freak show of Maltese public life', drawing ever greater numbers of readers and also an intensifying stream of online abuse. Just as my mother had discovered the 'miracle of the Internet' as a source of power, so had others.

Thousands, tens of thousands, of online trolls replaced the ranting phone calls to our house and the envelopes filled with shit. The trolls called for her to burn in hell. They shared memes of her as a witch, a characterisation long promoted by Labour. Sometimes she was depicted as an obese witch. Sometimes with green skin, sometimes with a hooked nose and broomstick. She was never depicted as she was: a human being.

One meme depicted her with satanic horns on her own funeral memorial card. 'With great happiness we welcome the death of Daphnie Caruana Galizia, known as the witch of Bidnija,' the meme read, 'who leaves to mourn her loss no one.'

Anonymous blogs went up, accusing her of being a lesbian or a transvestite. People wrote murder and rape fantasies about her. There were so many of these attacks that the barrage felt coordinated. She felt that way because many of the trolls appeared to be Labour supporters – they'd post party slogans and Muscat fan photos as much as vitriol against my mother – and many Labour supporters didn't read English. The trolls and blogs, in fact, rarely addressed my mother's actual writing. Their posts were almost always about her appearance, her family, or fake social media reports about her views fed to Labour's supporters by the party's own employees. A favourite lie was that she wanted all their children to die of cancer.

'They are meant to hate me, or dislike me, or despise me, or disagree with me, or whatever,' she said. 'Totally irrespective of what I write but as the person, as the figure that they are told to hate.'

The vitriol began to affect her health. She began eating more and putting on weight. She slept less and felt more alone. But she persisted, because 'you are not going to change amoral familism by pandering to it, or by making its practitioners believe they are right'. Assaulted by so much abuse, she in turn became less sensitive to how the subjects of her writing might feel. She described the Poodle's team as 'intellectually challenged', 'racist', 'kohlrabis' and 'dinosaurs'. Life under their rule would be an 'ineptocracy'. She mocked the way they behaved on Facebook, their fashion sense, the way they wrote and spoke. Above all, she felt disappointed that these politicians were even considered worthy of public office. It was because their supporters were 'brainwashed'.

After her blog post on the death of Mintoff, who was glorified by Muscat but who was to her 'appalling and hateful, an absolute sociopath', she received thousands of online death and rape threats. She said Labour supporters were now EU citizens, 'no thanks to their personal choices', but they still didn't understand concepts that Europe took for granted: 'free speech and open debate'.

But she recognised it was about more than the Labour Party. She criticised her fellow journalists, Nationalist politicians and many of the people she used to socialise with for not saying what they really thought about Mintoff – 'it makes them seem spineless, silly and even stupid (lack of rational thought and an inability to assess the facts)'. She said their self-censorship, an attempt to appear civilised, was evidence of the opposite: 'it is all about control through fear, and we thought we were done with all that'.

She felt among a 'small minority' in Malta. Many of its members passed on the usual tips and gossip that make their way to columnists. They were people who were raised in or who adopted along the way the beliefs and thinking that underpin democracy and liberal thought, 'the gold standard of "Europeanness"'. For the majority, the guiding principle was 'violent intolerance', no different to the fundamentalists who had threatened to blow up the Danish *Jyllands-Posten* newspaper office over its Muhammad cartoons or the ones who threatened to 'murder a writer for saying something they don't like'. The Maltese were, on average, 'ignorant', 'amoral' and 'avaricious'.

As my mother's writing became more caustic, the abuse directed at her intensified to the point where she felt unable to go out. She retreated into the enclosed garden of our house in the countryside. She planted new trees with my father. There were more olive trees by my old bedroom, more holm oaks and yet more olive trees further back. On the west side of the compound, a new row of lemon trees appeared, along with bergamot and some Seville oranges.

There was a principle at work here: a 'southern Mediterranean beauty, of nature, fields and buildings that blended in with both', she wrote. Other Maltese gardens, she thought, 'reflect a fear of nature, a love of concrete and hard surfaces that can easily be swept and washed with

---

disinfectant, a suspicion of trees, a lack of delight in plants, and an obsession with regimentation' because, she concluded, 'the ugliness of Malta's soul is synthesised in its gardens'.

In her own garden, she freed herself from the web of relationships, so tightly bound and interwoven in any small island nation, that made criticism difficult. In one way, she stopped caring. In another, her self-exile gave her a bigger stake. She could write even more freely and honestly about this 'distorted society of ours'.

But the more time she spent writing and tending to her garden in exile, the more they called her the Witch of Bidnija. And the more they cast her as a threat to the community, hiding out in the marginal countryside, the more the witch-hunt spread.

'It's like living in the play *The Crucible*,' she said, 'this witch-hunt in seventeenth-century Salem. And you watch and you think, "*Madonna*, this is like Malta but with different clothes."'

The house and garden had once been lively with company. A sideboard by the front door had been covered in invitations to parties, ceremonies and weddings. By 2010, the invitations had almost stopped coming. Many of my parents' friends felt my mother's writing had become too harsh. Those who had switched their allegiance to Muscat risked falling into her firing line. Others just didn't want to associate with a divisive figure. Fewer people came out to defend her.

The ostracism became almost total as the popularity of my mother's blog grew. But her readers and supporters there were mostly anonymous. The pressure on my parents' marriage became almost unbearable. They had always argued, and there were many times growing up when I thought they'd split. But the fights were now coming with increasing frequency and intensity. A shared life for them in Malta seemed to have become impossible. Yet neither wanted to leave. My father enjoyed his work and thought he could still have a life in Malta. My mother felt that leaving the country would be like giving up on everything she'd ever written for. They are the problem, she would tell my father, not me. Leaving would be like giving up on writing itself.

One fight, in January of that year, got ugly. My mother threw plates at the floor, and then a mug in my father's direction. It hit his head. The news made it to a dinner party hosted by a magistrate named Consuelo Herrera, with whom my mother had been in sixth form. It happened that my mother was in the process of investigating allegations of a romantic relationship between Herrera and a senior police officer. She would write that Herrera looked like the 'back end of a bus' and also like Worzel Gummidge, a scarecrow come to life in a television series from her youth.

Herrera told her dinner party guests that my parents' argument would be in the papers in a few days. One guest, shocked by the 'utter malice' on Herrera's face as she told the story, informed my mother by sending her a text message from the bathroom.

My mother responded by publishing tips she had been receiving on Herrera: that she had seen the love letters written by a senior police officer to Herrera when he prosecuted cases in front of her as a magistrate; that Herrera hosted parties at her house where politicians, businessmen and lawyers mixed, and where her guests would use cocaine, something she would deny in court.

Herrera filed a criminal libel suit against my mother, over what Herrera said were allegations that she had used drugs and was susceptible to corruption. She denied ever having had an affair with a senior police officer, and threatened my mother with a prison term. In an early hearing, she took issue with my mother's 'back end of a bus' description of her, saying, 'I'm no star, but . . .' Soon after, my father found a pair of police handcuffs in our letter box, which he never told my mother about.

My mother had no copies of any love letters herself, so my father advised her to call the senior police officer as a witness. Before he was made to testify under oath, Herrera dropped her suit. She claimed that evidence my mother gave during cross-examination amounted to a withdrawal of the drug use and corruption allegations, and so she had no interest in proceeding with the case.

While the proceedings were still ongoing, my mother combed through the libel cases on Herrera's docket and reported a number of them which she believed raised questions about possible conflicts of interest existing between the magistrate and parties involved. A short time later twenty-one of Herrera's cases were transferred to another magistrate. Many of them involved politicians and businessmen.

Keith Schembri was already very close to Yorgen Fenech when Muscat, as Labour leader, put Schembri in charge of the party's electoral campaign and asked him to act as its 'bridge to business'. Schembri had been making a success of his father's old print shop, importing paper, selling printing machines and eventually cornering the paper market. He called his business KASCO: the Keith Allen Schembri Company. With the Poodle's approval, Keith 'Kasco' Schembri began turning the Labour Party into a business.

He gave it a corporate structure, with an unelected chief executive officer who controlled the party and removed key elected posts, distancing it from party members and bringing it closer to his own office. He tried to remove party dinosaurs like Anġlu Farrugia, the police officer who had arrested my mother in 1984 and who had risen to Labour's deputy leadership. Farrugia was popular with the party's traditional base and had been elected deputy leader with two-thirds of the vote. But for the pro-business Muscat, these old socialists were a problem. Farrugia had shaved his moustache to freshen his image and acquired a law degree, but it was not enough.

Muscat kept Farrugia in the dark. At the Labour Party headquarters, he was put on the third floor and not given access to the boardroom level, one floor up, where Schembri and the Poodle perched. Schembri was always up there. Farrugia would see important businessmen and contractors coming and going to see him.

'I would ask,' he'd recall, '"What are they doing here?"'

They did not answer him. One day he had had enough. When he went up to the fourth floor, he found the door locked. A fingerprint scanner that Schembri had installed required a security code, which Farrugia had not been given.

'I almost broke the door down to go in. It made me feel uncomfortable.'

Muscat fired him as soon as an election campaign began in January 2013. It was a 'political murder', Farrugia told the *Times* of Malta in a big interview, 'in cold blood'. He said the party was too close to 'big businessmen and contractors' and that these were the people 'who wield power in the country'. He worried about 'corruption' and wondered whether those businessmen and developers were funding Labour's campaign.

My mother worried, too. She heard that Schembri was planning a slick campaign: a feature film, concerts, mini-feature television ads, and billboards that depicted my mother's face alongside opposition politicians. The conference kicked off with a press briefing about a new power station, Labour's central promise.

At the time, Malta's energy came from two sources, underwater cables connected to the Sicilian grid and a heavy fuel oil power station at Delimara, on Malta's southern coast. The promise was to develop a cheaper and cleaner power station there. It featured the Poodle and his 'star candidate', Konrad Mizzi.

Mizzi had come back to Malta after working in business in London. With his pink cheeks and pink lips and wide-set, vacant eyes, he was celebrated as young and new to politics. Behind the newness was a nothingness: motion without gesture, all disguising his one care, himself.

Mizzi said the plan was to convert the old heavy fuel oil power station at Delimara into a gas-fired station. A tanker containing liquified natural gas would dock on a jetty and pipe the gas directly into the new plant. According to

Labour's PowerPoint slideshow, the new plant would cut families' electricity bills by 25 per cent and water costs by 5 per cent.

Muscat talked of a woman from Delimara who had told him that her husband had died of cancer and that eight of her grandchildren were asthmatic because of the old power plant. 'She brought tears to my eyes,' he told the assembled press. 'Under my watch, I will close this cancer-and-asthma factory. We have to save these people. I don't want to hear of one child who gets sick.'

He reassured the journalists that he would personally take charge of the project's implementation, along with Mizzi. It would cost €370 million. Never mind the price, they said. They would make Enemalta, the state-owned energy company, buy the electricity the new power station produced on a ten-year fixed-term contract. There was 'strong interest' from the private sector as it was a 'safe investment', the Poodle said. 'This is not a done deal,' he added quickly. 'This is not a proposal belonging to any one company.'

My mother watched the press conference and, after seeing the €370 million figure, wrote: 'That was clearly the actual cost. And if they had the actual cost they probably had the supplier to quote it to them.' What she did not know then was that the proposal belonged primarily to Fenech, and that Fenech's team had made the same power station proposal to the Nationalists four years earlier, when they were in power.

'The decision is yours,' one of Fenech's associates had told the Nationalist Party's secretary general. 'We will do our bit if you do yours.' When the party official asked what

Fenech's associate meant, he was 'met by silence and a half-smile'. He ended the conversation, and Fenech's team took the unspoken offer – of a kickback in exchange for pushing the project onto the electorate – to Labour officials instead.

10

As my flight descended over the south of Malta, Delimara, where Muscat wanted to build his new power station, came into view. It was a day before the 2013 general election and I was on my way home from London to vote.

Matthew was stuck in Costa Rica, where he now worked for the International Consortium of Investigative Journalists. Andrew had returned from Berlin, where he was posted as a Maltese diplomat, a few hours before me, and he came to pick me up from the airport. He told me that our mother had meant to come, but she was busy writing. Over the course of that day, she uploaded twenty posts to her blog. She was typing when we got home. My father, worried, looked on.

There was a dead letter law in Malta that prohibited the publication of political content on the eve of a general election, but unlike my father, I did not think there was any real threat of the law being enforced. The Internet was replete with writing about Maltese politics. No one seemed to care, and the election was not much of a contest. A comfortable win for the Poodle's Labour Party was predicted.

At 7.25 p.m., my father was still looking worried as my mother uploaded a post she titled, 'Is this the man you want as your prime minister? Well, tough – it's what we're going to get.' The post contained a video of Muscat at an official function, evidence of my mother's assertion that he 'can't walk, can't stand to attention, can't lay a wreath with grace and dignity and doesn't even know that the wreath he's laid at the foot of the Independence monument should be upright, which is why it has that great big square stand at the bottom'.

Two hours later, my mother's adored mastiff Santino, a gift from a reader after the second arson attack, started barking at the garden gate. The doorbell rang. It was the police: a woman constable and two plain-clothes officers from the Criminal Investigation Department. One of the officers was Keith Arnaud, from the homicide squad. He moved towards the gate in a business like fashion, looking like he had better things to do than arrest a journalist.

The arrest warrant had been signed by a magistrate at the police commissioner's request. My mother noticed a discrepancy: the warrant gave her age as forty-nine, rather than her actual age of forty-eight. 'They were in such a great hurry,' she wrote, 'that they simply deducted 1964 from 2013 and didn't look at my birthday.'

She offered to give the police officers a statement in the house. They refused and called up headquarters to say she had refused to follow orders. My mother went into the house for a few minutes. When she returned, she asked me to lock up Santino and invite the police in.

She had called the press. A television crew arrived and, under the glare of its cameras, a compromise was reached. The police would take her to the Mosta police station, five minutes away, not the headquarters in Floriana, and interrogate her under arrest there.

The police interrogated her for two hours. They asked her why she called them 'trash' when they turned up at the house. She said they were 'perfectly civilised and nice', but their superiors had shown 'discriminatory and abusive political motivation' in ordering her arrest.

The police said they had come for her because they had received a complaint. 'Do you confirm,' they asked her, 'that you wrote and uploaded an article about the Leader of the Opposition, at around 7 p.m. this evening, with the aim of influencing people on how to vote?'

My mother asked the police if they had reacted because the complaint was about the Poodle who, in a day, would be prime minister. 'But while I was fuming at the shocking nature of the situation,' she later wrote, 'a part of me was laughing at this display of Joseph Muscat's insecurities.'

After Arnaud took down her statement, my mother walked out of the police station. A scrum of cameras and journalists got to her before us. So there they were: a dozen journalists reporting on the arrest of a journalist for breaking the 'Day of Silence' law on the day itself.

My mother was tired but running on adrenaline. She had left the house in one of my father's shirts and my old jacket. People watching the floodlit scene online said she looked like a man, that her hair was a mess, that she needed make-up.

We drove home. Apart from my father, none of us could sleep. I could hear my mother at her desk, writing into the morning. She steeled herself to leave the house for our polling station, but I could see how anxious she was. I could also hear it: she retched in the bathroom before we left.

If only her readers could have seen that she was a woman with the same vulnerabilities and anxieties as them. She never told them she felt 'churning, churning nerves all the time' or that there were periods when she thought, 'Oh my God, I'm going to get a stomach ulcer.' The bravura of her writing masked it, but she was afraid of what Muscat was going to do to the country – and to her.

It was the scale of Muscat's victory that surprised people. He won by a margin of more than 11 percentage points, thirty-nine seats to the opposition's thirty. The *Times* of Malta called it a 'historic landslide'. It was the largest majority in Malta's post-colonial history.

As prime minister, the Poodle knew he now had free rein. So did his supporters. They drove up and down the Bidnija road, shouting, 'Where is the witch?'

On his way out of the manic atmosphere of the counting hall, Muscat bumped into John Rizzo, the police commissioner. The two men shook hands. Before Muscat left he told Rizzo, 'I'll speak to you later, John.'

Rizzo was still at the counting hall when Muscat called and asked, 'Is Bidnija all right, John?'

'I hadn't understood what he meant by Bidnija at first, between the shouting and euphoria,' Rizzo recalled. 'I had paused and then I understood that he was referring to Daphne Caruana Galizia and I told him, "Rest assured. It is manned over there, coordinated, and I have police guards and everything."'

Muscat would use the exchange to claim he was concerned for my mother's safety. But it betrayed his sense that he could tell the police whom to protect and not protect. Rizzo didn't need to be told. He had increased the police presence near our house before. At the time of the second arson attack, he had begun sending frequent patrols to Bidnija, with squad cars driving up to the garden gate. He knew my mother found a police presence invasive, but said that he, not she, was the one who decided whether someone needed police protection.

A police officer who guarded his independence, Rizzo was about to file corruption charges against one of Muscat's personal consultants – the now former Nationalist MP who went by 'Johnny Cash' – when, not long after the election, the new prime minister called him again.

'The prime minister offered me "anything I wanted" as long as I didn't remain police commissioner,' Rizzo said. 'I told him I wanted to remain in the police as I hadn't done anything wrong.'

Muscat offered him a post with the Security Service, which, with the prime minister's sign-off, was the only authority that could intercept telephone communications. Rizzo felt uneasy. He asked for time to discuss it with his family. Muscat agreed, ordering him not to speak to the press in the meantime.

Rizzo did not really have a choice. Reasoning that the Security Service would be closest to his police work, he decided to accept the offer. He headed to the Office of the Prime Minister.

'But the next day I was met by Keith Schembri,' Rizzo said.

After speaking to the prime minister, Schembri, now Muscat's chief of staff, told Rizzo, 'There is no place for you at the Security Service. We need you at the Civil Protection Department.'

'You are going to make me look like a liar with my family,' Rizzo replied. 'I told them I will be joining the Security

Services. I am sorry, but this is not acceptable to me. Go tell the prime minister that I will not be accepting. I spoke with the country's highest authority and he gave me his word.'

Schembri came back to Rizzo with a sweetener. If he left quietly for the Civil Protection Department, a fire and rescue service, Rizzo could have the same salary, the same benefits and privileges as he'd had as police commissioner, and a €10,000 annual do-nothing consultancy.

Rizzo refused the consultancy fee on principle, but again he knew he had no real choice. As in colonial times, the premier could fire and hire police commissioners at will. He left the police force for the Civil Protection Department. The Labour crony who replaced him immediately dropped the corruption case against the Poodle's personal consultant.

In this way, Muscat and Schembri weakened institution after institution, consolidating power and control. They appointed their people to the bench, placed their moles in the anti-money laundering authority, and put more than half of all MPs, including some from the opposition, on the government payroll. And they pushed honest officials like Rizzo to the edges of the state.

Although marginalised, many could still see the rot in their institutions. And because they could no longer report it through official channels, now controlled by Schembri and Muscat, they began turning to my mother, who, in receipt of such intelligence, was turning into an investigative reporter. She used the information they supplied to show the Poodle's abuse of his office. His supporters hounded her for it.

The trouble had started just a few days after Muscat's election. My mother was on an afternoon walk in one of the villages with three of her friends. The village's feast was on and its decorations were out. She wanted to take photos of them for her magazine.

She and her friend fell behind the other two. A Labour Party mayor of another village, celebrating the feast with a nearby crowd, spotted her. He began calling out my mother's name and chanting Muscat's campaign slogan, 'Malta Tagħna Lkoll' ('Malta belongs to all of us'), at her. She ignored him and kept walking, turning round once to tell him that she'd call the police if he continued harassing her. He continued and was joined by two other people who began jeering at her. Soon, a group of people was following her down the street, shouting at her and ramming their phones in her face to take her photo.

Like it was 1985 all over again, she found shelter in a doorway, this time that of a Franciscan convent. Her friend made it in with her, and two monks from the adjoining friary slammed the door shut behind them. Outside, the mob began chanting in Maltese: 'Get her out of there! Get her out of there now! We have the power now! The power is ours! Joseph is our God!' One woman called out: 'Get her out of there by her hair, she is a bad woman!'

A group of police officers finally arrived. They took a statement from the mayor. They asked my mother if she wanted to file a complaint against him. She did, and they escorted her to the police station. The mayor, for a time, thought that my mother was the one being arrested, but he realised he was wrong when he was charged with harassing my mother soon after.

The lower court fined the mayor, but he appealed. The appellate judge overturned the fine for harassment but sentenced him to four days in prison for disturbing the public peace. The mayor then petitioned the president, one of Muscat's former ministers whom he himself had made president. The president consulted Muscat's justice minister, who had appointed the appellate judge. All agreed that the mayor should be pardoned.

The prime minister sometimes used his power more strategically. He flew a false flag of a 'civil liberties' programme – same-sex marriage, projecting rainbow lights onto Castille. And he spread patronage far beyond top public posts. He established a government customer care department in his office and put one of his cronies, Sandro Craus, in charge. The office centralised the distribution of government jobs and benefits to the Poodle's supporters and would-be supporters. By Schembri's own estimate, no fewer than sixty requests for government jobs came in every single day.

The government's wage bill grew. To fund it, the government sold state assets, privatised companies, and developed new products for new markets, including the sale of passports to the world's rich.

Other EU states offered residence to people who made substantial investments in their countries and who had spent a number of years living there. They didn't sell citizenship because it went against the bloc's spirit of cooperation. Malta was the first simply to trade its passports for cash, and there was no EU law to stop Muscat from doing this. If Malta sold a passport to a person, it gave that person rights in relation to the other twenty-seven EU member states. And it did something else: it made EU rights, in general, dependent on the size of someone's wallet. Muscat granted a monopoly on passport sales to a private company, Henley & Partners. He handed licences to firms of lawyers and accountants to act as agents of the passport scheme.

Europe worried. MEPs said Malta's passport scheme wasn't just against European values, but also represented a security threat. They worried that passport buyers – post-Soviet oligarchs, Chinese billionaires, sheikhs, a Vietnamese MP, people who had never heard of Malta – did not even have to live in Malta. Muscat, in response, ordered that passport buyers must rent or buy Maltese property.

My mother worried. The country was awash with dirty money, which was now the focus of most of her writing. Muscat shifted the banking sector's focus from the domestic to the international market, making it easier for foreign banks to establish themselves in the country. Under his premiership, the number of licensed banks would go from four to twenty-four, three of which were Maltese. His government attracted yet more online gambling companies through a combination of lower taxes, licence-fee waivers and re-location grants. It attracted cryptocurrency exchanges by reassuring the exchanges that their assets, wherever they came from, would be safe in Malta. Overseas earnings either weren't taxed or were taxed at a very low rate, meaning wealthy foreign individuals could buy a Maltese passport and pretend to live in the country to evade income taxes at home.

My mother had broken the story of Muscat's plans to sell passports at a time when he was trying to deport asylum seekers to Libya, illegally, on the grounds that Malta was too small for them.

'The poor get on ramshackle boats, packed in like sardines, and drown or spend 18 months in a detention camp trying to apply for asylum,' she wrote. 'The rich just swan in and buy their Maltese passport.' She called it 'an exercise in shameful hypocrisy'. Muscat, she reminded her readers, used to add to his speeches the Prayer of St Francis of Assisi, which begins, 'Lord, make me an instrument of your peace.' She published her own version. 'Henley, make me an instrument of your passport sales,' and, 'Where there is despair, let me profit from it; where there is darkness, let me give it a banking licence.'

The government worked with Henley & Partners to devise a response. Schembri's deputy emailed the company, advising it to first 'acknowledge the tragedy', then claim that Henley & Partners 'do not make political comments', and then 'if necessary' say that 'one group are seeking political asylum and the others citizenship'.

My mother wrote that the passport scheme debased Maltese citizenship and was unfair on the country's fellow EU states where passport buyers really wanted to go.

She found the basement flats and garages in which oligarchs claimed to live. They paid thousands of euros in monthly rent for the properties. Some basement flats had multiple passport buyers registered to them. She spoke to estate agents.

'But they don't even live here,' she told one.

'Isn't that better?' the agent said.

The estate agents benefited, as did landlords and property developers. Everyone benefited – not least Yorgen Fenech.

He got his power station. The government announced its decision to grant it to him on a Sunday when he told journalists that the specialised gas storage ship that would dock at Delimara had already been contracted. 'Perhaps the specialised storage ship administration offices operate on Sundays,' my mother wrote, 'and are not averse to whipping up a contract there and then.' When years later the opposition leader pointed to 'inconsistencies and changes' in the tendering process, saying its outcome had been 'predetermined', Muscat argued that if the decision had been pre-determined then changes and inconsistencies in the process wouldn't have mattered.

Everyone benefited. Our institutions were finally working. My mother was the problem.

Muscat was a success. He was busy with this idea of himself. He travelled to Berlin soon after his election to speak at a conference of the Social Democratic Party of Germany on the future of Europe.

Malta's ambassador to Germany managed to schedule a delegation lunch during the visit. Muscat had just fired him, so he was angling for a new post. The ambassador told my brother Andrew, his deputy, 'You should be at the lunch, too.' So the lunch was to include the prime minister, the ambassador he had just fired, a government press officer, Schembri and Andrew, who was not looking forward to it.

Andrew arrived early at the restaurant, a smart place that specialised in schnitzel. He waited at the entrance with the head waiter, convincing himself that he was doing this for the state. Muscat walked in first, shook his hand and said, 'Now, don't worry.' Andrew wanted to ask, 'Worry about what?' but Muscat went straight to the toilets. The rest of his delegation walked past, smiling at Andrew, and made their way to the table.

At the table, the ambassador talked about his time as a businessman in China. He had told Andrew he wanted to be posted to Shanghai. He did not know that Muscat had already given the posting to the Chinese wife of his shining star, Mizzi, the energy minister. The waiters all assumed that the ambassador was the prime minister and kept serving him first.

Muscat did not seem to notice or care. He took out his phone and fiddled with it while the ambassador talked. When the bread arrived, he grabbed at it and took large mouthfuls, sending bits of crust flying across the table. Andrew thought of his colleagues at other embassies, and how honoured they would feel to be included in such an intimate lunch with their countries' prime ministers. Schembri sat to his right, and Andrew tried engaging him in conversation. He was soft-spoken and deferential to Muscat. So was the press officer.

When the schnitzel arrived, Muscat wolfed his down. The press officer offered him the rest of his own schnitzel and he accepted, transferring the large slice of breaded veal to his plate. As he ate, fiddling with his phone, the lunch began to die around him. The ambassador had by then stopped talking, and they all just sat there in silence until the bill arrived.

Andrew walked over to the German secret service officer seated at a table near the exit and asked him to call the motorcade. As he waited, feeling underwhelmed by the men running Malta, he thought that at least he'd soon be joined in Berlin by one of his brothers.

Jessica, my girlfriend since my days at university in Malta, and I had visited Andrew and his girlfriend, Lucie, a few months earlier. We liked Berlin, and Jessica pushed for us to move there for a bit 'while we're still young'. The opportunity arrived in the summer of 2014 when she got a job at a start-up and I took up a fellowship at a university.

Life was good. I researched housing markets, gave a weekly seminar, and cycled, on my desperately hipster 1980s Motobécane, to Andrew's office for lunch and then to Jessica's after work for wheat beer by a canal. For months we lived easily and comfortably. I thought life in Berlin couldn't be improved.

Then, a few months later, Matthew called to say that he was driving into Berlin with his girlfriend. They had been living for a while on Lesbos, and once drove Syrians landing on the coast to the island's reception centre, but they found the place too desolate out of season. He told us they were now setting up in Berlin for good. So for the first time in about five years, the three of us would be living in the same place.

Matthew's apartment was in the city's leafy north. From a large pinewood dining-room table, he did his work for the International Consortium of Investigative Journalists. On the strength of his previous experience as a software engineer, the ICIJ asked him and his former colleagues to establish its data unit. In 2015, the unit received a major data leak. An anonymous source had found a back door into the document management system of Mossack

Fonseca, a Panamanian law firm that specialised in off-shore financial services. Using that access, the source acquired more than 11 million documents, which it shared first with reporters at the German newspaper *Süddeutsche Zeitung*. The leak was too large for the German reporters to manage alone, so they asked the ICIJ for help.

The ICIJ assessed the 11.5 million documents that became known as the Panama Papers and saw that it, too, needed help. The documents covered billions of US dollars in offshore financial transactions, many implicating politicians, going back to the 1970s. The leak would topple leaders, trigger criminal investigations, and allow the recovery of huge sums in unpaid taxes. But to get there, the ICIJ had to partner with media organisations across the eighty countries covered in the leak.

Matthew, who reviewed the documents early on, was concerned about some of the potential media partners in Malta. He had found in the leak that the managing director of the *Times*, owned a secret shell company linked to another secret shell company owned by Schembri. 'It was a classic kickback scheme,' he told me. It turned out that Schembri had sold Allied Newspapers a new printing press at an inflated price, a purchase approved by the managing director. Schembri then kicked a portion of his profits back to the shell company owned by the managing director. The price the company paid was so high that it brought the newspaper, Malta's biggest, to its knees.

When Matthew called our mother and told her about the scheme, she asked him to look up a few more names in the leaks. They found another of Schembri's companies: a Panama company, sheltered in a New Zealand trust. Then they looked up Konrad Mizzi, now managing the new power station project as energy minister, and discovered he also owned companies set up in the same way. Then they found that Mizzi and Schembri had used the same accountants to set up their respective companies, and that they'd done so in the same five-day period following Muscat's 2013 election victory.

The accountants set up Mizzi's and Schembri's companies as both officials attended the Poodle's first cabinet meeting. His government had marked the occasion by publishing a photograph. Muscat sits at the centre of the large mahogany table, beaming, and Giorgio Borg Olivier's portrait hangs above him. Many of his ministers, including one of the two women, are from the time of Mintoff. The younger ones are there: Mizzi's hair has yet to turn white. The economy minister, Chris Cardona, tries to get the prime minister's attention as Schembri, sitting in a corner, scowls at him.

'You can smell the whiff of corruption,' my mother wrote when she first saw it, 'right off this photo.' She had singled out Schembri, asking why he had left his printing paper empire for a government salary of €50,000 a year. 'It's obvious that he's done it for the openings it gives him,' she said, answering her own question, 'for more business.'

To her there had always been something suspicious about Schembri: it showed in the photo and now it showed in the leak. But it was still impossible to tell why Mizzi's and Schembri's companies had been created. She needed more time to find out, and in any case the ICIJ had embargoed all stories until April.

In the end, my mother couldn't wait that long.

On 22 February 2016, at exactly 1:00 p.m., she uploaded a post called 'If the (Panama) hat fits, wear it'. Alongside a stock photo of a man holding a Panama hat, she wrote that Mizzi had found one such hat.

She was rushing to get the story out because Mizzi was about to be elected deputy leader of the Labour Party, and she wanted to stop him. She had been hearing from sources that Mizzi was structuring privatisation deals purely to receive kickbacks. But none had provided her with the hard evidence she needed to publish. Twenty-one minutes after her post, she uploaded another one, cryptically referring to Mizzi's 'Easter lunch' and stating that he would be getting his lamb from New Zealand. She hoped Mizzi would understand from her posts that she knew he owned a Panamanian company sheltered by a New Zealand trust, and that knowing what she knew, he would withdraw from the election, saving everyone the pain and embarrassment. He did not, and her readers were left confused by her references.

So, breaking the embargo, she revealed what she knew explicitly. Mizzi, forced into commenting, said the set-up was for 'family planning'. He explained that his wife was Chinese and they had two children, so they needed an international set-up to manage their assets. People asked what would justify the set-up. Some noticed that in his assets declaration to Parliament, filed shortly after he took office, he had inflated his Maltese bank balance by a quarter of a million euros and suggested it was to pre-empt questions once the funds arrived.

'I have nothing to apologise for,' Mizzi told journalists. 'It is my money which I worked for.'

Muscat did not see any problems either. He pushed Mizzi's candidacy even after learning of his Panama company. Mizzi said Muscat had in fact approved an official declaration of assets that listed his Panama company. Muscat and Schembri had changed the Labour Party statute to enable Mizzi, an MP, to run for the post. The prime minister had even excluded other candidates.

'I look forward to working with him,' Muscat tweeted when Mizzi assumed the deputy leadership. 'Congratulations.'

They thought they had weathered my mother's report, but a few days later she revealed that Schembri had the same offshore financial set-up as Mizzi. And that it had been arranged by the same accountants.

The Nationalists seized on her findings and called an anti-corruption protest in Valletta. Thousands of people attended, waving Maltese flags and wearing Panama hats. My mother attended and was greeted as a celebrity, perceived now as being the real opposition to the Poodle. The Nationalists' leader gave a speech in which he said that Schembri had set up his Panama company with corrupt intent.

Schembri said his company never traded. Muscat defended Schembri as he had defended Mizzi, and he mobilised his party to discredit my mother. But the campaign against her hit a bump when the ICIJ finally lifted its embargo, exposing corrupt politicians across the world and adding credibility to my mother's reporting.

Politico nominated her as one of twenty-eight people 'transforming European politics, policy and ideas'. It called her 'a one-woman WikiLeaks, crusading against untransparency and corruption in Malta, an island nation famous for both'. The *Times of Malta* reported the news and referred to her as 'Controversial blogger Daphne Caruana Galizia'. Before the December ceremony in Brussels, she told *Politico* that corruption was accepted as normal in Malta and that she could not bear to see the corrupt rewarded. She emphasised what Europe meant to her. 'Over my dead body will my children be stuck on these rocks,' she said. She continued working.

The ICIJ released more of the documents, and my mother began digging around in the leak with the help of the organisation's partner journalists. She found an email from one of the accountants who had set up Schembri's and Mizzi's companies that mentioned another Panama company called Egrant. But there was no mention of Egrant's owner in the emails. 'It will be an individual,' one of the same accountants wrote, promising to give the Panamanian law firm, Mossack Fonseca, 'more details' on a Skype call.

My mother worked hard to uncover Egrant's owner, feeling it was the missing piece to the corruption puzzle involving Mizzi and Schembri. But as she wrote: 'No details of Egrant Inc are available in the Panama Papers because none were sent by email.' Egrant's ownership hasn't been established to this day, but the key company would turn out to be a different one altogether. It had come through a tip my mother had received from a Maltese source.

It was about a shell company called 17 Black, registered

in the United Arab Emirates and so not part of the Panama Papers leak. The source informed my mother, though, that 17 Black was a 'client' of both Mizzi's and Schembri's Panama companies. In February 2017, she uploaded a blog post headlined '17 BLACK – THE NAME OF A COMPANY INCORPORATED IN DUBAI'.

But she needed more than a tip to understand what the company was really for and who owned it. She needed documentary evidence, and that would have to come from an official investigation.

Muscat appointed one police commissioner after another, finding fault with each. The police force, already under-resourced, struggled to control crime.

Just two days before my mother's blog post on 17 Black, a car bomb was detonated at one of the country's busiest road junctions. It was 10.40 a.m. on a Monday. The target was a gang member called Romeo Bone, part of an under-world that was helping to smuggle fuel oil out of war-torn Libya and trafficking drugs and weapons into Malta. The gangs competed over markets for their illicit goods and bombed one another with impunity. 'And then the news: another bomb in another car,' my mother wrote after one incident. 'And I thought, there goes another diesel smuggler. Because the discernible pattern in criminal assassinations over the last few years in Malta is that diesel smugglers are blown up by bombs in their cars.'

Bone's car bombing was the sixth in about three years. All of them were unsolved because the police were weak against the gangs. Although Bone survived – the bomb had blown off his legs – he refused to talk, for fear of reprisals. But his associates knew what had happened: the car bombing was a retaliation. Their allegations were that Bone had shot another gangster twice in the head outside a bar close to St Aloysius college. The murdered gangster's two sons, who procured bomb devices from Italian and Albanian gangs and went by the family nickname Maksar, had then contracted the Degiorgio brothers from Marsa – described by one of their clients as 'the worst people in Malta' – to car-bomb Bone.

Yet most people didn't really care. They thought the gangs should be left to kill one another off. They thought they could live in two countries at once: daylight bombings and civil liberties. Or perhaps the experience of the bombings and violence throughout the 1970s and 80s left them maladjusted. In any country, but especially in a small one, you learn to live with anything. You learn to tread carefully because the past is painful, and peacetime is delicate. You wash away the violence and corruption with platitudes that close down discussions: *It was a different time*, or *All countries have problems*. Memories are edited and the truth disappears. Attempts to recover it aren't always welcome. The authorities do nothing and people get used to their ineffectiveness.

The fourth police commissioner the prime minister appointed, a man who once described Muscat on Facebook as someone with 'real balls', asked the attorney general what he should do about the Panama Papers, particularly whether he should investigate the accountants. The attorney general, who was both the public prosecutor and the government's legal adviser, advised the police against investigating, saying in an internal memo that they should 'thread very carefully' as action might be 'counterproductive'.

Frustration grew among the remaining people with integrity inside institutions such as the anti-money laundering authority and the police force. They were tired of seeing the internal reports they drafted, which ought to have triggered criminal investigations, being hidden away. They were tired of being told to stand down. They began leaking more information to my mother. And as she verified and published that information, Muscat's war against her intensified.

One of the Poodle's aides, Glenn Bedingfield, started a blog dedicated to harassing and slandering my mother during her Panama Papers reporting. He called it 'an equal and opposite reaction'. By the time February ended, just a week after my mother's first Panama Papers reference, he had uploaded 138 blog posts about her. He would write about her more than a thousand times from his government desk at Castille with the blessing of the Poodle, an old friend. When he wasn't at Castille, Bedingfield hosted a show for Labour's television station in which he depicted my mother as an insane, cackling witch – complete with a hooked nose, warts and a black conical hat – as she typed out gibberish, pausing to drink from a whisky bottle.

The last time my mother had gone to the beach, three years earlier, people had taken photographs of her, edited them to enlarge her arms and thighs, and then shared them online. Now, leaving home was being made impossible. A quiet café where she used to read the newspapers and write was raided and smashed up by the police under the guise of an audit. Even her now small circle of friends was harassed, to ensure total ostracism.

*

Writing and investigating became the only things my mother could do.

She raised the alarm that Malta was becoming a money laundering centre, that Muscat deprived institutions of resources or corrupted them, that journalists were being ignored and demonised. The public was at first uneasy. Some protested in support of her, others asked why she was sticking her neck out. Most saw her as trying to stop the good times. But she persisted. And like the officials who went from soliciting bribes from drug dealers in old Malta to soliciting them from oligarchs in hyper-globalised Malta, my mother, almost imperceptibly, moved from reporting on low-level Maltese corruption to grand corruption. The sums multiplied into the hundreds of millions, the criminal networks stretched from the Persian Gulf to Panama to post-Soviet states.

While still working to uncover more information on 17 Black, my mother began looking into Egrant again. A source at Pilatus Bank, a Muscat-era private bank in Malta whose business was laundering the money of Azerbaijan's elite, told my mother that a company controlled by the Azerbaijani ruling family had sent $1.017 million to Egrant's account at Pilatus. The source then showed her a document making allegations that Egrant was owned by 'Mrs Michelle Muscat', the Poodle's wife.

Michelle Muscat had once hosted the Azerbaijani dictator's daughter at a Maltese state palace. It was part of a new foreign policy that brought Malta so close to Azerbaijan that its oligarchs described Malta as one of their 'provinces'. The policy was shrouded in secrecy. Muscat and Mizzi's first visit to its capital, Baku, was revealed by the Azerbaijanis who, keen to be seen with representatives of an EU state, released a statement about it. It transpired that Muscat and Mizzi went there unannounced and without civil servants or press to sign a cooperation agreement, with Mizzi's ministerial discretion, in the field of energy. At the time, the EU was deepening its relations with Azerbaijan, having just agreed to invest in the country in return for some access to its oilfields. But my mother couldn't understand Azerbaijan's specific interest in Malta.

She suspected its oligarchs used it as an entry point into the EU for their dirty money, and the Egrant document she was shown at that time seemed to fit. When she transcribed and published it in mid-April 2017, the country was set alight.

'Serious crimes are being committed by those who have been elected to the power of government,' my mother reported to her readers. 'The country has reached a very dangerous turning-point.' Addressing state officials, she added: 'You must now give proper consideration to whether you have a greater responsibility towards your non-disclosure obligations than you do towards the rule of law and the future of our country.'

Muscat was more popular than his ministers and party. It turned out he was untouchable. He and his wife strongly denied the claims they had any connection to Egrant, calling my mother's report on the company 'the biggest lie in Malta's political history'. He fired up his party's media machine and supporters, saying my mother was trying to destroy his family. 'I hurt in a big way,' he would write, 'because the poisoned arrows reached my heart.'

On May Day, he summoned thousands of his supporters

to Castille for the Labour Party's usual celebration. 'Joseph, Joseph,' the crowd chanted. 'Joseph, Joseph.' He thanked them and then, using his powers as prime minister, called a general election for 3 June 2017. He told the crowd he had already informed the president of his decision. The election date was a year early, the economy was racing ahead, and employment was high. Sensing the crowd might need an explanation, without mentioning my mother's name or Egrant, Muscat said the early election was to settle her 'lie'.

'Others may try to tarnish Malta's name,' he yelled at the crowd, evoking past sieges and invaders. 'Because of their weak character, they have not understood that attacking Malta can only backfire.'

Five hours later, at about 11 p.m., Muscat was gripping his wife's hand and clenching his jaw as they stood outside the Labour Party headquarters. There they launched his campaign, under the slogan *'L-Aqwa Żmien'*, 'The Best Days'. Billboards were already going up across the country.

At a press conference, Muscat made the problem more explicit, saying Malta's reputation was being 'tarnished' from 'Bidnija'. The foreign press took him at his word. Global news reports said he had called the snap election to settle 'allegations of corruption' around Egrant.

My mother knew otherwise. She revealed that Muscat's campaign website had been registered in early April, by which point his election plan was, she wrote, 'already so far advanced that word was leaking out to me from producers of campaign collateral and others who had been commissioned to work on materials necessary for the election itself'. On the back of this information, she figured that 'something cracked in February, and in March he decided to call a general election'.

'We need to know what this thing is that they fear so much that they want it to happen after they are re-elected to another term in government, and not before,' she wrote. 'It is now more imperative than ever that we find out what cracked in February.'

If only she had looked back over her own blog posts from February. She would have seen the one about 17 Black, which simply mentioned the company. That mention would have been all it took.

Matthew had moved back home from Berlin to help my mother with a leak she had received. It consisted of more than 680,000 documents and emails from a company called ElectroGas, which had won the public contract to build and run the new power station at Delimara. It was the company directed and partially owned by Yorgen Fenech.

As they began working through the leak, my mother was still puzzling over Muscat's announcement of an early election. The prime minister was worried that problems at ElectroGas would damage his re-election chances. He told his officials he wanted to formally open its power station. Some warned him it was not ready – it still wasn't producing electricity – but, in need of a campaign boost, he went ahead. Amid a light show, a hologram and drones flying overhead, the Poodle high-fived children and announced a new dawn: clean energy.

According to ElectroGas's commercial director, Catherine Halpin, the event, which cost €100,000 of public funds, 'was purely political – it wasn't a real milestone for us, but the government wanted to have something to put on TV!' As engineers struggled to ready a single turbine in time for Muscat's speech, the prime minister declared the whole power station operational, meaning that its contract with Enemalta, the state-owned electricity company that had been forced to buy its power supply, came into effect. But as the power station was not producing electricity, ElectroGas had to pay large fines to Enemalta.

'Malta,' Halpin despaired in an email to her colleagues, 'will never change.'

To appear both successful and tough with ElectroGas, Muscat instructed his energy minister to say something in Parliament about the fines. 'The government will ensure every single penny of the damages due are paid,' Mizzi told the chamber, 'contrary to the approach taken by previous Nationalist governments.' But, secretly, Mizzi was in discussions with Fenech about first waiving the €18 million in damages, then allowing an interest-free payment after eighteen years, until he would finally agree to an annual 2 per cent interest rate on the damages over the eighteen-year deferment. Mizzi would then go a step further and again use his ministerial discretion, secretly, to waive eighteen years' worth of excise tax – valued at €46.5 million – that ElectroGas had agreed to pay on its importation of gas. Mizzi transferred that cost onto the state. He had reasons to protect ElectroGas's finances.

The company had already burnt through two loans. The Bank of Valletta, the nationalised successor to the bank my great-grandfather had run, still under government control, had led the financing: €110 million in 2014 and €450 million less than a year later. The government had guaranteed both loans and, as ElectroGas was approaching a default, the debt and any damages would be passed on to taxpayers. It needed new funding to survive.

Fenech, meanwhile, collected €1 million from Electro-Gas for securing the first loan and €4.17 million for the second – provisions he had written into his contract with the company. When Halpin asked for his invoices, she called it a 'success fee'. As success fees are what financial investigators and compliance staff call red flags for bribery, Fenech bristled.

'Please call it "development fee" NOT "success fee",' he emailed Halpin. 'Catherine it is important to refer to it that way even in electrogas records.'

There was little enough success at the company itself. On 25 May 2017 at 9.35 a.m., my mother reported that ElectroGas was struggling financially. 'Testing is scheduled to carry on until the end of September,' one source told her, 'if they manage to find finance to survive.' Another source told her the company was unable to meet its wage bill: 'the last payment run was on 28th March'.

Her blog post made it to Fenech by 2.03 p.m. In an email headed 'EGM on DCG' – ElectroGas Malta on Daphne Caruana Galizia's blog – Fenech sent instructions to his employees. 'Please do not react until it reaches mainstream media,' he told them. 'It is Fake News of course.'

It was a strange thing to say. My mother's blog had a greater audience than all the Maltese newspapers combined by this point, averaging hundreds of thousands of daily views and millions during election campaigns.

A day later, more news. The *Independent* published the conclusions of a leaked report from Malta's anti-money laundering authority as Muscat was debating the opposition leader on live television. The 120-page report, which was intended only for the police and would have been buried, showed that Schembri's and Mizzi's Panama companies were set to receive millions of US dollars from 17 Black once they managed – after being turned down by a number of financial institutions – to open bank accounts for their companies.

The report confirmed what my mother's source had told her when she had first heard about 17 Black – that it was a 'client' of Mizzi's and Schembri's companies. But the report still did not identify 17 Black's owner. It knew only that the money probably came from kickbacks connected to ElectroGas's FSU, the floating storage unit that kept gas in silos placed on top of the vessel and piped it directly from its jetty at Delimara into the power station.

A day later, Halpin emailed Fenech, saying that the 'banks are getting nervous'. The company's chief financial officer, a German, had warned his colleagues that 'a bank has already cancelled due to compliance'. He had watched a documentary news item about the story a week earlier, which he summarised to his colleagues as 'Interesting coverage in German TV about our FSU and bribery'.

The opposition leader said that if elected, he would end the ElectroGas project and buy more electricity from the Sicilian grid.

'Hogwash in my opinion but it will surely make new lenders really nervous,' Fenech emailed his colleagues, adding, in reference to the upcoming general election, 'I think we have to hold tight for a week.'

The week's wait was to see through Muscat's re-election. 'The people have clearly chosen,' he announced, 'to stay on the road to even greater results.'

His grandiosity did not prevent a simultaneous pettiness. Three weeks later, Andrew received an email from the foreign affairs ministry's permanent secretary. 'I wish to inform that in view of instructions that I have received, in terms of exigencies of the service, your posting in New Delhi is being terminated as of 15th July,' she wrote. 'I apologise for this short notice which is beyond my control.'

Andrew asked for a reason for his recall. She did not have one. At the ministry, she later said, there was no discussion about it, 'just that he was to come back within two weeks'. She asked him not to speculate on the reasons, nor upon why he had been given only the minimum notice to return. She had no explanation for why no one replaced Andrew or why he had to leave when his high commissioner plainly did not want him to.

There was nothing he could do. Andrew and Lucie started packing their bags for a return to Malta. He would now work in an archive in the annexe of the foreign affairs ministry in Valletta. His new boss had little for him to do. My father looked on, anxiously. 'At first, your mother refused to believe what had happened to Andrew was retaliation for her writing. She told herself that it was probably something else.'

It was the less painful thing to believe. But she knew Andrew's record was spotless. And although she never got to hear the foreign affairs minister's answer, a few years later, for Andrew's recall that 'I have nothing personally against *him*', she soon accepted that the government had used her son against her. At that moment, my father saw that 'she was really distraught'.

She stopped writing. She began to reassess everything. 'I have a sense of time running out,' she messaged one of her friends, 'so many things I wanted to do.' People began calling her to see why there was nothing new on her blog. They called my father to see if she was alive. Her blog had become part of their daily routine. As she had written, people visited the blog to 'feel normal in a sea of insanity where the crowd cheers the Commissioner of Police for failing to take action against a corrupt cabinet minister and the Prime Minister's chief of staff'. Under Muscat, her blog became 'a gathering-post or rallying-point for decent people who feel frightened and threatened at the rise, growth and spread of amorality'.

Andrew, too, was distressed by her sudden silence. That was what the government wanted. He tried to persuade her that his return to Malta would be good for him and Lucie. He told her that he was 'alive and unhurt'.

Two weeks passed before my mother returned to her writing.

Andrew was coming home, she thought, and Matthew was already there. She would never have said it, but she would have felt less isolated had the three of us lived in Malta. For all her talk of wanting us to leave and to explore, when it happened it had 'affected her really badly', my father said.

I booked a flight home in July that year. When I sent my mother the details, she said it would be just us. My father was away on 'some cycling trip', Matthew was collecting the rest of his stuff from Berlin, and Andrew was not yet back from New Delhi.

'It will be good to see you,' she wrote in an email. 'It's pretty gloomy here.'

She picked me up from the airport in the Peugeot she had leased after her old car had become so recognisable that people routinely scratched it, slashed its tyres and drove into it. We went straight to a restaurant for supper, taking a table outside. As we sat there, drinking wine and eating, I noticed the usual gawking, nudging and staring. I tried to ignore it.

The next time she suggested eating out, I told her I preferred staying at home in the garden. I instantly regretted keeping her home for yet another day and night. But she agreed.

On my last night in Malta, she bought a kilo of Maltese prawns – a rich red – and cooked them in white wine, butter and garlic. She asked me to lay the table out by the Judas tree. In spring and early summer, this short tree flowers deep pink. My father had told us, when we were boys, that Judas had hanged himself from one.

It was warm, but a cool breeze came up through the valleys. She lit citronella candles to keep mosquitoes away. She brought out a bottle of Catarratto from a Sicilian vineyard we had once visited on a family holiday. We talked about that holiday; how one afternoon Matthew, Andrew and I had sailed a small catamaran out from Sciacca in Agrigento, forgot to turn back before sunset, and had to be found and towed in by a speedboat.

She told me it was about time I asked Jessica to marry me. And she talked a little about herself: she wanted to travel more. Her spirits seemed to have lifted, at least in the moment, and we were outside long enough for the stars to fill the night sky.

The next evening she drove me to the airport. We had an established ritual for our farewells: she would walk me to the departures lounge, where I would walk through the first security gate and then take the escalator up to the gates. From the top of the escalator, looking down, you could see the lounge. My mother would always wait there, to my embarrassment and despite my pleas, to wave me off. This time, when I reached the top of the escalator, I turned to wave. She was not there.

I had so much to say.

Andrew and Lucie bought a derelict house in Floriana, a town just outside Valletta. Andrew would go to the house after work to scrape plaster off the walls, pull out old window and door frames and break off ugly wall tiles. Matthew would join him.

It was cathartic for my brothers: Andrew doing something constructive, Matthew taking a break from the ElectroGas leak. My mother would arrive, bringing food and drink, watching two of her sons work and joining in to scrape the paint.

One evening, she decided to go there with my father, as Floriana was having a town fair. She asked Matthew if he wanted to come. He said he couldn't, as he was going to meet his friends in Sliema later on. My mother told Matthew that he could take the Peugeot because she was going with my father in his car.

My parents got to Floriana by afternoon. Its streets had been closed to traffic for the day and its official buildings opened to the public. It was a rare outing for my mother.

People set out stalls in the streets. Some sold food, some bric-a-brac, and a man my mother knew was selling saplings of indigenous Maltese trees.

There is a photo of my mother buying some of the saplings. There is another of my parents sitting together on a park bench. The photos were shared online by an official from the Office of the Prime Minister, part of the harassment campaign the government subjected her to and that normally kept her at home.

Afterwards, my parents walked to Andrew and Lucie's house. Andrew was there on his own, going at the tiles.

My parents went into the house, and they chatted with Andrew for a few minutes. My father left to bring his car round and collect my mother and the saplings she had just bought.

Alone with Andrew, my mother talked about the pressure she was under. She was facing forty-two civil libel suits and five criminal ones. Most had been filed by Labour politicians and their donors, but four had been filed by the new Nationalist leader over her reports of his alleged involvement in money laundering for a prostitution ring centred on Soho in London. He had mobilised his party against her, so she was now getting it from both tribes.

The government was withholding advertising revenue from the *Independent*, promising to release it if the newspaper stopped carrying my mother's columns. In a meeting arranged by Schembri, the newspaper's owners had received a buy-out offer from one of Muscat's donors, who accounted for nineteen of the libel suits against her, and Yorgen Fenech. The attempts to hack her blog were becoming more sophisticated.

People increasingly recognised the depths of Malta's crisis, but it was easier not to see or speak of corruption. It was easier to blame Malta's Cassandra, our Daphne, for the country's problems. The narrative her adversaries pushed was that she sowed division and caused unrest to stop the country's progress. 'Scapegoating,' she called it. 'A classic case.' She said that she had grown used to the abuse, 'like a scar forms around a wound'. But now it went further than anyone could reasonably handle.

'*And*,' she told Andrew, 'they're trying to fry me alive.'

She gave him a long hug in the doorway, turned round to leave, then turned back and hugged him again. 'She had never done that before,' Andrew said.

12

The following day was a busy one. Matthew and my mother struggled to keep up with the ElectroGas leak and the calls they were receiving from sources. They were working by the dining-room's east-facing window.

Opposite the window, the large bougainvillea bled crimson paper petals to the ground. The sun had moved along its circuit and now hung above, casting them into sharp relief. They had not eaten any breakfast. Lunchtime came and went.

At about 2 p.m., my mother pulled herself away from her laptop by the dining-room window. She went to the kitchen and returned with a plate of tomatoes and mozzarella, seasoned and covered in olive oil. She placed it before Matthew.

The clock on her laptop kept clipping off the minutes. At 2.35 p.m., she uploaded a blog post. It was about Schembri, who was testifying in a libel suit he had filed against the former Nationalist leader. The leader had criticised him during his speech at the protests triggered by my mother's first Panama Papers blog posts. 'I swear on the cross that I am innocent,' Schembri had said on the stand.

'There are crooks everywhere you look now,' my mother wrote. 'The situation is desperate.'

Her bank called. It was about regaining access to her money, which had been frozen by the economy minister, Chris Cardona, and his aide as part of libel proceedings they had filed against her. The bank told my mother she was late for an appointment and must come now.

'Okay,' she told Matthew after hanging up, 'I have to go.'

She grabbed her bag and walked out of the front door, but moments later – precisely forty-four seconds later – she came back inside.

'Forgot my chequebook,' she explained, picking it up off the shelf right by the front door. 'Okay, now I'm really going. Bye, Matt.'

She slammed the front door behind her. The keys and evil eye amulet hanging from the lock jangled.

An elderly farmer who knew my parents was driving up the Bidnija road. He saw my mother coming the other way in her grey Peugeot.

'She must have felt something,' he said, 'because she stopped.'

He saw her pull up on the handbrake. White smoke began to emerge from her car. There was a bang and a flash.

'It was a small one,' he said. 'It was like a spark. Some debris was blown away from it and I saw her. I even heard her scream. A big scream.'

She screamed for around five seconds, then her petrol tank ignited.

'There was the big explosion and she became a ball of fire. She didn't have time, unfortunately, to escape.'

The second explosion sent the Peugeot, with her inside

it, shooting towards his car. It just missed him. The car landed in a field some fifty metres from where he had seen her stop.

He stepped out of his car and saw my mother 'was literally in pieces'.

He froze, and could not turn away, until he realised he had to stop oncoming traffic from running over her remains.

The noise of the explosion shook the windows of our house.

'I knew it was a car bomb straight away,' Matthew said. 'It couldn't have been anything else.'

Barefoot, he ran to the front door and opened it to blinding sunlight. The dogs had gone wild. He felt the blood drain from his face and thought that he might faint. But he ran to the gate.

He started down the white-gravel lane. Looking towards the Bidnija road, he saw, some 250 metres from the house, 'a tower of big black bubbling smoke. The kind you get when a pile of tyres is burning.'

And in that moment, he thought: My God, this is it.

He sprinted down the road, and when he got to the point where it dipped, he saw that the asphalt itself was on fire.

He was confused. He could see metal debris around him, but no car on the road. Then, in the neighbouring field, he saw a 'fireball'.

He ran to it. For a moment, the burning car looked white, not grey. 'Okay,' he thought. 'It's not her.'

But as he moved around the car he recognised the first three letters – QQZ – of its number plate.

The car horn blaring, toxic smoke filling his lungs, the heat from the blaze burning his face, he started running round the car, trying to find a way to open a door.

Narrowing his eyes to look through the smoke and flames, he could not see anything inside, not even a silhouette. 'There was nothing I could do,' he recalled. 'I've never felt so helpless in my life.'

He could hear the whine of police sirens in the distance, coming closer. A single police car arrived with two young officers. They stopped beside Matthew. They were in a panic, fumbling around with a single fire extinguisher.

One of them sprayed the blaze but then dropped the fire extinguisher. Matthew screamed and tried to grab it. The other officer burst into tears.

'Sorry,' the officer said. 'There is nothing we can do.'

Matthew looked around. He realised he was surrounded by our mother's body parts. He knew the officer was right.

'Who is in the car?' the officer asked.

'My mother,' Matthew said.

Before more police officers and the armed forces arrived to form a cordon, drivers got out to take photos. Within an hour, images of my mother's remains spread across private WhatsApp groups and fringe Internet forums.

My mother's sister Cora was the second family member to arrive at the scene. The car was still ablaze, and Matthew was still barefoot beside it. He got hold of a phone and began calling the rest of us.

Andrew was at his desk in the foreign affairs ministry in Valletta. Government officials were running around, giving staff little option but to donate money to a charity managed by Michelle Muscat, the prime minister's wife.

At around 3 p.m., the staff were asked to go to the building's courtyard for a speech about the charity. As Andrew listened, he realised that he and his colleagues represented the Muscats rather than Malta. He returned to his desk, dejected, and when he got there his phone rang.

'There was an explosion in Mum's car,' Matthew told him. 'You should come home now.'

Andrew's first thought: a mechanical fault, something to do with the engine. But before he could translate this thought into words, Matthew continued: 'Go tell Dad. I can't get through to him.' He rang off.

'I tried calling Matthew back,' Andrew said. 'But he was on the phone with someone else. Then I tried calling her, and . . . no answer.'

He got through to Matthew: 'Was she in the car?'

'Yes,' Matthew said. 'Come now.'

Andrew shot out of the ministry, ran the two hundred metres to my father's office, charged through the waiting area, straight past his secretary, and burst into my father's room on the first floor.

My father was in a meeting.

'We need to go,' Andrew told him. 'Something happened to Mum.'

My father picked up his car keys, apologised to his clients, and ran out with Andrew past more clients in the waiting room. He apologised to them too, saying there had been a family accident. The word he used for accident – *disgrazzja* – is normally reserved for fatal ones.

And all at once, with that one word, Andrew realised: Our mother had been killed, something my father had always feared.

The drive to Bidnija was interminable. People called and messaged. Andrew checked the news. As he tried to focus on the road, my father kept asking Andrew to repeat exactly what Matthew had told him.

'How bad is it?' he asked. 'Where is Matthew now?'

Police officers stopped them from driving up the Bidnija road. They parked and began to walk up. A homicide inspector, Kurt Zahra, realised who they were and approached.

'Did she die?' my father asked him.

'Yes.'

He continued up the road with Andrew, guided to Matthew by police officers. Andrew could not look away from the mangled and burnt chassis in the field to his left. He recognised one of the emergency doctors on the scene, an old friend. When she saw him, she brought her hands over her open mouth and burst into tears.

At last, they reached Matthew and Cora. Cora was on the phone. She had already called my grandparents and aunts with the news. Now she was fielding media calls, asking reporters to hold off running the story until all our family knew.

They walked together into the house. They sat around the dining-room table. Before they could speak to one another, a court official entered. She had been sent by the magistrate who was on duty that day, and so charged with running the inquest into my mother's death.

'I want to assure you that Magistrate Herrera is taking

this very seriously,' the court official told them. The duty magistrate was Consuelo Herrera.

It was around 2 p.m. in London. I was at a friend's house in the west of the city. We had just finished lunch and made coffee.

My phone rang relentlessly with a Maltese number that I did not recognise. The caller was so insistent that it disturbed me. If there was an emergency in Malta, I would have been called from a number I recognised.

I copied the number and sent it to my mother on Whats-App, asking whether she knew it. I noticed that the message I sent received one grey tick, meaning it hadn't been delivered. A message from a friend in Malta, an emergency doctor, came in: *Everything ok?*

Hurricane Ophelia? I replied. *Yes, fine.*

As I sat down with my coffee, Jessica rang.

'Paul,' she said, 'Cora just called me and said that Matthew's been trying to get through to you.'

I hung up and the Maltese number called again. I walked into another room, sat down on a sofa and answered. It was Matthew.

'Paul,' he said, 'there was a bomb in her car.'

And then, with each word separated by what felt like an eternity, he added: 'I don't think she made it.'

I felt my mind lift to the room's ceiling, so that I was looking back at myself, sitting on a sofa at a friend's house, listening to my brother tell me that our mother had just been assassinated.

'Paul?' he said.

'What do I do, Matt? What do I do?'

'Come home. Now,' he said. 'Get on the next flight to Malta.'

Outside, the sun was the colour of blood and the sky purple. Hurricane Ophelia had started near the Azores and reached London, blowing Saharan dust into the city, scattering the sunlight differently. Purple was my mother's favourite colour. Ophelia, who in *Hamlet* didn't realise the danger she was in until her 'muddy death', brought it to me.

Matthew met me and Jessica at the airport in a dark lounge suit. He explained that he had gone to court to ask Herrera to recuse herself on the grounds that she had filed criminal libel proceedings against my mother. He had gone with my father, Cora and the two lawyers my father had asked for help, Therese Comodini Cachia, who specialised in human rights law, and Jason Azzopardi, an expert in criminal law. Five hours on, she had not given them a decision.

We said little else. We cried into one another's shoulders and went outside, where my father was waiting in the car, and headed home. As we approached Bidnija, my father warned me of what to expect: a scene full of police officers and soldiers, lit with bright white floodlights.

Forensic officers guided us down the grassy middle of the white-gravel lane so as not to disturb any potential tracks to the house. It was warm and the air was still. In the garden, our dogs kept quiet.

I dumped my bag by the front door, and for a moment expected to hear the sound of my mother typing. We sat at the kitchen table and waited for the homicide inspectors to come.

Zahra, the officer who'd met my father at the crime scene, and Keith Arnaud, the head of homicide, entered. I recognised him as one of the officers who had arrested and questioned my mother in 2013 and felt that, with him and Herrera, we had little hope of solving the murder.

We moved to the living room. They asked about our whereabouts and for our phone numbers, in order to start tracking down calls made in the area that day.

When I looked around the room, I saw we were all lost. Matthew was running on adrenaline. He went through the details of the day. He told the police officers that whoever had triggered the bomb must have used the Tarġa Battery, the old British artillery battery facing Bidnija Hill, as a lookout. The gun post provided a direct line of sight into the dining room through its east-facing window.

'We're already on it,' Zahra told him.

Zahra and Arnaud said the police had called in Europol agents and the Netherlands Forensic Institute to help. A counterterrorism police officer had thought to call the FBI to help analyse cellphone data in the area, which was an unusual procedure for a murder in Malta, where the police force didn't have the technical capability to sift through and trace such data and so previous car bombings went unsolved. They left. Night passed; dawn came.

Matthew published a Facebook post in which he described Malta as 'a mafia state'. The Maltese had never thought of themselves in this way, and some responded by saying he was just overwrought. The government's supporters said he was damaging the country's reputation.

We heard drones flying overhead. Police officers marched around our garden. Forensic officers in white suits combed through the fields around the house. A group of journalists gathered at the end of the lane, waiting for us to emerge. Phone calls, a never-ending stream, came in.

One was from our lawyers. Seventeen hours after they had asked for Herrera's recusal, she had agreed to step away, decreeing that justice needed to be done and seen to be done, and the case was transferred to another magistrate.

With this news, I tried convincing Matthew to eat. He was refusing to, feeling that it would mark an acceptance of our mother's death; that by not eating he was holding time. I said we needed to eat to carry on. My father busied himself in the kitchen. We ate and walked outside.

We sat at the northern edge of the garden, where we had once flown our bicycles into the air. A few metres away, near the white mulberry tree, two young police officers played games on their phones as they sat on a bench that my mother had bought.

We went to the front of the house, where Matthew showed us the indigenous saplings my mother had bought in Floriana the day before she was murdered. A large old pinewood table was blanketed with them. Matthew told us she had wanted to plant a Maltese garden.

The saplings, just leaves attached to twigs, were small, vulnerable things. But what promise they held. A mighty holm oak. A tough bay laurel. A towering Aleppo pine. I could not bear to look at them. We went back inside.

13

Cora came to the house to help with the flood of media requests. Reporters kept asking us whether my mother's murder was related to her work on the criminal gangs who smuggle fuel out of Libya, using Malta as a base. We could not understand the questions. Aside from a few passing mentions on her blog, my mother had never investigated them. We wrote and sent out a fact sheet about her. It moved from my mother's early opinion columns to, as Malta's institutions were 'systematically taken down' and the country welcomed 'volumes of illicit financial flows', her reporting on 'the links between Maltese politics and the country's criminal underworld'. We asked journalists to focus on the real subject of her investigations: government corruption.

The prime minister appeared on television, smirking, saying that he would 'leave no stone unturned' in bringing the perpetrators to justice. Through various intermediaries, including the president, he asked us to endorse a €1 million reward for information on the assassination. There was no need for us to endorse it other than for it to show that we were on the same side as Muscat. We heard that he wanted to announce the reward at a scheduled meeting in Brussels three days after the murder.

Before he landed there, my brothers and I uploaded a joint Facebook post. It was our first public intervention and would set the tone for all that would follow. We wrote: 'The government is interested in only one thing: its reputation and the need to hide the gaping hole where our institutions once were. This interest is not ours. Neither was it our mother's.' Before signing off with 'We are not interested in justice without change', we called for the resignations of Muscat, the attorney general and the police commissioner.

The police commissioner gave his first press conference on the murder that day. He was the same man that, in a Facebook post, had admired Muscat's balls. He was inarticulate and uninformed. The journalists present were aghast. Afterwards, they described it as a train wreck. The government said the press conference 'could have been better' and never allowed another. They must have expected some issues because they had placed the police commissioner's deputy, Silvio Valletta, by his side.

We were shocked by Valletta's presence. Not only had he been on the board of the anti-money laundering authority while it suppressed reports on the government corruption my mother had been uncovering, but he was married to one of Muscat's cabinet ministers. My father wrote to the commissioner, asking what Valletta's role in the investigation was, but received no reply. Our lawyers, Therese and Jason, found that Valletta, as head of the criminal investigations division, was overseeing the entire murder investigation. They advised us to write to the commissioner again, saying that Valletta couldn't ensure an independent and impartial inquiry, given his conflicts of interest, and must be removed.

While we waited for a reply from the police commissioner and continued to field media requests, the coroner called my father. He explained that identification, so far, was circumstantial. My mother was unrecognisable. Forensic officers investigating the explosion found that her car was completely burnt down. The bomb contained the equivalent of three to four hundred grams of TNT, enough to ensure death for the person in the driver's seat and capable of rupturing eardrums in the surrounding area. The forensic officers examining my mother found most of her burnt body was still in the car. The officers considered using an adhesive to reassemble her head but found it too fragmented. It had begun falling apart in a doctor's hands at the scene.

Her right leg and left foot were missing. The officers found them on the road. By the left front wheel, they found part of her right hand and a fragment of bone, both heavily burned.

The officers had removed what there was of my mother's body from the car and put it on a sterile blanket, and then into a body bag. They packed the rest of her remains separately and sent everything for DNA analysis at the morgue.

The coroner told my father that he needed a DNA sample from my brothers or me to match with her remains. My father said he would bring the three of us to the morgue. We were scared to get in a car. My father pleaded with us. 'It's a twenty-minute drive,' he said. 'Boys, please.'

It was the first time since her death that we'd left the house together. Matthew sat in the front passenger seat. I sat in the back with Andrew and held on to his arm.

When we arrived at the morgue, we did not know what to do with the car. We did not want to leave it unattended. We worried someone would tamper with it or attach a bomb. The bombing had pushed us into a world where anything was possible. We left it near a car park attendant and agreed to check its underside and seats for devices when we returned.

Inside, a plain-clothes officer guided us to the coroner's office. We were late, but the coroner was not there. We waited for him in silence. He barged in, shook my father's hand, and made small talk about knowing one of my father's cousins.

'I'm sorry,' Matthew said. 'This is totally inappropriate.'

The coroner and my father looked embarrassed.

'Matt,' my father pleaded. 'Please.'

'No, enough,' Matthew replied. 'It's not the time for small talk.'

The coroner lowered his head and explained he needed to take a swab of saliva from one of our mouths.

'Is this really necessary?' my father asked. 'She had pre-existing fractures in her left arm and right ankle. Can't you use those?'

'Yes, friend,' the coroner said, 'but there are a lot of fractures.'

Matthew was still agitated, and Andrew was trying to support my father, so I told the coroner he could take the swab from me. I signed a document, and he took my photo. I glanced at it on the way out but looked away before the image of myself, wan and unshaven, could fix in my mind.

Outside, we checked the underside of my father's car before returning to Bidnija.

The bomb site was cleared, but I felt unable to visit. Matthew would sometimes go, as late as three or four in the morning. One of the police officers stationed outside our house told my father. It worried him, but he did not know how to talk to Matthew about it.

People laid flowers and placed candles and banners during the day. My mother's parents began to bring flowers as well. My mother once wrote that when she heard of somebody who'd lost a child, her mind shut down at the thought that the same thing might happen to her. 'Those who have children are never safe. They are forever haunted by fear.'

My grandparents tried to visit the bomb site when no one else was around. But on one visit, they met the Bidnija brothers, an electrician and a plumber, who owned the field. They had worked on Dar Riħana and knew my mother. Their father, a farmer, had passed the field down to them. They told my grandparents that he had always left that part of the field to wild flowers, only working the soil around it.

It seemed unlikely. The bomb site was in the middle of the field. But what else could they say to my mother's parents as they walked through the dry cracked soil, to lay down their flowers?

Condolence letters and cards piled up in the house. One, a heavy envelope with a Roman postmark and addressed simply to 'Matthew Caruana Galizia, Bidnija', contained a card with a message of condolence, a black ribbon and a single leaf of bay laurel.

The bay laurel's waxy leaves are hard to tear. The shrub evolved in an unkind Mediterranean environment. It anchors deep in arid soil and can withstand both dry heat and cold winters.

My father, who still found it difficult to speak to my brothers and me about our mother, saw us puzzle over the leaf. He sat down, cards and letters scattered around us, and for a few moments we were three boys again, listening to our father tell a story.

Daphne, he told us, pursued by the lovelorn Apollo, begged her father, a lesser god, for help. His solution was to turn her into a bay laurel. My father went to my mother's books, pulled one off the shelf, and opened it to a passage from Ovid: 'A heavy numbness seized her limbs, thin bark closed over her breast, her hair turned into leaves, her arms into branches, her feet so swift a moment ago stuck fast in slow-growing roots, her face was lost in the canopy. Only her shining beauty was left.'

Apollo's unrequited love for Daphne was now impossible. He broke twigs off the Daphne tree, as the Greeks call it, and made himself a wreath, which he wore on his head. He vowed that Daphne, like him, would have eternal youth. Her leaves would never wither and fall.

As my father talked, I looked out of the living-room window at the bay laurel my parents had planted years earlier. Sunlight played on its leaves. It had grown tall, as tall as the old Aleppo pine near it. We went into the garden and cut off one of its branches.

We sent some leaves from the branch to the activists, a group of women who called themselves Occupy Justice, who had begun camping outside Castille on the night of the murder. One of Muscat's senior advisers called them prostitutes, adding, 'I'm sure that they will find someone to warm them up if they feel cold.'

*

We sent more leaves to the thousands of protesters who joined them, six days after the murder. They moved from near Castille to the Parliament building, where they roared, 'No change, no justice.'

Opposite Parliament, another group of women activists called il-Kenniesa – the Sweepers – unfurled two white banners. They were splattered with red paint like bloodstains. The first read 'MAFIA', and the second, 'STATE'. Police officers pulled them down. The activists put them back up.

The crowd of protesters applauded and began marching down Valletta's main street. They carried Maltese flags and placards emblazoned with my mother's last published words: *There are crooks everywhere you look*. Many wore T-shirts with her face on them. They stopped at the courthouse and hung on its gates a large banner with 'No Change, No Justice' written across the face of the police commissioner. I watched it all on the television at home in Bidnija. I recognised old school friends hanging the banner.

There were also current pupils from our old school who were there with their parents. The children carried flowers and cards with messages for my mother and left them at the foot of the Great Siege Monument opposite the courthouse, which commemorated the Maltese who'd died fighting the Ottoman siege five centuries ago. Its three bronze figures symbolise faith, valour and civilisation. It became a memorial to my mother, the site of monthly evening vigils held in her memory.

We cut another branch from the bay laurel for the Archbishop of Malta. He had come to the house to talk about my mother's funeral. The president had already been harassing us about the arrangements, calling my father's mobile repeatedly and, when he did not answer, trying from a different number. She was pushing to attend the funeral. 'The country needs unity,' she told my father. 'We must present a unified front.'

When we declined, she turned to the archbishop to press her case. My father was persuaded by his argument that the president, in her ceremonial role as head of state, wasn't part of the government my mother had been investigating. But as with the prime minister and the opposition leader, whom my mother had investigated and who had both sued her, my brothers and I refused to have her in attendance. None of them, we pointed out, had tried to stop the collapse of Malta's institutions that had enabled her death.

The archbishop turned to my father and said: 'They really take after their mother.'

'Yes,' my father replied. 'It's like having three wives.'

The archbishop did get us to agree to having the funeral at the Rotunda of Mosta, a big church not far from Bidnija, so that the whole country could mourn. I felt uneasy. My mother had never liked dramatic Catholic funerals, although she had once written that 'in extraordinary circumstances' funerals were important for the living, as with Paolo Borsellino and Giovanni Falcone, the anti-Mafia judges who had lost their lives to bombs in Sicily.

The second time we left the house together was for a libel hearing. At the start of 2017, my mother had reported an eyewitness's account that the economy minister, Chris Cardona, and his aide had gone together to a brothel while attending an EU conference in Germany. It was for this that the two of them had sued her for libel, getting the court to freeze her assets in anticipation of damages. My mother's readers had crowdfunded €70,000 to cover her legal costs. Cardona had responded that crowdfunding was a good idea because he was about to 'hit her' with more lawsuits.

This was nothing new for my mother. The cost of filing a libel suit is low in Malta, and there are no penalties for frivolous and vexatious lawsuits. Claimants rarely turn up in court; their goal is usually not to establish truth or justice, but to use the court as a means of harassment. In one case Konrad Mizzi filed against my mother, his lawyer argued that she was just a blogger and that she did not have a press card (she refused to use one), so her sources should be stripped of their protection under law. The Labour Party donor who had filed nineteen separate suits against my mother over the same story cost her €7,000 in court fees just to file her responses. In an earlier hearing of Cardona's case, my mother wrote how his lawyer's tone 'seethes with savage hatred and anger, with contempt, and above all, with extreme irritation that a woman not only opens her mouth without stroking egos (or something else), but then won't shut up'.

With her death, under Maltese law the Cardona suit now passed on to us. A few claimants had dropped their civil suits – and the criminal libel suits dropped automatically, as the police couldn't prosecute a dead person – but the rest kept pursuing their cases to claim damages from my mother's estate. We could get out of them by not registering as her heirs. But we did.

We knew the eyewitness in the Cardona case, and we had all the evidence, right down to the locker number he had used at the brothel. The eyewitness could not believe that Cardona, a lawyer himself, had committed perjury to sue, placing at risk his warrant to practise law and his parliamentary seat. 'After all,' the eyewitness said, 'it was just a brothel.'

Cardona was set to present his case first. A hearing was scheduled for a week after the murder, three days after our trip to the morgue.

A security official collected us from Dar Riħana that morning in a Land Rover. My father, in the front passenger seat, kept thanking him. I saw how he, like my mother, had grown unused to ordinary kindness.

We entered the courthouse through the back, thinking we would avoid people that way. But inside the place was packed – registrars, marshals, lawyers, victims, suspects. As soon as they saw us, they stopped talking. Their arms fell to their sides and they looked at us as if we were ghosts. My father, unaware of the effect we were having, walked over to his fellow lawyers as though nothing had ever happened. We pulled him into the courtroom.

The presiding magistrate had been reading out a decree to the registrar when we entered. The registrar looked at us and began to weep. The magistrate noticed us, paused and, with his mouth slightly agape, followed us around the room with his gaze. My father sat at the bar with our libel lawyer, and we sat on a bench behind the bar.

'The court offers its condolences,' the magistrate said.

Cardona had not showed. His lawyer asked the magistrate for an adjournment. Our lawyer shook his head in disbelief.

Matthew stood and walked to the bar. 'Sorry,' he told the magistrate, 'I want to make a statement.'

There was no procedure for such an intervention. My father and our lawyer looked anxious, but the magistrate allowed Matthew to speak.

'I want to make it clear that we want the case to continue,' he told the court. 'Chris Cardona has an interest in not allowing the case to go forward.'

Cardona's lawyer flew into a rage. He told the magistrate that despite our 'strong emotions', it was not fair that we had been given the chance to make a statement.

'I am not emotional,' Matthew replied.

The magistrate ruled that it was up to Cardona whether the case continued. For the time being, he had no choice but to adjourn the case. We would have to wait to present our evidence.

To lighten the mood on our way out of court, our lawyer began telling us a story about our mother at one of her many libel hearings. It was summer, and she was wearing sandals. The security guards told her that she could not enter the courtroom in open-toed shoes. Inside, everyone was waiting for her, and the magistrate was ready to find her in contempt of court. Our lawyer called her and she explained her dilemma. He called my father at his office, two streets away. My father went to the courthouse door and swapped shoes with her. She entered the courtroom wearing oversized black leather loafers, and he went back to his office in a pair of women's sandals.

I felt myself crack into a smile for the first time in days. Then I thought about what it must have been like for my mother to swim upstream for thirty years.

The security official who had taken us to court hurried us back into his Land Rover and took us to the airport. We were on our way to the European Parliament. Andrew's friends in the Parliament and in diplomatic missions in Brussels had set us up with meetings, and the president had scheduled a plenary debate about media freedom. With Maltese institutions so compromised, it was plain to us that justice would have to come from outside the country – and from us.

From room to room at the Parliament, delegation to delegation, like representatives of big tech in our suits and ties, we lobbied. We told the socialists that Muscat's government was betraying its values. We told the Greens that corruption was wrecking Malta's environment and widening inequality. We told the Eurosceptics that Malta was an example of EU dysfunction. And we told conservatives and liberals alike that the rule of law in Malta was in crisis; that the EU was only as strong as its weakest member, and Malta had become its back door to illicit money. We said that if the EU could not handle Malta, then it had no hope with the democratic crises unfolding in Poland and Hungary.

Presenting Malta in that way surprised them. No one had ever really thought about us. When they did, it was with affection: we were a small, sunny island nation. The country's institutional collapse, its rampant political corruption, seemed to have gone unnoticed. The dissonance between their idea of us and the murder of my mother helped catch their attention. Journalists were not supposed to be murdered in Malta. That was something that happened in Russia. Hadn't Europe consigned car bombs to history? A French bureaucrat we met described my mother's killing as 'spectacular'. The MEPs took notes, asked questions and treated us like witnesses of a crime scene.

The next day was the plenary debate, with all the members in attendance. The focus was to be how to improve the safety of journalists working in the EU in light of our mother's murder. At the beginning of the session, the president introduced us and asked for a minute's silence in her memory. The seven hundred or so members stood, hands clasped in front of them, heads bowed, as the long seconds passed in silence. When the minute ended, they turned to where we sat in the public gallery and began to clap. The noise rolled up from the benches like thunder.

Then the members began speaking. A Green MEP called my mother's murder 'a brutal demonstration of power by those who consider themselves above the law'. He said she was killed, rather than a police officer or magistrate, because she had had to take on the functions of such officials. A Dutch Liberal MEP argued that if a member state did not 'uphold the European standards when it comes to the rule of law', there was in effect 'no rule of law in the European Union'.

The three MEPs from Malta's Labour delegation, including the party's former leader Alfred Sant, submitted a joint statement that warned 'there are those' who were exploiting my mother's murder to damage Malta's democratic credentials. When the Parliament debated a resolution to intervene in Malta, his delegation voted against it. The Maltese MEPs who supported it were labelled traitors. They were in good company. The resolution passed with 466 out of a possible 751 votes.

The European Parliament sent a cross-party delegation to Malta to investigate its 'serious concerns' about the country's rule of law, democracy, media freedom, and the independence of its police force and judiciary.

On our return from Brussels, we drove straight back to the house. I wandered through it as though in haunted ruins. I heard Andrew crumple onto his old bed and cry. In my room was the desk that had been mine since I was a boy. I found a box with rolling papers that my parents had never discovered, and the books they'd given me two Christmases before. Here I was again, a boy, a teenager and a grown man of twenty-eight, all at once.

It was in this room that my mother had read to me, and stayed with me after a nightmare. It was in this room that we had argued about my grades and my smoking. I thought back to one of her refrains, said in exasperation: 'A mother's love doesn't reward mothers; it empowers her children.'

Matthew was on his laptop in his room. He was looking through the ElectroGas leak our mother had begun receiving at the start of 2017, a few months before her murder. It was still live.

Almost three weeks after my mother's death, the magistrate overseeing her inquest released her remains for burial.

The day of her funeral was cloudless and warm; it seemed like an earthly indifference. Black suits, black ties, black hearts. We walked slowly from the cortège and into the church, behind my mother's closed coffin. The hundreds of people gathered outside broke into applause, and the hundreds of people inside continued it, the sound echoing and re-echoing around the oversized dome until the coffin was laid in front of the altar.

Below it lay the flowers and wreaths people had sent. Spotting one labelled 'Anġlu Farrugia' – he was now the speaker of Malta's Parliament – Matthew grabbed it from under the coffin, ripped up the label, and kicked it away. The archbishop, with his mitre and his swinging censer, and the dozen priests and former bishops pretended not to see as they took up their positions above the coffin.

Behind our extended family, I could hear the sound of weeping mixed with choral song. Our friends and our old teachers were there. There were farmers from Bidnija. There were former presidents and prime ministers, the chief justice and judges.

The archbishop directed some of his homily towards journalists: 'Never grow weary in your mission to be the eyes, the ears and the mouth of the people.' And to the murderers: 'However hard you try to evade from the justice of men, you will never escape from the justice of God.' He then turned to my brothers and me. 'Your beloved mother died a cruel death by the hidden hand of someone who valued darkness over the light, for his actions are evil. See that you will always be the children of the light.'

I wondered how we could be children of the light in what felt like complete darkness.

Matthew and Andrew helped carry my mother's coffin out of the church and into the hearse, while I walked alongside Jessica. The crowd began to clap again. The sound filled the square and then it stopped. In this wide-open space, with its main roads blocked to traffic and its shops and cafés closed, all that could be heard was the sound of my brothers' footsteps as they moved slowly towards the hearse.

Then out of the silence came a man's voice. 'Justice! We want justice!' he shouted. As we drove away, I could see in the rear-view mirror people raising two fingers in the shape of a V, an Allied symbol of democracy and victory, and I could hear them singing the national anthem.

'It was the first time,' my grandfather Michael told me, 'that I felt Maltese.'

I flew back to London a few hours after the burial, leaving my brothers behind. In our garden, Jessica and I planted a bay laurel.

14

I felt easier leaving Malta so quickly after my mother's funeral because I knew that my aunt Cora and my brothers would soon join me. The New York-based Committee to Protect Journalists, one of the NGOs working on my mother's case, had organised security training for us near London.

A former Special Air Service soldier picked up Cora, my brothers and me at Heathrow airport and drove us to a country house outside the city, where two more former soldiers met us. They taught us how to detect car bombs, do counter-surveillance and perform first aid. Then we had a session on grief and trauma. One of the soldiers spoke calmly about the mutilated bodies he had seen in combat but cried when he spoke about the natural death of his elderly mother.

Matthew was still working on the ElectroGas leak. We asked him to give it a break, but he told us that the leak was important; it was the one major investigation our mother had begun but did not get to publish. He had brought a hard drive containing all the leaked documents, including ones that kept coming in after the murder. He showed us an email chain among the company's employees about my mother's murder.

'It's a big one!' one employee wrote. 'I used to think she was untouchable . . . looks like some things are changing.' In another chain from the day of the murder, employees were told to 'slow it down on Portomaso' – the business tower where Yorgen Fenech, their director, had an office. They were trying to get hold of him, but he had called in sick that day.

Cora told us we had to pass on the leak. It was dangerous and insane, she said, for Matthew to work on it or even to keep the documents.

'So, what the hell do you want me to do?' he asked.

What he did was contact Stephanie Kirchgaessner and Juliette Garside from the *Guardian*, whom he knew from working on the Panama Papers, and told them that we had some data they should see.

They drove to the country house where we were staying that night, and Matthew copied the leak onto a hard drive for them. It was enough work for dozens of journalists. Juliette and Stephanie took the hard drive and went back to the *Guardian*'s office.

The following day we met Stephen Grey, a reporter from Reuters. Stephen took down the details of our discussion in shorthand. He said he wanted to work on the story and would collaborate with the *Guardian*.

We all met in the *Guardian*'s investigations room in London on our way back home. The newspaper's engineers showed Matthew their technology to organise and search through leaked material. We talked to Stephen and Juliette about what they could expect from us as sources. We understood that when we left the room, we would be shut out of the editorial process. We wondered what would come of the journalists' project.

*

My father was still in Malta. He hadn't received a reply from the police commissioner about Silvio Valletta, so we instructed Therese and Jason to sue the police to force Valletta's removal from the murder investigation.

In our court filing, we argued that Valletta's involvement breached our right to an independent and impartial investigation, which was protected by the European Convention on Human Rights. The murder was a 'targeted killing' of a journalist whose work focused on members of the same cabinet Valletta's wife belonged to and on Valletta himself, as a board member of the anti-money laundering authority. We added that the police force wasn't keeping us informed of progress in the investigation, even as stories about it were being fed to newspapers.

My brothers and I were still in London. It was late November, and my twenty-ninth birthday came and went. I was distributing a dossier that I had written, anonymously, about Malta's corruption crisis to journalists and public officials around Europe. Over its fifty-three pages, institution by institution, I described how the country's rule of law had collapsed since Muscat had first been elected, falling even faster than Hungary's and Poland's. It started with the judiciary: Muscat had made fifteen appointments to the bench, eleven of whom were connected directly to the Labour Party, out of a then total of twenty-two judges and twenty-two magistrates.

My brothers set up more meetings. We spoke to the board of Reporters Without Borders UK, which made our mother's case central to its campaigning work. Its board included a barrister named Caoilfhionn Gallagher. After we spoke, she'd rushed up to us like a hurricane and offered to help us pro bono. We went to meet with her at her firm, the internationally renowned Doughty Street Chambers. We had no idea how to pronounce her first name, so we simply asked for 'Ms Gallagher' and even got that wrong, as the second 'g' is silent. She met us with her junior, Jonathan Price, in a room full of leather-bound legal tomes. The two of them ran us through an international legal strategy, then immediately started helping Therese and Jason on the Valletta case.

Keith Arnaud, who as head of homicide reported to Valletta, would call our legal action 'a hit below the belt' in a Facebook post. To us, it seemed like more evidence that Arnaud wasn't grasping the political context of the murder. The investigation felt even more hopeless.

Muscat's officials and the pro-government press said our case was an attempt to derail the murder investigation. And the investigation, they said, was making progress. But they didn't bother to tell us how.

Muscat scheduled a press conference for the morning of 4 December. He spoke in English for the international press about a major breakthrough: eight Maltese men had just been arrested in connection with my mother's murder.

The police commissioner was nowhere to be seen during the press conference. Muscat stood alone at a podium, saying that investigators had trailed the men for some time and believed them to be the ones who had carried out the car bombing. He opened the floor to questions.

An employee of the Labour Party's media organisation asked Muscat whether the murder had anything to do with fuel smuggling. He demurred. A journalist asked whether the investigators believed the suspects to be the master-minds behind the murder.

'I really wish I could answer that question,' the Poodle replied in Maltese. 'I have a very clear idea in my mind about that question.' But he went no further, saying that to answer would prejudice the case. He said the investigators' work would be made public if and when the compilation of evidence, the court process in which a magistrate ruled on the strength of the prosecution's case, began. He ended the press conference. Soon after, Muscat tweeted that another two men had been detained in connection with the case, bringing the total number of arrests to ten. It was all news to us. We were learning of major developments in our mother's case along with the rest of the country.

Footage of one raid carried out by the authorities was given exclusively to the public broadcaster and to the Labour Party's television station. It was spectacular. It involved soldiers, heavily armed police officers and plain-clothes officers; army trucks, dinghies, a drone and a helicopter. It was on a decrepit shed, once used to store potatoes for export, on a wharf in Marsa, not far from the horse-racing track. It seemed to have served as the suspects' hangout. The footage captured empty beer cans, fish tails and jawbones, a Spider-Man doll hanging from the roof, and an old wooden cable drum used as a table.

Soldiers moved towards the shed on a dinghy, climbed up, and pointed their machine guns at the silhouettes of two men. They ordered them to lie face down on the ground with their arms stretched out. They did, seeming resigned to their fate. Two large white vans pulled up on the other side of the shed, and armed police officers poured out of them.

Some ran in to secure the area, others surrounded the men. The footage then switched to the arrest of a third man outside the shed. He faced a parked car, his arms splayed against it, as a plain-clothes officer searched him. The footage then cut to officers searching the area and the men, with cable ties around their wrists, in different locations outside the shed. The footage ended.

It was impossible to make out the identities of the men from this short, disjointed footage. They were always filmed at a distance and their faces were blurred out. But not long after these first news reports, the identities of all the arrested men were leaked to the same media.

Seven were released on bail. The police alleged that they were involved in procuring and supplying the bomb used to kill my mother. The police kept the remaining three – the ones arrested at the potato shed – in custody. These men were suspected of planting and detonating the bomb. They were known to the police – their mugshots were also leaked to the press – but their names and faces meant nothing to us.

We asked around and heard that they were involved in a lot of recent car bombings, including the attempted murder of Romeo Bone. That they were involved in the gangs, centred on Marsa, that trafficked drugs and helped smuggle fuel out of Libya. They were the brothers Degiorgio – Alfred and George – and their associate Vincent Muscat. Alfred was known as il-Fulu, the Bean. George Degiorgio's associates called him ic-Ciniz, the Chinese. Short, scruffy, middle-aged Vincent Muscat, whose skull was distorted by an old gunshot wound, was called Kohhu.

The police took the three men to court the following afternoon for their arraignment. They pleaded not guilty to murder, conspiracy, forming part of a criminal gang, using explosives to kill, being in possession of explosives, and recidivism.

The compilation of evidence against the three men was scheduled to start a little more than a week later. The first magistrate declared to the court that she'd been at St Dorothy's with my aunt Amanda. The defence asked for her recusal and she agreed. The police took the three men back to prison and brought them to court again four days later.

The second magistrate told the court that my mother once mentioned her in a blog post about Muscat's appointments to the bench. She recused herself. The police took the men back to prison. Thirteen of the thirty days for a magistrate to decide if there was a case for the men to answer had already passed.

It was the first hurdle, and already it felt like we were falling. I could tell my father was suffering a double disappointment: over the case and at the realisation that the justice system he had spent more than thirty years of his life working in was so weak. But he was in court the next day, along with the three men and our lawyers, for the third magistrate.

The defence searched through my mother's blog, the country's corruption encyclopedia, and found a mention of the magistrate's husband. It was praise for his work at the planning authority. They asked for her recusal. She rejected their request, and the proceedings, at last, began.

The prosecution – Arnaud, his deputy Zahra and the

attorney general – began presenting their evidence in court. The interrogation transcripts revealed that it was George, the Chinese, who had made a series of crucial errors that led to the arrests.

Arnaud and Zahra had begun interrogating the Chinese at 8.25 p.m., the day after his arrest, in room 122 of the Floriana police headquarters. The Chinese would not even confirm the year of his birth as 1962, give his father's name, or indicate if he wanted a lawyer. He was no stranger to these circumstances. He had been convicted of threatening a police officer and charged with possessing unlicensed weapons, cocaine, and lock picks. He knew he had a right to remain silent, and he used it.

Arnaud told the Chinese that the bomb was detonated with an SMS and presented him with a photograph of a reproduction of the detonation device. He explained how the device worked and then said, 'we have the evidence showing that you were the person who sent the SMS'.

The policeman laid out what his team – including Europol agents, the Netherlands Forensic Institute and the FBI cellular analysis survey team – had found against the Chinese. They had pieced it together carefully.

The three hit men had struggled for weeks to get the bomb into my mother's car because she had no daily routine and because she shared the Peugeot with Matthew. Alfred – the Bean – watched my mother's movements from his lookout at Tarġa Battery, the old artillery post facing Bidnija. Forensic officers found his DNA on a cigarette butt there.

Unlike the rest of us, my mother always parked in the garden, where the car was protected by the two-metre-high boundary wall that had been built after the first arson attack. Our two dogs roamed around in the garden.

On the evening of 15 October, Matthew had returned from Exiles, the beach in Sliema where my parents first noticed each other, around 6.30 p.m. Thinking that either he or my mother, who was already home, would use the car again later that evening, he left the Peugeot outside the walls. As it happened, neither of them went out again that night. The men got their chance.

They waited for nightfall, then collected the bomb the Maksar brothers supplied from a garage in Żebbuġ, in the south of Malta. Forensic officers traced the TNT used in the bomb to this garage. The men headed back to Bidnija to plant it. This time, the Chinese went to the Targa Battery lookout. Koħħu took a position at the top of the Bidnija road.

The Bean levered open the Peugeot's rear window on the passenger side, opened the door, and placed the bomb under the driver's seat. He switched on the device. Then he went to spend the rest of the night at the Targa Battery while his brother headed to the shed in Marsa. At 1.41 a.m. the detonation device was armed remotely.

At 6.14 a.m., the Chinese switched on the burner phone that would be used to trigger the bomb. He gathered his things, including a second burner phone to communicate with his brother and Koħħu's burner phones, and a Samsung Galaxy phone registered to his name, and climbed aboard his brother's cabin cruiser, *Maya*, moored close to the potato shed. Unbeknown to him, this Samsung Galaxy phone was being tapped by the Malta Security Service because of his suspected involvement in another crime that wasn't disclosed to the court.

At 7.55 a.m., he set sail, passing out of the Grand Harbour, then west past Sliema and St Julian's, before turning back east towards Valletta again. The Chinese liked to fish, and had told friends that he was going fishing on this day.

Just before noon, the Chinese realised the trigger phone did not have any credit. Using his personal Samsung, the one tapped by the Security Service, he called a friend from the boat to ask him to add €5 in Vodafone credit to the trigger phone. The friend was hunting in the countryside and could not help. Still using the Samsung, the Chinese called another friend with the same request.

'Don't take long, if you can,' he told this friend. Soon the phone credit arrived.

At 2.55 p.m., he was idling in a stretch of water sheltered by the breakwater at the tip of Valletta's peninsula, under a monument to the victims of the Second World War bombing raids of the city.

It was here that his brother's burner phone called his. The Bean, positioned at his lookout at Tarġa Battery, told him my mother was leaving the house. Precisely forty-four seconds later, the call ended. My mother had gone back into the house to collect the chequebook she had forgotten.

The Bean called his brother again and stayed on the phone with him for one minute and forty-seven seconds, as he described my mother's movements. This time, she really was leaving. She got into the Peugeot, started the engine and drove down the lane, turning left to head down the Bidnija road.

Soon after the turn, the Chinese sent a text message to the bomb. At 2.58 p.m., the message – '#REL1=ON' – activated a circuit on the device.

The Bean heard the first explosion while he was still on the line. The Chinese began sailing back to Marsa. Using the Samsung phone, he called a friend and, laughing, told him, 'I've caught two big fish today.'

Then he texted his girlfriend at 3.30 p.m. *Buy me wine, my love*, he told her. She replied: *OK*.

By 4 p.m., he was cruising to the *Maya*'s mooring near the potato shed. He took the SIM card out of the Samsung and threw it into the harbour. He chucked the burner phones, too. They sank to the seabed, settling among several other burner phones and SIM cards.

Arnaud told the Chinese that he was simply recounting what the hit man did, and the mistakes he made. He told the Chinese that it was those mistakes that got him caught.

Arnaud had questions. Why, he wanted to know, did the Chinese have the number of his girlfriend written on his hand? Why had all three men thrown away their personal phones right before the raid? Why was the Labrador they usually had chained to the old potato shed, the one the police had always seen during their surveillance, not there on the morning of their arrests?

'Did you know we were about to arrest you?' he asked.

The investigators did suspect that the men had advance knowledge of the raid, but the one question they couldn't answer was the most important. Before closing the interrogation, Arnaud asked the Chinese a simple question – the one he didn't have an answer to yet: Why did you kill a journalist?

*

The evidence against the three men presented in court appeared strong. But the prosecution struggled to connect the murder to my mother's journalism, and so did we. Her constant theme had been the corruption of Muscat's government – white-collar crime, involving accountants and shell companies, not car bombs and Marsa gangs.

The theory that diesel smugglers were behind the murder, given the involvement of these three men, took on new force. But we just knew it didn't end with them. We pored through my mother's twenty thousand blog posts and three decades' worth of columns, searching for a connection. Any optimism that they would lead us somewhere disappeared soon after their arrests, like a match struck in the dark and quickly extinguished.

Our campaign continued.

We at least felt encouraged that the delegation of MEPs that came to Malta after our first campaigning trip to the European Parliament had proved effective. They said they arrived 'seriously concerned' about the rule of law in Malta and left 'even more worried'. They reported authorities' apparent reluctance to investigate and prosecute major cases, which created a 'perception of impunity'. They singled out the failure to prosecute corruption and money laundering. It was a damning assessment and cast my mother's murder in the context of a dysfunctional state. The MEPs submitted their report to the European Commission and said they'd pursue a formal audit of the rule of law in Malta, which could result in the suspension of its rights as an EU member state if the picture deteriorated.

The Maltese government and its supporters accused the MEPs of foreign interference. Some suggested that my brothers and I had been feeding them 'poison'. They pointed to the ongoing criminal proceedings against the three men as evidence against there being a crisis in the rule of law. They used the proceedings to try to put a lid on the murder.

During the last parliamentary sitting of the year, an opposition MP tabled a motion for an inquiry into my mother's investigations of corruption, including her reporting on the leader of his own party, the Nationalists. His motion called for the appointment of three retired judges trusted by at least two-thirds of the house to have access to all the evidence held by the state and the power to summon witnesses.

Muscat, who had the power to convene such an inquiry, did not attend the session. The MP gestured to the prime minister's empty seat and repeated what history records King Henry II saying to his courtiers about the Archbishop of Canterbury – 'Will no one rid me of this turbulent priest?' – who was then murdered in his cathedral. Every single Labour MP present voted for an amended version of the motion that replaced calls for an inquiry and any reference to my mother's reporting with praise for Muscat and what he'd achieved with the murder investigation.

My brothers and I watched it unfold from a safe house, once an orphanage, in the north-west of France, which we used as a base for our campaigning trips around Europe. There was a trip to Vienna for a meeting with the Organization for Security and Co-operation in Europe, where we gave a speech on my mother's case to ambassadors from across Europe, and more trips to the European Parliament, where we met more MEPs. The safe house was by the coast, and when we weren't travelling we'd punctuate our long cold days of calls with politicians, NGOs and journalists with long wet walks along a grey promenade. I felt we were becoming increasingly isolated and, with piles of documents and diagrams spread around us, were starting to look like obsessive, unshaven conspiracy theorists. Our father came to stay for a few days. He cooked for us and fussed over the state of the house. He was worried that the three of us had given up our jobs to campaign on my mother's case full-time, relying on him for financial support.

My father was back in Malta when Parliament rejected the judge-led inquiry, and in court the next day to testify in our case to remove Valletta from the investigation. The judge had encouraged us to come to an out-of-court settlement with the government, on the grounds that the very existence of the case was causing damage to Malta. We pointed out that we had written to the commissioner before filing the case, but he had never answered.

The judge didn't like the case and he didn't like the 'Urgent Advice' that our Doughty Street lawyers had published at our request ahead of the hearing. The lawyers had argued that the government was in flagrant breach of our rights and demanded urgent action to remove Valletta. The judge described this as an 'attack upon the independence and impartiality of the judiciary'.

His reaction matched that of the government. 'The undertone of the so-called "Urgent Advice" is that the State was itself involved in the murder of Daphne Caruana Galizia,' a government press release stated. Its 'irresponsible allegations' were based solely on the 'open contempt' that the Caruana Galizias held towards Malta and 'cannot be made or taken lightly'.

As the judge seemed partial to the government's argument, my father was nervous before he testified that morning. The judge asked him why he had filed the case. 'Duty,' my father said. 'Out of respect to my wife and her memory.' And, his voice breaking: 'I cannot find peace.' The judge then asked him why he thought the murder was 'a political killing'. He replied: 'She was murdered for what she had written or what she was about to write.'

The hearing ended; judgment wouldn't come for months. But the case and the attempt at convening a judge-led inquiry in Malta gave us the idea for a new campaigning goal. We could use the human rights law underpinning our case, of the need for an impartial and independent investigation, and the law that the Nationalist MP tried using to start a judge-led inquiry into my mother's work, to campaign for a much broader inquiry.

Leaving Andrew and Matthew in France, I went to London for regular meetings with our lawyers at Doughty Street Chambers about it. We were still locked out of the police investigation – relations with Arnaud and his team remained tense – and locked out of the magistrate's inquest because, by law, he operated in secrecy. Even so, both inquiries focused solely on criminal culpability when there was a wider and more serious question: whether Malta could have prevented my mother's assassination.

As a signatory to the European Convention on Human Rights, Malta was obliged to answer that question. Its second article, 'Everyone's right to life shall be protected by law', places an obligation on states to protect life; to have laws and institutions in place that protect individuals. The obligation is heightened for specific individuals whose lives are at risk, people of whom the state should be aware. But there is another obligation on states: not to take life – and we suspected that the state, in the standard human rights language, was, or may have been, implicated in my mother's assassination. She was a journalist investigating state corruption. It was state officials, and those close to them, who had had the greatest motive to kill her. So, we needed an inquiry that was both independent and public.

Malta had never convened a public inquiry before and, although our lawyers advised that our laws allowed for one, the power to order one rested solely with the prime minister. We kept coming up against the same problem: that Malta's post-independence constitution had effectively renamed colonial governors as prime ministers. It was another long shot. But what else could we do?

In London, I hoped to spend more time with Jessica. Like my brothers' partners, she worried about my health and the long stretches I spent away. But the meetings at Doughty Street about the public inquiry were increasingly frequent. And I began travelling again, sometimes with the Doughty Street team, trying to convince other governments to pressure Muscat into convening the inquiry.

The diplomats and foreign MPs and other officials I met with all said they were doing so behind closed doors. I explained that Muscat, who was then trying to become president of the council that defined the European Union's political direction and priorities, was sensitive to how foreign politicians saw him. He had to be publicly embarrassed into acting.

When I returned to London, I was too tired to do anything. One night things came to a head. Jessica asked me when things would return to normal. I said never. She started to cry and I did not know what to do.

Friends tried to draw my brothers and me out for drinks or holidays; to get us, as the phrase goes, to move on. But that was an impossibility to us. We could not have a drink or go on a holiday without thinking about our mother. Each moment we spent away from the case was a moment we felt further from her. In this private world, we were one another's buoys. One sinking, the others swimming, in changing configurations of trauma.

At times, our quest seemed no more than an act of mourning. Keeping going felt like a way of honouring our mother, of not giving up on the idea that justice in Malta was possible. This was the legacy she had left us. Her quest had become ours.

15

In January 2018 my brothers and I went to the Council of Europe, which is a non-EU body that enforces the European Convention on Human Rights, to call for a special rapporteur to our mother's case. The idea had come from Bill Browder, the investor and human rights campaigner whose accountant, Sergei Magnitsky, had been killed in state custody in Russia. During a phone call from our safe house in France, Bill told us that a special rapporteur, like the one he had lobbied to have assigned to Magnitsky's case, could interview sources, collect evidence, and then write a report that might recommend sanctions against Malta, as a member state.

Aside from the Magnitsky case, the Council of Europe had only ever assigned a rapporteur in two other murder cases: that of Anna Politkovskaya, the journalist and human rights activist, who had been shot dead in her Moscow apartment block in October 2006, and that of Boris Nemtsov, Russia's opposition leader, who had been gunned down outside the Kremlin in February 2015. The odds were long, but we were willing to try for it.

On an afternoon train from Paris to Strasbourg, while talking on the phone with Tony Murphy, our solicitor in London, my brothers and I wrote the motion for a special rapporteur, based on the Nemtsov motion. In three hundred words, we called for 'an examination of the full context of the assassination, including institutional failures and the systematic targeting of Caruana Galizia for her work'. For a rapporteur to be appointed, we would need the support of at least twenty members of the council's parliamentary assembly, which is comprised of MPs from the council's member states.

In Strasbourg, we walked around the council building, handing out flyers and putting up posters on noticeboards. The Maltese government delegation removed the posters whenever they found them, and we kept putting them back until we had to stop to prepare our speeches.

A young Maltese assembly member, an MP from the Nationalist Party, stopped by the table where we were working and told Matthew that things in Malta looked so bleak he was going to leave politics. He said he planned to grow pomegranates in Gozo because a German doctor had told him they could cure cancer.

I saw that Matthew was about to give him both barrels. Andrew and I pulled him away and headed to the event room, where we were to be hosted by two MPs, one a Dutch Conservative, the other a German Socialist. Soon journalists and MPs filled the room.

Matthew spoke first. 'Our mother's death warrant could have been signed two years ago,' he said. After her first major corruption reports, he said, 'It was like watching her death unfold in slow motion.'

'If justice isn't done in her case,' Andrew added, 'it would be like killing her a second time.'

'Please find that motion,' I said, 'and sign it and ask your colleagues to sign it.'

After our speeches, our hosts asked the audience for

questions. 'Did your mother ever encounter any difficulties of freedom of expression during her lifetime,' one of Muscat's MPs asked, 'or was she able to write whatever she wanted?'

The room fell quiet.

'I'm sorry,' Matthew replied, 'but your question is outrageous. She was killed for what she wrote, for God's sake. How can you possibly say that she was free to express herself?'

We took more questions, thanked everyone for their time, and left to collect more signatures for our motion. We did not know how many we had by the time we returned to our hotel, exhausted. By this point, we had all burnt through our savings and were relying completely on our father for money, so Andrew had booked just one room, with three beds. It turned out to have only a double bed and a single.

'I'll take the single,' Matthew said.

Andrew and I collapsed onto the double bed and checked our phones for news. Our motion had received 114 signatures by close of day, which meant that more than a third of the assembly had signed it. 'I've never seen so much support for a motion,' a council bureaucrat told us the next day. 'I could only wish my children would do this for me, if . . .' He trailed off.

The official explained to us that the next step was for the council to elect one of its own MPs as the rapporteur. Pieter Omtzigt, the Dutch MP who had hosted us, was a candidate. His colleagues called him a 'pit bull' because he never let things go. The Maltese government lobbied against his candidacy, but he won.

*

Our next Council of Europe stop was an obscure agency called Moneyval, a group of experts on fighting money laundering and the financing of terrorism.

Moneyval works by conducting regular assessments of its member countries' financial systems, checking whether they comply with laws and standards on financial crime. It has no enforcement power, but its strength lies in the result of its assessments, which carry ratings. Financial institutions, small to large, use those ratings to determine where they can operate in a country and whether they should accept its financial transactions.

If a country is blacklisted based on a Moneyval assessment, its financial sector is shut out of the global economy. Malta's financial sector, which had ballooned and globalised under Muscat, accounted for a large share of the economy's rapid growth by this point. This gave us leverage for our campaign.

We met the Moneyval team responsible for Malta. It seemed strange that four youngish bureaucrats in collared shirts and V-neck sweaters could wield so much power. We talked to them about our mother's investigative work and provided them with as much documentation and evidence as possible.

We presented the same set of allegations that my mother had put together not long before her murder: that the prime minister's chief of staff and his energy minister had 'set out to cheat us and lie to us, to defraud the government they run, to defraud us'. Schembri and Mizzi took ownership of Panama shell companies, using the same accountants and lawyers, shortly after being elected. Mizzi and Muscat awarded a privatisation contract to gasify

Malta's energy supply to Fenech's company in a deal that profited him enormously at the public's expense. A United Arab Emirates shell company, 17 Black, linked to the new power station but of unknown ownership, was a client of Mizzi's and Schembri's companies. Another Panama company, Egrant, had an account at Pilatus Bank, the Azerbaijani laundromat, but it was unclear whether it was part of this same picture. What was clear, as my mother had pointed out, was that Schembri was 'the common factor' lurking behind every part of the picture. It was even Schembri who had ensured that Pilatus got its banking licence.

The Moneyval analysts wanted to know if he had resigned.

No, we said.

Ah, so he was fired, they said.

No again.

But surely the police were investigating him.

Not that either.

We understand, they said.

Next came GRECO, the council's anti-corruption body. We gave the analyst responsible for Malta the same documentation, the same talk. It was by this point coming easily, like a well-rehearsed sales pitch.

Back home, government officials and supporters said we were shaming Malta. Across the Labour Party's radio and television stations, its newspapers and social media channels, in Parliament, they called us traitors, said we had a hidden agenda, and that we were exploiting our mother's death for money, fame, or something. Matthew bore the brunt of the abuse, in the same way that our mother had. 'The Son of the Witch', they called him.

Muscat's officials wove conspiracy theories around Matthew, who began spending more time in Malta. They repeated the lie that he had left the Peugeot outside our garden wall the night before her murder so that the hit men could find it. One of Muscat's supporters told Matthew he'd send him a 'jigsaw puzzle' of our mother for Christmas. Another, spotting Matthew as he drove past the bomb site, mimicked the sound of an explosion.

The ugliness in Malta had always been difficult to explain outside the country. It was expected and self-perpetuating. The dehumanisation of a journalist allowed for her murder, and her murder allowed for the erasure of her work and whoever carried it on. The norm shifts, the floor falls, the ugliness deepens.

The campaigning continued. Matthew travelled so much that he always seemed to be in the same clothes. On one trip, some German federal agents who were investigating individuals in the Panama Papers leak noticed that he'd been wearing the same outfit the last time they'd seen him. After their meeting, they dropped him off at H&M.

The German federal agents had acquired data from my mother's devices on the Panama Papers. They were wary of handing it over to the Maltese magistrate running an inquiry into my mother's report on Egrant, fearing that the data, in the hands of Maltese authorities, would jeopardise her sources. The Germans said they'd answer any questions on it but, to protect her sources, would not hand over the data. 'Why do these people have something to hide?' wrote Bedingfield, Muscat's aide who had blogged about my mother relentlessly. 'Is there interest simply in leaving this murder unsolved, so that they will be able to blame the Labour party?' And: 'Maybe we will start seeing some banners asking, "Where is that laptop?"' Within hours, large printed banners, in English and Maltese, appeared at a busy road junction: 'Why is someone hiding Daphne's laptop?' On social media, alongside photos of the banners, Muscat's officials used my mother's final words against us: '#thesituationisdesperate'.

In London, I found myself struggling to explain why my family had to campaign for justice day and night, and why Maltese society was so partisan that it could not come together even to condemn my mother's murder. I would tell people about the secret Facebook groups of Labour Party fanatics that were uncovered by *The Shift News*, a new group of Maltese journalists. The Facebook groups had 60,000 members, including Muscat, his officials and the president. Here was where the trolls that my mother had always suspected were working in coordination had planned their harassment and slander campaigns against her. The day of her murder, thousands of them had celebrated her death. 'Fuck her blood,' one wrote. 'Let her burn in hell.' A police sergeant who my mother had reported on years earlier said on Facebook: 'Everyone gets what they deserve, cow dung! Feeling happy :)' Others shared memes of clinking champagne flutes and witches burning at the stake. Some even claimed my mother had organised her own car bombing to shame the country.

I felt safer outside Malta. Matthew decided to move back in March and immediately began campaigning there.

He had three questions printed on an enormous vinyl banner: 'Why aren't Keith Schembri and Konrad Mizzi in prison, Police Commissioner? Why isn't your wife being investigated by the police, Joseph Muscat? Who paid for Daphne Caruana Galizia to be blown up after she asked these questions?' His friends hung it from the second floor of the Valletta town house belonging to my father's family. It was torn down within hours. Matthew reported the act to the police as theft. Then they printed and hung another banner, with an additional sentence: 'This is our second banner – our first got stolen.'

And then, after he learnt that the planning authority had torn down the first banner, we instructed Therese and Eve Borg Costanzi, another human rights lawyer we had added to the team, to sue the planning authority for breaching our right to freedom of expression. The case would win us damages and would be the first constitutional precedent we set as part of our campaign.

In the months since we'd met with Stephanie Kirchgaessner and Juliette Garside from the *Guardian* and Stephen Grey from Reuters, they'd been joined by reporters from eighteen organisations in fifteen countries, under the banner of the Daphne Project. In April 2018, they began publishing their first stories.

The *New York Times* carried a front-page report about my mother's assassination. Reuters published a special report about it on its homepage. *Le Monde* wrote about Malta's role in laundering Azerbaijani money. *La Repubblica* and the Organized Crime and Corruption Reporting Project wrote about fuel smuggling and the Italian Mafia's infiltration of Malta's online gambling sector. *Süddeutsche Zeitung* carried a long interview with my father.

France 2 and Radio France reported that Chris Cardona, the economy minister who was suing us over the brothel story, regularly drank with the Bean at a bar in the south of Malta. They had been spotted there together shortly before the Bean, his brother the Chinese and their associate Koħħu were arrested for my mother's murder.

The Daphne Project had begun to expose the web of government corruption that had made my mother's murder possible.

In response, Muscat's supporters spread out across the Internet, posting slogans including 'Proud of my Prim Minister'. In his comments to the press, Muscat claimed the Daphne Project's stories were 'rehashed'. Subtext: they were my mother's stories. He summoned his supporters to a rally outside his office at Castille, distributed placards that read '#JOSEPHMUSCATPROJECT', and then delivered an angry speech to the besieged in which he warned of consequences for those 'caught lying to smear Malta's name'.

In the *Guardian*, Juliette Garside had reported on the leak of ElectroGas files, revealing that Malta was losing money 'hand over fist' under the terms of the government's contract with the company. ElectroGas's chosen supplier, Azerbaijan's state-owned energy company SOCAR, was selling gas to ElectroGas at far above the market price, and for a fixed ten-year term. SOCAR, having none of the kind of liquefied natural gas the ElectroGas power station needed, had bought it from Shell and then added a mark-up before selling it on to ElectroGas. Over the first year,

SOCAR bought the gas for $113 million and sold it to ElectroGas for $153 million – nearly twice the open market rate. ElectroGas passed the $153 million cost of the gas on to Enemalta, Malta's state-owned electricity company, and then charged it even more money to convert the gas into electricity.

'The arrangement is unusual,' an energy expert Juliette quoted in her report said, 'and typically one would expect the LNG supplier, in this case Shell, to contract directly with the project.'

Not contracting directly with Shell had cost Malta $40 million in one year alone. The arrangement was clearly good for SOCAR, which owned a third of Electro-Gas and thus was getting paid double by Enemalta: once for the gas and again for the electricity. It was good for ElectroGas, which had locked Enemalta into buying its production for many years. But it was clearly not good for Malta.

In a six-page letter to the *Guardian*, Mizzi, as energy minister and the project's lead, claimed that the arrangement was not at all unusual. In fact, he said, the ElectroGas deal was a good idea, and he was a good minister. When, a few days later, Grey and Jacob Borg, a young reporter on the *Times of Malta*, uncovered more evidence that Mizzi's and Schembri's Panama companies were set to receive €5,000 a day from 17 Black, Mizzi denied any links to the company. But Schembri did not deny his connection to 17 Black. Instead, he claimed that the evidence Grey and Borg had found was just a 'draft business plan'.

A week later, Borg revealed that Schembri's and Mizzi's

accountants, the ones who'd set up their Panama companies, sat on the official selection committee that awarded
the public contract to build and run the new power
station to ElectroGas. The government had long refused
to disclose the selection committee's members, citing
commercial confidentiality. In his report, Borg pointed
out that the government had commissioned these same
accountants to draw up a feasibility study for a new
power station – and that they were now auditors for
ElectroGas.

There was an even more secret agreement that Mizzi
had signed at SOCAR's insistence, the one that had set
the terms of the unusual gas purchases Juliette uncovered
but that no one had access to at the time. It said that
if ElectroGas couldn't afford to pay for the gas it
needed from SOCAR, then Enemalta would step in to
pay for it.

The government knew that this agreement violated EU
law on state aid, which stopped governments from giving
unfair subsidies or grants to companies in their jurisdiction. This guarantee that Enemalta would step in to cover
ElectroGas's multimillion-dollar obligations to SOCAR,
and save the company from insolvency, was effectively an
enormous government grant.

Fenech, as ElectroGas's director, conspired with Mizzi
to hide the agreement from the European Commission
when its officials began a routine evaluation of the deal.
The Commission then approved the deal, so Muscat was
able to tell the electorate, over and over, that ElectroGas
was a Europe-approved project.

Fenech and Mizzi even tried to hide the agreement from the banks supporting the project. Mizzi declined to share it over a secure website, the normal procedure for commercially sensitive documents. The lead lender, HSBC, insisted on seeing it because its compliance team had grown nervous over twenty months of back and forth in which ElectroGas, and Fenech in particular, kept refusing to hand over the agreement.

Finally, HSBC's lawyers – two experts on state aid – were permitted to view it in person, in a secure room at SOCAR's office in Geneva. It was an approach so complicated it cost ElectroGas €10,000 to arrange.

When the two lawyers finished reviewing the agreement, they immediately advised HSBC and the rest of the lenders to stop extending credit to ElectroGas, recognising that the agreement violated EU law. Mizzi and Fenech then tried lying to the banks, saying that the European Commission had reviewed and approved it. But it didn't wash. The banks, which were already nervous about the corruption stories emerging from ElectroGas, refused to provide the credit the company needed to survive while the agreement was in place.

At this point, everything hung in the balance: Muscat's original electoral pledge that saw him rise to power, the country's power supply, the hundreds of millions of debt pushed onto Maltese taxpayers, the tens of millions that Fenech was set to make.

The Maltese government rushed to replace the secret agreement with one that didn't breach state aid law, and it managed to do so – in secret – by the first week of December 2017, a few weeks after my mother's murder. The banks were reassured, €360 million of new credit flowed into ElectroGas, and the balance was restored.

To celebrate the deal, Fenech gave a party at his VIP club on the twenty-second floor of the Portomaso tower in February 2018. Muscat was a guest of honour and had wanted Fenech to give a speech, until his aides shot that idea down.

'Today they advised that they think we should avoid speeches altogether,' Fenech told the ElectroGas board, 'and just get on with the party.'

The Daphne Project's reporting gave our campaign a boost, but we were still nervous about our case to have Silvio Valletta removed from the murder investigation as it came up for judgment in June.

The government had told the court that the case was not in our interest. It said we were derailing the investigation and it would be better if we just dropped it. The judge seemed, at times, swayed by its argument. But in the end, he ruled that the government was 'arrogantly wanting to dictate to [the victim's family] what they should say' and 'seeking to intimidate them'. Its argument exceeded the 'limits of acceptable legal behaviour' and it merited 'the utmost level of censure'. We had never expected such a strong finding.

He accepted our arguments that Valletta was a politically exposed person through his marriage to one of Muscat's cabinet ministers; that he had been the subject of my mother's writing; and that he was a board member of the anti-money laundering authority, 'the subject of focused analysis by the assassinated victim'.

In conclusion, the judge ordered Valletta to 'desist from continuing or in any way participating in the investigation' and that 'every act and decision taken in the investigation must be re-examined by his substitute'. He awarded costs against the government. The judgment made clear that Muscat had ensured that, for nine months, the murder investigation had been conducted in contravention of the Maltese constitution and the European Convention on Human Rights.

Muscat told the press that the ruling had 'repercussions at every level'. His government gave notice of appeal, which wouldn't succeed in reinstating Valletta. Arnaud said, on Facebook, that rather than supporting him we were 'purposely making these dangerous hits!' We still felt we had done the right thing, but our elation was short-lived.

At the start of July, we heard that the magistrate assigned to the inquiry into Egrant, the shell company that my mother had linked to the Muscats, had found there was no evidence to substantiate the claim that Michelle Muscat owned it, and that the document shown to my mother had been forged. We knew what this meant. It would allow the Poodle to claim he had been exonerated and that my mother was a liar. We did not appreciate just how aggressive his PR campaign would be.

Muscat convened a press conference. He stood in front of a podium, his full parliamentary group behind him. 'This was a web of lies intended to hurt me and my family,' Muscat said. 'They wanted us to face court with a twelve-year prison term. They wanted to harm me and the Maltese economy.' And then he paused, raised his hand to his face, and cried. He recovered. 'We cried together,' he said about his family, 'not understanding who would lie about us in this manner. The day of truth has finally arrived.'

Muscat called for the former Nationalist Party leader who had made Egrant a central focus of his 2017 election campaign to resign his seat in Parliament and for the new Nationalist leader to expel him from the party. The new leader suspended him from the party and asked him to leave his seat, but he refused. The opposition was divided: one side loyal to the new leader, the other to the old. Muscat had succeeded in destroying whatever parliamentary opposition to him existed.

Muscat's wife, who my mother had previously accused of having received money in Egrant's bank account at Pilatus, gave an interview to *Malta Today*, an English-language newspaper whose editor had called the Valletta ruling 'a golden opportunity to evade justice'. He headlined the interview 'REVISITING THE NIGHTMARE'.

He asked Michelle Muscat: 'Now that the Egrant inquiry has vindicated you, do you feel it time to "ride the wave", as the expression goes?'

'I always rode the wave,' she replied.

'It's an uncomfortable question to ask,' the editor said, 'but what about Daphne Caruana Galizia? What are your feelings towards her?'

'If there is someone who wants Daphne Caruana Galizia to be alive today,' she replied, 'that is me. When I heard the news about what happened to her, I think I was more sorry than her own family. Her family could go on to make her a saint; but at the time I said to myself: "Now I will have to live with her lies.'"

The truth was that neither we nor the press had access to the full Egrant inquiry report at that time. Protocol required that the magistrate hand over his report to the attorney general. This he did. It was then the attorney general's duty to review the findings and initiate prosecutions. And it was his duty to share that report with prosecuting officers. This he didn't do. The report was never shared beyond Muscat's immediate circle. And, it would turn out, the report contained a great deal that Muscat had decided not to reveal.

After a meeting at Doughty Street Chambers in August 2018, some nine months after our first formal request for a public inquiry, our solicitor Tony Murphy organised interviews with the main British broadcasters for me to say we were preparing to sue the prime minister into convening the inquiry.

'It's sad it's come to this point,' I told the BBC's chief international correspondent, 'where we have to be more forceful in our request for a public inquiry.' We could not 'rule out' the government's involvement in the assassination, I told ITV. 'We want the truth,' I told Channel 4.

The following morning, we all met at Malta's High Commission in London. We delivered a formal call for a public inquiry and walked outside, where television crews were waiting for us. I told them that Muscat 'has nothing to fear but the truth'.

The reaction in Malta was quick and typical. One of the Poodle's MPs, a former bodybuilder, said that the call for a public inquiry was part of 'the mission of Caruana Galizia's children to derail the investigation'.

In November 2018 Matthew was awarded the Prize for Impact at an awards ceremony of the organisation Reporters Without Borders in London. 'He has worked tirelessly to obtain justice for his mother's murder and for the crimes she exposed,' his citation read, and 'to galvanise the international community, and to hold the Maltese authorities to account'.

I had just returned from a campaigning trip to Bratislava, where a young journalist named Ján Kuciak and his fiancée had been murdered to stop his investigative reporting on a fraud by a Slovak oligarch. I arrived just in time for Matthew's victory speech. He talked about our fight, all the people who had helped us, and what we still had to do. People clapped and cheered.

After his speech, at the reception, Juliette Garside told us that Stephen Grey and Jacob Borg had learnt of a report drafted by Malta's anti-money laundering authority that had uncovered the owner of 17 Black. Frustrated by the inaction of the police in the face of the report, someone had leaked it to the journalists. Grey and Borg's story about it was scheduled to run the following day on Reuters and in the *Times of Malta*. 'It's big,' said Juliette.

The next morning Matthew and I read the headline together: 'MYSTERY COMPANY NAMED BY MURDERED MALTESE JOURNALIST IS LINKED TO POWER STATION DEVELOPER'.

'Yorgen Fenech,' I said. 'It's Yorgen Fenech.'

It had taken almost two years since my mother's first

blog post on 17 Black in February 2017 to tie it to Fenech. He had named the company after his father's favourite roulette number. The clue had been there all along.

What cracked in February? our mother had wanted to know, puzzling over Muscat's snap election. Now, at last, the cracks were opening up.

16

My father had been asking me to visit. 'You're being funny about it,' he'd say. 'You can't avoid Malta forever, you know.' Andrew was still in France with Lucie, but he had visited Malta a number of times. Matthew had moved back. A year and a half after my mother's funeral, I gave in.

I boarded my flight with an almost physical sense of dread. Somewhere over Italy, the plane began to shake. Jesus, I thought, this is all we need. Why had I listened to my father?

Before my mother's murder, Jessica and I had returned to Malta often. After, Jessica had said that we'd spent enough time in Malta. She was right, I thought. Malta had taken enough from us. I was tired of the place. I was sure it held no more nostalgia for me.

But when I stepped out onto the tarmac in the warm night, all my memories rushed to meet me: the heaviness in the air, the limestone terminal with its inverted arches and, inside, the glistening tiles and smell of detergent. By the time I walked out of the terminal I felt tired, as though I had travelled a much greater distance than the 1,300 miles from London.

After all that, my father hadn't come to pick me up. He had sent a typically abrupt text – *At school reunion. See you at home.* Matthew came to the airport instead. Still, I was happy to see my brother and, in a way, relieved. My father's driving was nausea-making – corners taken with wide swerves, hills with stop–start acceleration.

Halfway up the hill, at the bomb site, was a kind of altar to my mother, full of flowers, candles and a banner with her portrait on it. Matthew and I fell silent as it came into view. I imagined him driving past it each time he left home and returned, determined to look ahead but unable to look away.

At the house, Matthew brought my bag to my room. Andrew texted to ask whether I had arrived.

Before I closed the window shutters against the morning sun that would soon come, I looked across the dark to the coast, where an illumination of hotels, cars and apartment buildings stood out against the black sea. On a boat lifting and falling on the swell, a man had once sent the signal that detonated the bomb under my mother's car seat.

Waking early in my old room, I lay in bed until my father opened the door and then knocked.

'You can't stay in bed forever, you know.'

'Why not?' I asked.

'I suppose you can, but your brother wants to go swimming.'

My father was just lowering himself into the driver's seat when Matthew called out, 'I'll drive – don't worry – I'll drive.'

We drove to the coast north-west of Bidnija, an area rugged enough to keep the crowds away. We walked down the clay hills, moving through spring's clover and thyme, to get to the shore. The work made us feel good; we were earning our peace. We sat on a limestone slab jutting out into the sea, the sun slowly burning overhead.

The heat comes early to Malta, but the sea that April day was still cold and rough. The waves overtook one another, breaking one after the other. Behind them the swell was like a body breathing.

Matthew jumped in. 'It's perfect.'

My father took a step back, folded his arms behind himself in his usual way, and looked out at the waves crashing beside him. What was he thinking?

The last time I had felt like this I was nine years old, sitting on the sandy beach one headland south along the coast, watching my brothers swim and waiting for our parents to take us home. Home to tea and peaches so ripe that they melted in your hands as you peeled them. It felt for a moment as if nothing had happened in between.

We went to Valletta once, to see the memorial to my mother at the Great Siege Monument. People still left candles and flowers daily and held vigils on the sixteenth of every month. Some government supporters had begun harassing the people – mostly women – who left the flowers and candles. They called them whores and said they were destroying a national monument. They'd steal the flowers and candles at the end of the day. They ripped up photos of my mother that were placed there and threw them in a bin. They once placed photos of Karin Grech, the girl who was murdered in 1977, Raymond Caruana, the young carpenter murdered in 1986, and Mintoff at the memorial.

Whatever these men didn't manage to erase was handled by the government. The justice minister's portfolio included 'local culture'. Under those auspices, late every night, he'd send cleaners to clear all traces of my mother. But the flowers, photos and candles would return each morning.

So the minister, Owen Bonnici, ordered vinyl banners that read 'Great Siege Monument' to be put in front of this memorial. He said it was in preparation for restoration work. People laid their flowers and candles in front of the banners. Bonnici then blocked access to the banners and surrounded the area with steel barricades and plywood hoarding.

It would be weeks before any restoration work was done, on a monument that had only recently been restored. It would be months before protesters won a case against Bonnici, claiming he had breached their rights to peaceful assembly and free speech. Bonnici's behaviour, the judge would rule, was 'absurd', 'divisive' and 'born of pique', and each of the hundreds of times he had ordered the memorial's clearance was indeed a breach of human rights.

When I saw the memorial, it reminded me of the one to Boris Nemtsov. Activists had set it up at his murder site near the Kremlin, and they restored it each time pro-Kremlin thugs dismantled it. They called it a living memorial. As one Russian journalist wrote, totalitarianism first kills people, then the will, and finally it kills memory.

We spent the rest of my visit moving between the house and the coast, eating and swimming. On our last day at the beach, I realised that from the sea, the first settlers' view of the island was still here. The rocks around us were created out of the boulders those Sicilian farmers would have seen. The short juniper and oaks they cleared would have looked like the trees around us now, stunted and twisted by the same winds that brought them in. A little more sailing would have taken them to the easier part of the coast, near the natural deep harbour that would give Malta its name. I imagined a version of history where no one came after those first farmers or the Phoenicians. It was a story in which the Maltese might have never existed.

But it was hard to hold on to this way of thinking. Too much had happened. Behind us, away from that coast, the air was thick with the dust and noise of construction. The roads had changed. The buildings had changed. Nothing stayed the same.

During a phone call, Andrew told me that he felt we had lost both Malta and our mother. He would stay in France. I felt the same. I thought of something my mother had written on her blog after another bruising hearing in the Chris Cardona libel case. 'I survived in Malta,' she'd said, 'because I had no choice, and by keeping myself to myself. What kept me going was bringing up my sons to know that what they saw around them in Malta and Maltese society is not normal, and the knowledge that they – unlike me – could and probably would leave, which they did.'

But for Matthew, I could see that something else had happened. The murder that drove away Andrew and me had made it impossible for him to live anywhere else. Perhaps it was because for him the trauma had been so immediate and vivid. He couldn't look away. He was determined to stay, feeling that real justice involved changing Malta itself. And his bond to the country had widened. It was Matthew who had found this hidden part of the coast where we swam. He had taken up scuba diving to explore yet more of the country.

My father was, as always, harder to read. When he drove me to the airport for my flight back to London, he looked worn down, as if the hope had seeped out of him. I told him that, whatever I felt about the country, I was feeling better about the case after the Daphne Project's revelations.

He said 'perhaps' we would get somewhere. But he could not shake the feeling that my mother's case would end, or never end, like the cases of Raymond Caruana and Karin Grech.

I told my father I thought something would happen here. The truth might have been buried, but it was only gathering force down there. 'Perhaps,' he said again. He was managing my expectations more than his own. He did what he always did in such situations – he changed the subject.

As we walked into the airport's departures area, he talked about his work in Valletta and how supportive some people he met there were. Some surprised him. 'I bumped into Ray Fenech of the Tumas Group a few days ago,' he told me. 'He said, "Someone like you, I need on our board."'

The exchange angered me. Fenech's ownership of 17 Black, the shell company set up to funnel money to Mizzi's and Schembri's Panama companies, had been exposed. His uncle knew, like everyone else in Malta did, that my mother had been investigating 17 Black. His approach to my father seemed to me like an attempt to use him to launder his reputation. I was even angrier that my father couldn't seem to recognise this. He kept saying, 'It might not be what you think.' He'd represented clients who'd dealt with Ray Fenech and had had meetings with him at Portomaso himself, so there was some basis for the approach. It made me think how, in Malta, people are so close that they have to compartmentalise one another to extreme degrees. In any case, I had little right to feel angry. My father lived there, unlike Andrew and me, and living there required constant moral and ethical compromise. Andrew had once said that enough time in Malta would leave you 'deformed'.

I left my father in the departures area. From the top of the escalator, I looked down and saw him. He was carrying out my mother's farewell ritual. I waved goodbye.

Waking in London the next morning, I reached for my phone. There was a text message from our criminal lawyer Jason: *Can I please call? Urgent.*

It was cold outside, and condensation had collected on my bedroom window. I was tired. I lay there and thought about not replying. With Jason, who was determined and energetic, most things were urgent. But I told him to call.

'Paul,' Jason began, 'I love your brothers like my own, but I can't tell them what I've just heard.'

I imagined he had tried them first. The urgency in his voice, though, felt real. I sat up, grabbed the notebook and pencil I keep on my bedside table, and said, 'Tell me.'

Jason said he had gleaned important information from a source he couldn't name. I suspected it was someone connected to Koħħu. By this point, rumours were flying around that Koħħu had started speaking to the police as far back as April 2018 in the hope of a plea deal. But we had never had any confirmation of the rumours – and there had never been any shortage of rumours – or any idea what Koħħu might have told the authorities. I listened and took notes.

Initially, the plan was to shoot my mother through the dining-room window at the Bidnija house. But the guns they got hold of weren't good enough. They imported a bomb from Italy. At one point during their surveillance, they had been thrown off course by a random police road-block next to their lookout at Targa Battery. The men devised a leash to control our dogs, in case they needed to jump over the garden wall.

Koħħu was roped in to help the Bean and the Chinese at a later stage, mostly to drive them around. He tried get-ting out of the job, but the brothers managed to force him back in. And, crucially, Jason told me that the police had found a middleman – a man who contracted the three hit men on behalf of a mastermind. I asked Jason for the names of the middleman and the mastermind.

'I don't have them,' he said. 'Arnaud knows. He's trying to break a wall of silence.'

As I lay in bed listening to all this, my notebook pressed against my lap, I remembered how my mother had joked that my handwriting was like a serial killer's. After the call with Jason, I read and reread each sentence I had written, making sure I could read it all. I had to tell my brothers and father – it was the first major step in the investigation since the December 2017 arrests – and I did so on Signal, an encrypted messaging service.

Then I leaned back onto my pillows, and felt my head

A DEATH IN MALTA

spin. I looked out of my bedroom window, wiped the condensation, and saw the bay laurel that Jessica and I had
planted after the funeral.

A more public kind of progress began at this time. The
Council of Europe's anti-corruption authority, GRECO,
reported that Malta's criminal justice system was 'at risk of
paralysis' and that senior government officials enjoyed
impunity for corruption. It was another damning assessment that supported the picture that the delegation of
MEPs had painted a few months earlier, of a crisis in the
country's rule of law.

A few weeks later, in May 2019, Pieter Omtzigt, the
Council of Europe's special rapporteur, finished a draft of
his report. It had to be approved by the council's human
rights and legal affairs committee, which was meeting in
Paris. Andrew, who was living in Geneva at the time,
rushed there to observe the vote and hear Omtzigt's findings: deep-rooted corruption and institutional failures, a
country in need of urgent constitutional reform, and political interference in the murder of my mother. Omtzigt
highlighted that corrupt officials 'enjoy impunity, under
the personal protection of Prime Minister Muscat', called
for a public inquiry, and gave Muscat a September 2019
deadline. If the prime minister failed to convene one by
then, Omtzigt recommended sanctions against Malta by
the Council of Europe.

'Malta's weaknesses are a source of vulnerability for all
of Europe,' Omtzigt said. 'If Malta cannot or will not correct its weaknesses, European institutions must intervene.'

All members of the committee, except for Muscat's

representatives, approved the report. 'I'll never forget the moment all those hands went up in support of the report,' Andrew recalled. 'She never gave in. It was the state that fell apart.'

When Omtzigt took the committee-approved report to the council's parliamentary assembly for final approval in June, almost all members, apart from the Azerbaijani delegation and Muscat's representatives, voted in support. Malta would now have to convene a public inquiry by September or face sanctions. We put the lawsuit we were preparing against the prime minister on hold and kept it ready in the event that Muscat didn't comply.

And then Moneyval, the council's anti-money laundering authority, finally reported that Malta had 'failed' its test. It gave the government a year to fix the problems it had identified, including the absence of investigations into 'high-level and complex money laundering cases related to financial, bribery and corruption offences'. If it failed to fix those problems, Malta would face economic ruin. The warning was enough to throw Malta into a fresh crisis.

The pressure on Muscat's government was becoming unbearable, as people began to fear for their livelihoods.

In London, at least, things were calmer. I resumed something of a normal life. I joined a new journalism company called Tortoise and began reporting for a living. It felt both strange to be following in my mother's footsteps and overdue. It was the first time in my life I felt I was doing work that I should be doing. And I was able to spend more time with Jessica, after a year in which our life together had seemed suspended while I lived in perpetual motion, travelling with my brothers from one parliament or another, from one conference or another, week after week, in what began to feel like one long day.

Jessica had always understood that my mother was more than her reporting. In fact she had avoided talking with her about it, because she sensed that my mother was trapped in it. Sources were always calling, the readers always demanding more, more, more, the subjects of her writing always hounding her. Instead, she had talked about my mother's magazines, or about food, a shared love.

Jessica helped me to see that since her murder, I had abstracted my mother to her journalism alone. It had made the endless campaigning for justice bearable, especially the moments when I had to talk about her. Jessica felt the loss of the complete person. On one of our walks from south to central London, she pointed out the shops and restaurants my mother had liked to visit when she came to see us. London had reminded her that in some places, being a journalist was 'a normal job' and where 'every newspaper has five like me'; where she felt the relief of being 'ten a penny'. There she could be invisible.

Our route took us past Westminster Cathedral, with its red-and-white-brick spire that resembled a minaret. I had never been inside. Jessica insisted we enter. We lit a candle for my mother, and then walked around its eleven chapels. One was dedicated to St Paul. Above the chapel's altar, there was a Latin inscription that read, 'The Lord gives us the Law.' On one of the walls, there was a mosaic of Paul's shipwreck in Malta. He looked terrified at where he had landed. Jessica saw me looking at the figure and pulled me away.

When we decided to marry, Jessica wanted our wedding to be in Malta, where our families and most of our friends lived. I couldn't countenance it, so instead we chose a chapel carved into a hillside in eastern Sicily.

Not long after the wedding, in July 2019, police in Houston, Texas were notified that a passenger on a flight from London appeared to be taking drugs on board. On arrival at Houston's Intercontinental Airport, the police arrested the passenger. His name was Yorgen Fenech.

After the Daphne Project had revealed his ownership of 17 Black in November 2018, Fenech had stopped showing up for board meetings at ElectroGas, despite his fellow directors' requests for him to attend. 'My concern was 17 Black,' one board member would recall more than a year later, fearing the shell company had been used as a vehicle for kickbacks. But 'during that period Yorgen was hardly around.'

Not even Keith Schembri could find him. 'Sometimes,' Schembri would say, 'I'd call him and he wouldn't answer.' He was away from Malta for months. 'He might have had some health problems. Nobody had told me what those problems could be.'

'Those problems' turned out to be an addiction to cocaine. It escalated after the 17 Black report. We heard from multiple sources in Malta that his addiction was spiralling out of control. He was consuming ever greater quantities of the drug, buying it from the dark web.

The Fenechs sent Yorgen to a rehabilitation centre in London. The centre expelled him after it found him taking cocaine on site. That was when his family booked him onto a flight to Houston, where they had arranged for him to enter a different rehabilitation centre.

He took cocaine with him: 8.43 grams of it. Some he put in his checked bag and some in his carry-on, in Ziploc bags concealed with a plastic wrapper, concealed in another, smaller zipped bag.

But a flight attendant had noticed him taking cocaine on board and notified the Houston airport police.

He told the officers who arrested him that he was in Texas for 'stress therapy'. They searched him and his bags and found the cocaine. He admitted it was his, gave the police his personal details, and told them that his next of kin was 'Schembri, Keith'. They jailed him, found more cocaine in his checked bag, and the following morning brought him before a judge to face a charge of personal possession. He pleaded guilty, and received a month-long jail sentence, later converted to a stay at a medical facility. His family wanted him to stay in Texas, far from Malta. But the moment it was over, US Immigration and Customs Enforcement would deport him.

When Muscat was told about Fenech's arrest and conviction, he said he was 'concerned about him and his family'. But not even Muscat or Schembri could help with the US Department of Homeland Security. Nor could the expensive Stetson-wearing lawyer the Fenechs hired after the public defender they were assigned. In August 2019, Fenech finished his sentence, packed his bags, and boarded a flight back to Malta.

17

I was cycling to meet Jessica at a pub in south London when the Maltese government announced a public inquiry into my mother's death. It was September 2019, five days before the deadline Pieter Omtzigt had set.

Our Maltese lawyers immediately sent us the government's press release. It said the board would be chaired by a respected retired judge. But the government had included one of its own lawyers and a minor official as wing members who could outvote the chair. All our campaigning for a public inquiry was in danger of being used against us: to cover up rather than to throw light upon the assassination.

Matthew was flying back to Malta from Bangkok, where he had given a seminar to prosecutors on investigating shell companies. Cora was in Brussels, speaking at an event on the abuse of defamation laws. I got through to Andrew, and with our solicitor Tony Murphy we planned a statement in response.

We said that the composition of the board of inquiry was still under discussion. The international press ran our statement. The government buckled and said, for the first time, it would meet us to discuss the inquiry. Crisis averted; a sigh of relief.

When at last I put my phone away, locked my bike to a lamp post, and walked towards the pub, Jessica came out and said, 'You're fucking late. And I didn't even want to go to the pub.'

She stalked off to our house and I followed. The next morning, the smoke had still not cleared. Jessica had already gone out by the time I woke up. I went to Battersea Park and lay down on the grass below a pagoda overlooking the Thames. I wondered how we could stop the public inquiry from becoming a whitewash. I tried to understand why my wife was so upset with me. My phone buzzed.

It was a message from Jessica: *I didn't want to go to the stupid pub because I'm pregnant idiot.*

I promised her that I would make only one more trip. An Italian publisher had brought out a collection of my mother's journalism and had organised a publicity tour in Milan and Rome for my brothers and me to promote it. After Rome we were going back to Malta, for more events – a protest, a Mass – in honour of the second anniversary. And to meet the justice minister in Valletta about the public inquiry.

The second anniversary of my mother's murder arrived like a punch to the gut. The Italian publishers were kind and took great care of us. But I felt the continual publicity was starting to drain us and, worse, make our mother into a kind of abstraction. We were always repeating the same things about her and the case. We now had a series of damning reports on Malta, a possible public inquiry and three men in custody, but so far, it added up to nothing. Nothing was coming out of all these fragments.

Our father met us at Malta airport, car keys in hand, jingling. 'Boys,' he called. '*Boooys.*'

As we drove into Bidnija, my father told us that people would be gathering at the bomb site to mark the second anniversary. I did not feel up to it. I could barely look at the site as we went past, and I stayed at the house when my father and brothers went back to the vigil.

The Mass that evening was to be held at St Francis on Republic Street, Valletta's main street. A crowd greeted us there. It was my first time in the church. I was relieved to find the pews full, and behind the pews a crowd of people, and behind the altar, another crowd of clerics and laymen.

We sat at the front, with our grandparents and aunts behind us. The Mass was to be celebrated by the arch-bishop's delegate and an Italian priest who had founded an anti-Mafia organisation. They had asked us to give the same readings that we had given at the funeral.

My parents had never taken us to church growing up, so my brothers and I were guided through the ceremony by my father and a hovering priest. The readings were in Maltese, which made them sound ancient to us. Matthew spoke first, repeating the passage from Ecclesiastes that my mother had once said was 'engraved in my heart'. Wickedness in place of justice. A time for everything. A time to be born and to die, to kill and to heal, to mourn and to dance.

I had thought that time would never come. I thought it still as I walked to the altar. My reading was from Revelation. Looking at the text set on the stand in front of me, I saw how fevered it was. A woman clothed with the sun; a dragon cast onto Earth to persecute her.

Walking back to our pew, I saw that my father's face was

contorted, halfway to crying. I sat next to him. 'Good,' he told me, 'but you mispronounced a few words.'

The Italian priest approached our pew to give us the sacrament of the Holy Eucharist. My father indicated that we should stand and accept it. I put my hands out, right over left, and the priest placed one piece of the Host in them and then another, saying, '*E questo è per la mamma.*'

Outside, we led hundreds of protesters down Republic Street. We were carrying a banner with the words '*Verità u Ġustizzja*', 'Truth and Justice'. Apart from the slow heavy drum beat, and the refrain of *ġustizzja, ġustizzja*, the city was silent. People watched from the sides of the street or from balconies.

We walked to my mother's memorial at the Great Siege Monument, which the government was still sending cleaners to dismantle daily. There were flowers and candles and banners, as well as more people. There was a stage and floodlights, and a series of speeches.

Standing in the small crowd, for the first time I sensed that the mood was different from what I remembered of Malta. This was not hopelessness or despair. There was a sense of anger mixed, strangely, with optimism. There was some reason for it.

About a week earlier, the *Sunday Times of Malta* had run a front-page splash on the murder investigation. Citing 'two sources close to the investigation', the article said that a 'major businessman' was suspected of being the mastermind, but he hadn't yet been questioned, as evidence was still being gathered. One of the sources told the journalists my mother was murdered 'because of what she wrote or what she was about to reveal'. The case against this person wasn't strong enough yet, so the police were focusing on a middleman who might have been connected to the gambling scene. This middleman, they found, had drawn up a will shortly after the hit men were charged in court.

The report made it feel like something was finally happening. My family and I had our own questions – ones that Matthew asked Arnaud to come to the house the following day to answer – but for the protesters it was the first real sign of progress they'd seen in two years. And they had campaigned for justice so long, and had survived so much intimidation doing so, that these steadfast believers had developed a sense of togetherness around the idea that justice might still be possible.

When the vigil ended, people were slow to leave the square. Some old school friends stayed behind. We drank beer out of plastic cups and talked. The talk was light and full of hope. My grandparents accompanied my brothers, my father and me back down Republic Street to our cars. As we left, the activists were packing away the lights, speakers and stage. Soon the public square would be empty again.

The next morning, my father, Andrew, Therese and I went to the office of the justice minister, Owen Bonnici, to discuss the public inquiry into the murder.

Matthew had flown to Brussels straight after the vigil to speak at the European Parliament. In any case, he and my father had already met Bonnici along with Muscat to discuss the public inquiry. Preparations had been made through an intermediary. Muscat had wanted to know in advance whether Matthew and my father would shake his hand, whether they would sit near him, opposite him, or nowhere near. He had wanted to know whether he should greet them at the door to his office or just inside. My father could not believe the questions. Since that meeting, at least, the terms of the inquiry had been developed. The first objective was to determine whether the Maltese state had facilitated or failed to prevent my mother's assassination. The second was to establish whether there was impunity for serious criminal offences in Malta. The board in charge of the inquiry would have the power to access all information held by the state, take evidence on oath and recommend prosecutions. But the composition of the board – three judges – remained an issue for this second meeting.

On the way through the reception, we spotted Bonnici and the deputy attorney general waiting for us at the top of a flight of stairs. The deputy attorney general said hello, then stepped behind Bonnici. A short man, Bonnici had a nervous smile fixed on his face. He shook our hands and asked if we had ever met. He did not mention the memorial or why he had it cleared every day. He did not mention my mother at all.

We sat on opposite sides of a large square table in his office. The ceiling was high, making Bonnici look even tinier. I sat between my father and Therese, who attended as our human rights lawyer in Malta.

We had agreed on the chair, the respected retired judge, but Bonnici wanted to pick the wing members. Attempting a compromise, he suggested that he pick one and we could then pick the other. He argued that this arrangement would conform to the way the two political parties always shared power when appointing government boards.

There was a problem, Therese said. The board must be independent of both the government and the victim's family.

'Yes, you are right,' Bonnici said quietly. 'Of course,' he said. 'Of course.'

He began proposing names of judges and making notes on his pad of yellow Post-its.

Therese and my father reiterated that the criteria were clear: independence and impartiality. Yet Bonnici kept coming back to one name, a retired judge married to a vocal Labour Party politician who, just before retirement, had kicked an inquest into the corruption of Muscat's officials into the long grass.

'Please,' Bonnici kept saying, 'you'll make my life easier.'

It all became clear. Bonnici's notes were for Muscat. And more: it was not Bonnici who wanted to have the memorial to my mother cleared every night, but Muscat. Bonnici had no real power.

I could see my father was becoming tired. Therese and Andrew were becoming irritated. The deputy attorney general remained quiet. I looked at Bonnici and said, my voice raised, 'Stop suggesting this judge when he is obviously and totally inappropriate.'

Bonnici looked down and fidgeted with a Post-it note. He said he had to 'refer back', but didn't say to whom. On the way out of his office, my father chided me. 'You really didn't have to shout at him, you know.'

Matthew returned from Brussels that night, and in the morning when I woke, I could hear him making coffee upstairs with my father and Andrew. We had one final meeting planned for our trip to Malta. Keith Arnaud was on his way to the house to update us on the murder investigation, after Matthew called him to speak about the *Sunday Times of Malta* splash from a week earlier.

Arnaud arrived with a young sergeant. On his way into the house, he stopped to look at the old pinewood table covered in new saplings. Matthew had planted the small trees my mother had bought at the fair in Floriana the day before her murder, and had bought new ones. Arnaud asked if they were bay laurels. I realised he had been following our campaign more closely than he'd ever let on.

We sat in the living room upstairs, the same room where we had met him two years earlier, on the day after the murder. My father brought in the coffee, and we asked Arnaud why there had been no further arrests beyond the apprehension of the three hit men in December 2017. We wanted to know who the 'major businessman' and the middleman the article had mentioned were.

Arnaud said he would explain, though he warned us that he could not name any individuals.

He didn't dispute anything in the newspaper report. It was, effectively, the first confirmation we had from an official that the person who had ordered my mother's murder was known to the police. How long had they known? Who was it? I would have been angry that we were kept in the dark for so long had I not been relieved to hear of the progress.

Arnaud's sergeant looked around the room but kept quiet. Arnaud drank more coffee. 'Be patient,' he said. 'Things are at a delicate stage.'

They knew that the middleman had recorded some of

his conversations with the mastermind, so they needed to get hold of those. With Europol, they had looked into the middleman some more. He was a taxi driver, but his main source of money was an illegal gambling business. He took bets on everything, mostly horses, at the Marsa horse-racing track.

'So,' Matthew said, 'why don't you arrest him for that, and use it as leverage?'

'Your words,' Arnaud said. 'Not mine.'

Arnaud said that the anti-money laundering authority had already opened an investigation into the middleman. The police would then arrest him for money laundering and raid his properties, thereby seizing the recordings. With the recordings in hand, and the threat of money laundering charges, Arnaud hoped to pressure the middle-man into confessing to his role and giving evidence against the mastermind.

He said that Europol was helping them on the case and pushing them to act sooner rather than later. But his team needed more time to determine whether there was enough evidence for the raids and to make sure the recordings were either on the middleman or at his properties.

Two hours passed as Arnaud talked. Even though the investigation was at a 'delicate stage', I could see that he was feeling optimistic about it. He seemed less business-like than usual.

One last thing, Arnaud said as he rose to leave: the only reason it had been he who came to arrest my mother that night before the 2013 election, when she had written about Muscat, was that he had happened to be on duty in the area.

'On that point,' he said, 'are we okay?'
'Yes,' we said.

A month passed. The Council of Europe was about to convene a discussion of its concerns about the impartiality of the government's proposed board of inquiry. A few hours before it did so, the government announced a new board: the chair to whom we had agreed, alongside a former chief justice and the first woman to be made a judge in Malta. At last we had three individuals we all considered to be of integrity and ability.

The investigation now also had the right name: the Independent Public Inquiry into the Assassination of Daphne Caruana Galizia. Its proceedings would be public, as would its final report. Its board would recommend changes to Maltese law so that nothing like this could ever happen again.

It was what my brothers and I had once told a journalist it should be: 'Malta's first truth and justice commission'. It was a declaration that our mother's death was a concern for all Maltese. It didn't matter whether they were for her or against her, Labour or Nationalist.

18

Matthew was with me in London for the annual human rights awards ceremony named in honour of Sergei Magnitsky. Bill Browder hosted the event every November, the month that Magnitsky died, inviting a packed room of dissidents, journalists and lawyers.

Caoilfhionn was at our table. Her client Maria Ressa was onstage collecting the award for outstanding investigative journalism. Ressa had founded a news organisation in the Philippines reporting on Rodrigo Duterte's increasingly autocratic rule, while his officials and trolls harassed her. A year later, in a Manila court, she would be found guilty of 'cyberlibel'; the year after that, she would be jointly awarded the Nobel Peace Prize with the Russian journalist Dmitry Muratov.

Ressa spoke about her work and the work of others, whom she said had suffered even more. The Iranian journalist Jason Rezaian, she said, had been imprisoned in Iran for close to two years. He had become so used to his tiny prison cell that when he was finally freed, he found himself walking around in cell-shaped patterns outside.

'And then, of course,' Ressa said, 'there's Daphne.'

She spoke about my mother's work, and about Matthew witnessing her murder. Her voice broke as she said that our campaign for justice gave her 'tremendous hope'.

Feeling overwhelmed, I reached into my inside jacket

pocket for my phone to distract myself and saw that I had a message from our criminal lawyer Jason: the Malta police had had the middleman in custody for two days and he was now talking. His name: Melvin Theuma.

The police had asked Theuma who his lawyer was. He gave them a list of lawyers with known Nationalist Party ties. He even asked for Jason who, aside from being our lawyer, was a Nationalist MP. Theuma was nervous about anyone linked to Muscat and Schembri, and the Labour Party more generally. The police would soon know why.

Theuma's was the first arrest since that of the three hit men two years earlier, who were still in pre-trial detention. But we knew how delicately poised things were, so we guarded ourselves against disappointment. I busied myself with my work.

I normally reported on fraud cases for Tortoise, but now my editor asked for a report on my mother's case. He wanted a podcast, so I went to Malta with a young audio producer. We picked a week when few court hearings were scheduled, so that my family and others connected to the case would have time to speak to us.

Before leaving London, I met Jessica at the hospital for her last prenatal scan: she was carrying a boy.

The landing in Malta was turbulent. My father picked us up at the airport, and we drove to Valletta for something to eat. Through the big glass window of a pasta place, as we talked about Malta's smallness, two old friends walked past, saw me and waved.

We dropped the producer off at his hotel, and my father swerved us home to Bidnija. It was late, and we had to be in Valletta early for a pre-trial hearing in the case against the three hit men. 'I'll wake you up,' he said. 'And no wasting time. The traffic's become really bad.'

I felt as if I had slept for five minutes when my phone came alive with messages at about 6 a.m. *17 Black's boat being raided*, the first read. *Yorgen Fenech under arrest*, the second.

The second message came with a photo of Armed Forces of Malta soldiers and police officers boarding Fenech's motor yacht. It was his black-and-white 75-foot *Gio*, normally anchored in the Portomaso marina. I was now fully awake.

My father opened my bedroom door. 'Ah, good,' he said. 'You're already up.'

About seven hours earlier, between 10 and 11 p.m., Fenech's yacht captain was preparing *Gio* for departure when he noticed a photojournalist wandering around the marina. The captain knew the photojournalist from kitesurfing circles and asked him what he was doing. He said that someone in a Portomaso apartment had tipped off the *Times* that Fenech was readying his yacht to leave the country. The captain told him that there was no such plan.

In fact, the plan had been hatched a few days before, soon after Theuma was arrested. Fenech had contacted two lawyers. One had represented the drug trafficker accused of attempted murder about two decades earlier, who had sued my mother over her description of that case as a 'Pandora's Box of stinking sleaze'. The other lawyer was her son, a St Edward's College contemporary of Fenech's. The older lawyer advised Fenech that he might want to take a break, to rest his mind, in another country. Her son suggested that it would ideally be where extradition was not possible.

Yorgen's uncle Ray Fenech, the chairman of the family conglomerate who had suggested a board position to my father a few weeks earlier, had asked that Yorgen check with Schembri as to whether the airport was safe enough that he could get the family's private jet out through the low-security VIP area. Yorgen checked, instead, with an airport official. *Don't worry*, he messaged the official, *not escaping but need to go for some days . . . No way to make it discreet, right?* The official replied: *Not really, habib*. So Fenech felt safer taking his yacht to Sicily, then picking up a small truck there that belonged to his French horse trainer, so as not to hire any vehicle in his name, and driving to the trainer's stables in a remote part of Normandy to lie low. He asked Ray to take care of his children. Then he put his plan in motion. At his request, the captain asked the Sicilian ship-yard where *Gio* was due for repairs in December whether he could bring the yacht earlier. The captain managed to secure a slot at 8 a.m. on 20 November, meaning they'd have to leave Portomaso before sunrise. As he typically sailed out when it was still dark, the captain assured Fenech their departure wouldn't look 'fishy'.

The captain persuaded his friend the photojournalist who had turned up that night to leave the marina. He then went up to Fenech's apartment to warn him that he had found 'paparazzi' hanging around. Fenech said, 'When you see that they've left, tell me and I'll come down.' The captain walked around the marina a couple of times until he felt sure that there were no other journalists there. Then he went back to Fenech and said 'The coast is clear'.

At 1 a.m., Fenech quietly boarded the yacht. He brought €7,000 in cash, enough to get going and too little, by his standards, to look suspicious. His uncle had advised him not to use credit cards, which would be traceable. He also brought twenty-one SIM cards. He settled into his cabin while the captain continued preparing the yacht for departure. It was all going smoothly until a Portomaso security guard, effectively one of the Fenechs' employees, saw a person walking around the marina at 3 a.m. The guard messaged the captain who then messaged Fenech about it. Fenech replied, *They're saying that we are going to make a grand escape.*

More journalists descended on the marina over the next two hours, waiting, watching. It was beginning to look as if the escape plan was a very badly kept secret. The security guard told one of the journalists that he had to leave because he was on private property. The journalist said the public had a right to access the marina. They argued. The guard said he was going to call the police. *Gio*'s lights went on at about 5.15 a.m., and its engine purred.

'Call the police!' the journalist said. 'He's leaving. Call the police now!'

The police already knew. The person spotted at 3 a.m. was a member of its Criminal Investigation Department. 'We had sensed suspicious manoeuvres by Fenech,' Keith Arnaud would recall. He had put agents on watch at the marina, the airport, at sea, and at the ferry service to Sicily, and had called in the Armed Forces of Malta. A patrol intercepted *Gio* about a mile north of Portomaso, ten minutes after it had left the marina, and its officers arrested Fenech on suspicion of murder as its flashlights broke through the dawn sky.

'I thought it was a fisherman, caught poaching tuna,' one of my father's colleagues said when we got to his office. 'I was out jogging on the Sliema front, and suddenly I just saw these flashlights.'

Matthew had gone to the United Arab Emirates with Stephen Grey to collect more information on 17 Black. My father called him with the news.

Matthew already knew. Stephen Grey had been following *Gio* on an online vessel tracker and saw when it started moving out of Portomaso. Matthew was on his way back to Malta now.

My father rang off and gave me a tie, required for men in court, from the collection he kept in his office for visiting reporters and sons. We met the audio producer and walked past heavily armed police officers into the courtroom.

I stopped to hug my grandparents, who were sitting in the front row, as always. They were just four metres behind the Chinese, the Bean and Koħħu, who had not sat next to his accomplices since he had started talking to the police almost two years earlier. Now he sat far to the side of them, behind his own lawyer, who was playing with a green highlighter.

The lawyer for the Chinese and the Bean tried to argue that the evidence against his clients was invalid. He asserted that the message – '#REL1=ON' – used to arm the bomb was the same kind of message you might send to switch on a water heater remotely.

After we left the courtroom, the audio producer and I went to Portomaso. *Gio* was still there, guarded by a young police officer as people streamed along the marina for a look at the yacht.

Back in Valletta, a crowd gathered in front of Castille. 'The prime minister has blood on his hands,' an activist yelled. 'Blood on his hands!' The crowd began shouting 'Mafia' at the prime minister's office, but Muscat had not yet appeared. No one knew what to do or where to direct themselves.

We walked to the memorial to my mother. The crowd drew in more people as it moved down Republic Street. The faces around us registered anger.

For two years, the Maltese people had been told that my mother's death was 'just a murder'. Muscat's head of communications had cautioned them not to call it an 'assassination' because the word was 'very politically loaded'. They had been told that my mother's work was all 'fake news' and 'fairy tales'. But Fenech's arrest that morning had shown the propaganda for what it was: a big lie.

The Daphne Project had already revealed to people how Fenech had structured the ElectroGas deal to pay enormous kickbacks to Schembri and Mizzi. It had already shown people that my mother had been uncovering, piece by piece, a national fraud. The piece she had been missing was Fenech, so when he was arrested for her murder that morning it had suddenly become clear: she was killed to stop the Maltese people from knowing they were being defrauded by their own government.

Like petrol poured onto a smouldering fire, the realisation that they had been lied to and lied to fuelled the collective sense of rage about the murder. People were not in the mood to stand in silent observance at the memorial.

Nor was I. I felt my jaw lock. I had never experienced this before: being too angry to talk. People in the crowd walked up to my father and me and shook our hands, but we could not find the words to speak.

'They're in Parliament!' an activist shouted. 'The government's MPs are in Parliament!'

Moving as a single entity, the crowd turned back down Republic Street to the Parliament building. They besieged it, circling the building as they chanted, '*Assassini, assassini.*' The chant had a cadence that made me feel as my grandfather Michael had felt during the national anthem outside my mother's funeral: Maltese.

We pushed closer, past steel barricades and a handful of police officers. We were just approaching the building's main entrance when the justice minister, Owen Bonnici, emerged, on his way out of the chamber. His aides scrambled him into his chauffeur-driven car. The crowd surrounded the car, shouting, 'Justice, justice.'

'Why don't you clean the memorial now, Mafia?' they cried.

People began throwing coins at his car, kicking and banging at it. My aunt Amanda pressed a photo of my mother against the car's back window where Bonnici was sitting. 'You see this? This is my sister's face; you should see it before you go to sleep every night.'

A group of people squatted in front of the car, blocking it from leaving. Others, still shouting, began banging out a rhythm on the car: 'Justice, justice'. For half an hour, they chanted and banged: 'Justice, we want justice'.

They reluctantly dispersed and, at last, the car began to move. Eager to leave, the driver ran straight over a police officer's leg. She howled and was pulled away by another officer as the minister's car sped off. The Poodle's officials were on the run.

The truth was on the march, and nothing would stop it. Day and night, the protests continued.

One night outside Parliament, there were more steel barricades, row upon row, and more police officers. The police officers and barricades blocked the Parliament building's open ground floor, which a foreign architect had designed as a statement about transparency in government. The police officers kept the protesters at a distance. But there were even more of us now, chanting 'Mafia, Mafia', and then '*ħabs, ħabs*' – 'prison, prison' – at the MPs inside.

Some tried to flee through an emergency exit at the back of the building, but for a while, they couldn't figure out how to open it, so the protesters were treated to the sight of its governing class scurrying down a narrow passageway and then huddling against a door they couldn't open.

Muscat, defiantly, left through the main entrance. He was surrounded by a group of men who rushed him, on his short little legs, into his idling car. We pelted him with eggs and coins and fake banknotes as he was hurried to the car. In the light rain, the egg mixed with the fake banknotes to make a green muddy slick that spread across the Parliament's square.

It was this, above all else, that surprised me. A population with no tradition of civic society had been inspired to spontaneous protests. They raged across the country.

Protesters carried portraits of my mother. They wore T-shirts printed with her face on them and those now-famous last words she'd written: 'There are crooks everywhere you look now. The situation is desperate.'

'Daphne,' I heard one yell, 'the crooks are coming out, and now *their* situation is desperate.'

One night outside Parliament, I met my aunts and a number of friends. They wished me a happy birthday. I had forgotten. I cannot remember sleeping that week.

As health organisations warned that the political crisis was becoming a mental health crisis, with the population angry, confused and unable to work, a group of protesters stormed Castille. They forced themselves in and sat in one of its halls, chanting and playing drums as more protesters tried to get inside. It was a new idea: Castille at last used by the Maltese to express a civic feeling.

And then, as though a supernatural force was at work, a ship dropped its anchor on the underwater cables connecting Malta's electrical grid to Sicily's, ripping them up. The ElectroGas power station was unable to cope. There were national power cuts. Alarms went off.

In Valletta, people poured out of their offices and

shops. When Muscat told them the situation would have been worse without ElectroGas, another bolt of anger surged through the crowd.

It felt as if what I'd told my father had come to pass. The truth had been buried underground, growing and building force, and now it blasted everything away. The explosion that had killed my mother had changed my family forever. This second one, I hoped, might change the country for good.

19

In court, we heard how the operation Europol had code-named 'Blue Elephant' happened. Arnaud's team had been monitoring the hit men's calls from prison. Each of them called only their families.

The Chinese would call his brother Mario. On one call, Mario passed the phone to his wife who told the Chinese: 'I'm praying for you every day. Come on, let's get you out of there.' The Chinese would always ask Mario whether he had met with 'that guy'. His brother would say yes or no in response, clearly understanding who 'that guy' was without his name ever being mentioned.

In January 2018, just a few weeks after the hit men's arrests, the police had begun a surveillance operation on Mario to find 'that guy'. During a call on the evening of 21 March, Mario asked the Chinese to tell the Bean to call him the next morning at 9.45 a.m.

The Bean called from a prison phone, three minutes late. After they greeted each other, Mario passed his mobile to another Maltese man. 'Have courage,' he said. It was 'that guy'.

The guy said he would start passing on cash for the brothers' lawyer through Mario. The money would come from the person who had paid for the murder. He said he would also pass on food – rabbit, rib-eye steaks and little cheeses made from sheep's milk – so they could eat well in prison.

Arnaud's team closed in. They put cameras and long-range microphones outside Mario's house. They waited for a guy whose visits coincided with the tapped calls from prison to materialise.

He did turn up. First in a white Jaguar, later in an SUV. The cars kept changing. His identity remained elusive.

Then, one day in April, the Bean called Mario, who told him that Koħħu had begun talking to the police, seeking a plea deal. Koħħu had told the police that the three of them had been contracted to murder my mother, for which they had been paid €150,000. But he claimed they did not know who the money ultimately came from.

In prison, the Chinese and the Bean could not believe it. They had worked with Koħħu for years: shootings, a bank heist, murder. They'd always got away with their crimes, in part because they never spoke. The Chinese, incredulous, asked Mario how he knew this information. Was it from that guy whose name begins with 'M'? His brother said yes.

As the police puzzled over 'M', they were approached by an informant from the criminal underworld. The informant told them 'M' was Melvin Theuma.

Melvin Theuma – 'that guy' – had one of the few taxi spots at Portomaso. He had another taxi that he subleased to a friend. The friend noticed that Theuma had been looking anxious and unhealthy. He had not been himself since December. Something or someone was bothering him.

He had advised Theuma to start recording his conversations with whoever was on his back. If they keep bothering you, the friend said, let them know you have the recordings. Theuma heeded that advice, and then began talking to people about the recordings he had made. One was the informant, who began wearing a wire after talking to the police. Arnaud's team now had the middleman, and they knew that the middleman had material evidence on whoever had contracted him.

Melvin Theuma was a teenager when his father died. The Marsa racing club became his family. He started there as a groom, then was taken on as a scout by a bookmaker who laundered his proceeds through a used-car dealership.

The Marsa horse races, which began under colonialism, were no longer glamorous. The stone balcony overlooking the track where royals once sat was crumbling. Where once thoroughbreds had galloped, trotting horses now pulled sulkies, two-wheeled carts with drivers.

Theuma worked the stands, full of men calling bets, waving banknotes, swearing. He was good at it. He ran his own gambling ring from a shop opposite the Fenech family's stables and began taking bets for Fenech and his uncle Ray, whom Theuma called Mr Ray. The orphaned Theuma revered Fenech.

'He knows everyone,' Theuma thought, 'and I don't know anyone.'

He ran Fenech's errands, fetching bread and rabbits for Fenech family lunches at their country house. Fenech and Mr Ray, in return, granted him one of the ten prized taxi spots at the Hilton at Portomaso.

A few weeks before Muscat announced the early election in May 2017, Theuma had worked that spot all day, making it home at around 4.30 p.m. He parked his car in his garage and went upstairs to make some coffee.

Fenech called. He wanted Theuma to come to Portomaso, so that he could speak with him.

'I'm coming,' Theuma replied.

'Come to the Blue Elephant restaurant,' said Fenech, referring to a Thai chain within Portomaso.

Theuma went to the restaurant and called Fenech to let him know he was outside.

Fenech came out. 'Do you know George the Chinese?' he asked. 'Because I need him.'

'I know him, but I don't have his contact details,' Theuma said.

'See what you can do to get them,' said Fenech, 'because I want to kill Daphne Caruana Galizia, because she's going to release information on Mr Ray.'

Theuma said he'd find the Chinese 'and see what I can do'.

On his way back home, Theuma called a friend and asked for the number of the Chinese's brother the Bean, to whom he was closer. As soon as he got it, he immediately called the Bean. They agreed to meet at 2 p.m. in Marsa, at the old storage shed once used to keep potatoes for export.

Theuma arrived at the potato shed half an hour late, which upset the Bean. 'I'm *time time*,' the Bean told him.

'I have a person who wants to kill Daphne Caruana Galizia,' Theuma said.

'But does this guy pay?' said the Bean.

'Would I have come if he didn't?'

'Let's meet in two days.'

The Bean didn't seem to know what killing such a high-profile journalist meant. Theuma couldn't understand

English and had never read her work, but their paths crossed once: my mother's tyres had been slashed near the Hilton at Portomaso and Theuma, seeing her stranded, offered her a lift home without, he said, charging her a fare.

Two days later, Theuma and the Bean met at Busy Bee, a popular café known for its ricotta cannoli. The Bean did not want Theuma to visit the potato shed again. Theuma ordered an espresso, the Bean an orange-flavoured soft drink.

'On that,' the Bean said. 'I spoke with my friends. €150,000. But €30,000 in advance and €120,000 after. So, if I start working and you stop me, the €30,000 is lost.'

'All right,' Theuma said. 'I'll get back to you.'

That same day, Theuma went to Fenech and gave him the price.

'Now, we'll talk,' Fenech said.

'All right,' Theuma said.

A day or two later, Fenech called him. 'One Sandro Craus is going to call you, from Castille.'

'From Castille. What for?'

'Hang up.'

Sandro Craus was the Labour crony who headed Muscat's customer care department, distributing jobs and favours to supporters. As soon as Fenech rang off, Craus called Theuma. He said, 'Tomorrow at three p.m. you have an appointment with Keith Schembri at Castille.'

Theuma was stunned. He had never been to Castille. On the day, he wore a smart pair of trousers and a jacket. But he did not know how to enter the building. Embarrassed to use the front door, which was guarded by a soldier and reserved for ministers, he called Fenech for advice.

'Where do I get in from,' Theuma asked, 'the front or side door?'

'The front door,' Fenech said, 'where there'll be a soldier.'

Theuma went in through the front. Halfway up the steps, he was greeted by Schembri. They had met once before, at Schembri's country house. They shook hands. Schembri gave him a tour of Castille. In the cabinet room, its walls covered with portraits of former prime ministers, Theuma took a photo of Mintoff's. They moved on to Schembri's office.

Schembri made Theuma an espresso. They had their photo taken together, arms around each other, in front of a silver-framed photo of Muscat and Schembri in the same pose. Schembri then sent Theuma to Craus.

'The government is going to give you a job,' Craus told Theuma.

'But I work as a taxi driver,' Theuma said.

'Don't worry,' Craus replied. 'They will still give you a job.'

He sent Theuma to a nearby ministry, Theuma did not know which. He just referred to it as the ministry opposite the old theatre, the ruins of a neoclassical opera house built by the British, which had been destroyed in the Second World War. The building housed the family affairs ministry.

Ministry officials interviewed Theuma. 'Do you know how to send an email?' one asked him.

'Yes,' Theuma lied. He had never used email before.

'You got the job.'

The interview was over in two minutes. Theuma was

now a government driver on €967.09 a month. He told the officials he already had a taxi job and would not be able to come to work. He never did. They paid him anyway.

'If you had to ask me where I worked,' Theuma would testify later in court, 'I wouldn't even know where to say.'

For Fenech, this was about showing Theuma that he had Castille's protection. Theuma did not understand at first. He called Fenech, who said simply, 'Isn't an extra pay cheque better? Good luck.'

It was another kind of luck Fenech wanted to discuss when he next called Theuma. It was 1 May 2017, and Muscat had just announced the early election, which Fenech already knew was coming because Castille had informed him about it. Fenech told Theuma to pause the murder plot and place a bet, on his behalf, on Muscat winning by the same margin as in 2013. Fenech told Theuma to put down €150,000, the price of the murder. He stood to win €300,000.

Theuma placed the bet and went to the Marsa potato shed in search of the Bean. He saw him, signalled, and they met at the Busy Bee. He told the Bean to pause – not stop – the murder. He gave him €2,000 of his own cash – 'not to look bad'. The Bean suspected they had found another squad for the hit.

'Make sure,' the Bean told Theuma, 'that if this person gets you again, you come to me.'

'Of course, I'll come to you,' Theuma replied.

'All right.'

It was not long before Theuma was back. Muscat won the early election with more or less the same majority. Fenech won his €300,000. Theuma waived the usual 5 per cent fee he charged on bets because of their 'friendship'.

Fenech called him the day the electoral result was announced.

'There,' he said. 'Start moving again.'

'Where?'

'To kill Daphne.'

Fenech was drunk. Theuma, recognising the alcohol in his voice, took no notice of the order. A week later, when he delivered Fenech's cash winnings in an envelope, there was no mention of the murder or any sign of the €30,000 deposit the Bean had demanded. Theuma let it pass, returning to his taxi work.

Some weeks later, Theuma picked up Fenech from Portomaso to take him to the airport. Fenech came down with a bag, opened it, pulled out a brown envelope, and handed it to Theuma.

'What's this?' Theuma asked.

'The money,' Fenech replied, 'to give to that guy to kill Daphne Caruana Galizia.'

Theuma drove Fenech to the airport, then drove to the potato shed and signalled to the Bean. Once again, they met at the Busy Bee, where Theuma gave him €30,000 out of the €150,000 in Fenech's brown envelope.

From that day on, Fenech called Theuma incessantly. 'Call after call,' Theuma said. 'Call after call. He'd say, "Go tell him before she releases this information."'

'This isn't for Mr Ray,' Theuma realised. 'It's him who wants to kill her. The information is on him.'

The pressure continued. 'Go hurry him,' Fenech told Theuma, 'so he kills her. Go hurry him, so he kills her. Go hurry him, so he kills her, because she's going to get this information out.'

On one call, Fenech had another instruction for Theuma. 'Tell him, "Make sure what happened to Bone doesn't happen here." That they don't kill her. Because we'll have more problems.'

Theuma went to pass on the message to the Bean, finding his brother the Chinese was also there and had been brought into the job.

'So many bullies died,' the Chinese told Theuma. 'Do you think she won't?'

'Rest assured,' the Bean said.

They had another kind of problem with my mother. They could not establish her routine, because she didn't have one. To avoid being harassed or stalked, she often did not leave the house. She had started using the rental Peugeot when her own car became too recognisable. The hit men asked Theuma for tips. Theuma, in turn, asked Fenech, who passed on the names of some cafés she'd been seen at and some dates when my mother would be out of the country, information he got from one of Muscat's ministers.

The hit men once followed her to the airport and, on another occasion, to a hotel near Valletta where she met Andrew for his birthday. They followed her to the same hotel a few days later for my grandparents' anniversary dinner. Matthew and my father were also there.

The hit men considered placing the bomb there and then, but Koħħu worried my mother wouldn't return to her car alone. The Bean and the Chinese told Koħħu, 'We'll go ahead, even if others are with her in the car.'

After the dinner, Matthew, my father and my grandparents got in the car with my mother – almost my entire family. But the hit men hadn't managed to get the bomb in before they emerged from the restaurant.

The delays frustrated Fenech. 'If she releases that information,' he told Theuma, 'it will be for nothing, all this.'

Theuma had no more to pass on. The hit men gave no dates. He once went to Bidnija with them and examined their hideouts and progress to report back to Fenech. He tried to get on with his taxi work and bookmaking. On 16 October 2017, he finished work at 3 p.m. and headed home.

'I switched on the television and *pupp*,' he said, 'I saw it. From that point in time, I became scared of everything.'

He managed to meet Fenech the following day. He had seen in the news that the FBI was assisting the murder investigation. The Bureau had been called in by a Maltese counterterrorism police officer, although Schembri and Muscat would later claim it was they who had done so. The FBI's cellphone analysis team happened to be in Europe, and they landed in Malta within hours.

The FBI's arrival worried Theuma. He hurried up to level twenty-one of the Portomaso tower, where Fenech kept an office. He found him sitting at a long table, in a meeting with SOCAR's Azerbaijani representative on the ElectroGas team. Seeing Theuma, Fenech got up and pulled him into another room. He told him not to worry about the FBI.

'At the end of the day, isn't the Malta police going to investigate?' he said.

Fenech had reason to be dismissive, given that the man in charge of the police's Criminal Investigation Department was Silvio Valletta, the deputy police commissioner.

When we filed our case in November 2017 to have Valletta removed from the murder investigation, we had only argued that he was married to one of Muscat's cabinet ministers and that he had failed, as the police force representative on the anti-money laundering authority's board, to prosecute the crimes my mother exposed. We did not know that he was Fenech's friend. And that they used to drink together at Fenech's country house, go to European football cup finals together, hold the hands of each other's children – even after his subordinates had identified Fenech as the prime murder suspect.

We did not know that Valletta had told his officers not to question Fenech over his ownership of 17 Black. We did not know that Fenech and Theuma used to call him 'Valletta l-Oħxon', Valletta the Fat. Nor that Fenech would say, 'God forbid they remove him,' before the appeal court finally sided with us a year after we had filed the lawsuit. Arnaud and his team, who thought so poorly of our lawsuit, didn't know any of this either – until they heard some of it from Theuma and, later, found a video of Valletta fooling around in Fenech's Rolls-Royce Wraith, a €250,000 car. 'I trusted Valletta with my life,' Kurt Zahra, Arnaud's deputy, told us.

Luckily for him, Fenech had other sources on the investigation into the murder he had commissioned. Schembri, he said, began giving him confidential details 'within a week' of the murder, which he provided 'continually' and in 'real time'.

When the police and the Malta Security Service went to Castille to brief Muscat on the murder investigation, Schembri made sure he was present, even though he had no reason to attend. There was nothing in law or custom that said it should be so. He attended the briefings even though Muscat knew he was a close friend of the prime suspect.

So when the FBI found the '#REL1=ON' message that detonated the bomb, and shared it with Maltese authorities, which Schembri controlled, the information – including the message itself – went straight to Fenech, who passed it on to Theuma.

'There,' Fenech said, 'we have trouble.'

'Shall I tell the Bean?' Theuma replied.

'Of course.'

Theuma told the Bean, and later warned him about the coming raid on the hit men's potato shed. It was information that Fenech gave him, which Fenech got from Schembri. That was how the hit men knew the police were coming that December 2017 day when Theuma, scared that he would be eliminated because he knew too much, had a new will drafted.

Fenech even learnt who the bomb makers were, something that Theuma, the middleman, did not know. *Don't panic*, Fenech told Theuma in a message. *They got to Maksar, who already said the bomb was made at their garage.*

Theuma could not keep calm. He became suicidal. He came close to jumping off his roof. He began drinking heavily and taking sedatives to help him sleep. He had never had Fenech's sense of security, his proximity to power or his wealth. Fenech sent him on holiday, gave him whisky, tried keeping him together.

When Theuma saw Muscat's officials claim that my family was hiding my mother's laptop to stall the murder investigation, and then saw those 'Where is the laptop?' banners go up around the country, he went to see Fenech about it. He wanted to know whether the Maltese authorities getting their hands on the data would be good for them. 'It would be better for me because Daphne wrote about many people,' Fenech said, 'and they would certainly not have any clue who was behind it.'

But there was only so much reassurance Fenech could give. When he told Theuma that Koħħu had begun talking to the police in search of a plea deal and had given the police Theuma's name, something they already had through surveillance of the hit men's prison calls, Theuma flipped.

'It's not true!' he told Fenech. 'It's not true about Koħħu!'

'So how do they know about the Busy Bee meeting?' Fenech replied.

It was at this point that Theuma began recording his conversations with Fenech, as one of his friends advised. Theuma was the only person the hit men knew. He had never given them Fenech's name – 'Never, never!' He was exposed. But one time, he called a fellow taxi driver and told him 'that guy of the tower' – Portomaso – had 'betrayed' him. He used his normal phone line, which had been tapped by the Malta Security Service as part of the investigation.

Details of that intercepted call were given to Fenech. He was angry with Theuma for the loose talk. 'It's not right, my friend,' he told him. 'I was always a man with you.' But he understood that Theuma feared for himself and his family and, Fenech said, 'Family comes first.'

Using Signal, the encrypted messaging service, Fenech

ordered Theuma to call his taxi driver friend back. Theuma was to tell his friend he felt 'betrayed' because Fenech had promised him an additional taxi spot at the Hilton at Portomaso. He had even bought another taxi, he was to explain, but Fenech then reneged on the deal under pressure from his uncle Ray.

'Think it over,' Fenech told Theuma about this plan. 'Study it well.'

Theuma took screenshots of his messages with 'Yurgin', which were set to auto-delete as a security measure, including one where he told Fenech, *Us, we are helping each other, my friend.*

If we are strong together, Fenech later messaged Theuma, *they can kiss our balls. If we break down we will have big problems.* But in the end, it was Fenech who let the side down.

His cocaine addiction worsened. 'I told him,' Theuma said to one of their associates: '"Yorgen, with that, you don't solve anything."' He was away from Malta at rehab for months, ending the security he provided Theuma. Before he disappeared, he told Theuma, 'I know I did everything exactly right about the power station, but I'm feeling trapped about the murder.'

In Fenech's place, Theuma began relying on one of Schembri's henchmen for information. This man worked for Muscat's personal security team, on attachment from the Security Service, and it was he who told Theuma that the Malta Police Force was under pressure from Europol to investigate his bookmaking business. And Europol was after Theuma's bookmaking business because it had learnt about his recordings of Fenech and his role in the murder from a confidential informant.

Schembri's henchman tried reassuring Theuma that the hit men would get bail. They had a judge, he told him, the same judge whom the justice minister, Owen Bonnici, had tried to impose on the public inquiry's board. One of Fenech's friends also tried reassuring Theuma that the investigation into his bookmaking case would go to a police officer in Fenech's pocket.

The officer in question was Ray Aquilina, second-in-command at the police economic crimes unit. He was to prepare his questions for Theuma and send them to him in advance. He was to say what Theuma needed to counter the police's evidence, and how to explain away his cash holdings. He was to receive a €5,000 bribe or one of Theuma's used cars. Fenech's friend advised Theuma against the used car.

'He'll keep coming to you,' the friend told him, 'and asking for more money, for parts and that.'

The friend, after reassuring Theuma that Aquilina could be trusted, then tried persuading him to destroy his recordings. The friend knew about the recordings because Theuma had sent them to Fenech to show that he had dirt on him.

Fenech messaged Theuma. He apologised that he was unable to stop the investigation into Theuma's gambling ring, but reassured him that Aquilina would handle it. Then added: *Be one hundred per cent sure everywhere is clean.*

Theuma refused to delete the recordings. He had wheeled and dealed for Fenech for years. 'I was hanging out with a lion,' he said, 'and I'm a mosquito.' He had once felt that he owed Fenech for the taxi place at the Hilton at Portomaso. Times had changed.

'I used to think he was my best friend,' Theuma said, 'but after he got me involved in this, I consider him the worst person in Malta, in the world.'

In the end, it was not Aquilina who turned up to arrest Theuma. It was a group of officers. Theuma was driving his partner's Toyota when the officers surrounded him. An old plastic ice-cream container, about the size of a shoe-box, was on the passenger seat. 'This box,' Theuma told the police, 'never leaves my sight.' Now, he clung to it like a lifeline. Seeing the officers but no Aquilina, he realised they had come two days earlier than what was agreed, and thought: They did it, they betrayed me.

He told the officers he wanted to speak to Keith Arnaud 'about the murder'. Before stepping out of the Toyota, he grabbed the ice-cream container. He refused to let go of it until he got to the interrogation room. His lawyers gave the container to the duty magistrate. At 3 a.m., the container was on a flight to The Hague for safe keeping with Europol, as Arnaud's team continued questioning Theuma.

His lawyers insisted on an agreement, signed by the police commissioner, the attorney general and Muscat, that Theuma would receive a pardon of all his crimes in exchange for testifying to the container's contents.

Inside the container was the photo Theuma had taken with Schembri at Castille, along with pen drives that stored his recordings, and a handwritten note: 'I Melvin Theuma am providing this information that I was the middleman in the case concerning Ms. Caruana Galizia. I am relaying this proof so that you will know who hired me and paid for the bomb. I am doing this because I realised that these two people, Yurgen Fenech and Keith Schembri il-Kasco, were working to get rid of me as well. So I prepared this proof so that if I am eliminated you will know the entire story.'

For days, Muscat delayed signing the agreement. A copy made it to Schembri and then to Fenech. When Fenech saw that Theuma was about to be pardoned for both the murder and his bookmaking, he went into a blind panic.

Fenech used an unhelpful mixture of cocaine and sedatives, and his behaviour grew even more erratic. Fenech's family doctor arranged for him and his brother Franco to spend time at his country house in Gozo. He packed more sedatives for Fenech, who was now delirious and babbling, and drove him there.

In Gozo, the doctor overheard Fenech and his brother, both out of their senses, plot escapes from Malta. There was talk of a boat to Tunisia and then a flight to Dubai, where there was no risk of extradition. There was talk of a submarine and a rocket. The Fenech brothers asked the doctor if he knew anyone with a boat, although they had plenty of their own. The doctor called a friend and asked him about his boat while Fenech transferred his company directorships to his brother. Nothing else was agreed.

They returned to Malta, and hid. Fenech developed his plan to escape to Sicily, on the pretence that his yacht needed repairs.

Muscat instructed Schembri to call Fenech on the day of his planned escape. Schembri, who said he was 'ready to step into the fire for Yorgen', asked him, 'Do you really think it's a good time to leave the country?' He spent twenty-four minutes on the phone trying to convince

Fenech to stay and not draw more attention to himself by leaving. He said he would help him, but that he must be ready to fight aggressively. Despite this offer, Fenech insisted on leaving. 'I spoke to my lawyer,' he told Schembri, 'and she said, "There's no problem, you're not under arrest, go . . . and we'll come up with the narrative."'

Fenech was taken to the police headquarters in Floriana a few hours later. He asked for his family doctor, who 'administered some tranquillisers'. The doctor left.

He was called back when Fenech complained of chest pains. Detainees often made this complaint in order to be referred to the hospital. Fenech was given some morphine at the hospital and a burner phone. Using that phone, he called the doctor again and told him to go to Schembri's villa in Mellieħa to collect something.

The doctor obeyed. He was greeted by Schembri's wife, and they chatted for twenty minutes while Schembri was having a shower upstairs. Schembri came down, and they made small talk, but 'not about the case'.

Then Schembri nodded at some A4 papers on the corner of a desk, and told the doctor, 'Do me a favour, take them to Yorgen.' The doctor folded the papers in four and went to see Fenech, who was now out on bail, under armed guard at his Portomaso home.

'I just took the papers and headed to Portomaso,' the doctor recalled. 'Keith Schembri and his wife were in a hurry, on the way to a party.'

When the doctor got to Fenech's luxurious apartment, he was shocked to see armed officers there. Fenech's wife was there, as were his maid and one of his lawyers. He tried to hand the papers to the lawyer, but Fenech snatched them.

'He was very agitated,' the doctor said. 'He asked me for a biro and then began to scribble all over the papers.'

As the doctor prepared to leave, he heard Fenech say, 'If I go down, I'll take everyone with me.'

Schembri's papers contained an elaborate defence strategy for Fenech. It was a detailed plan to pin the murder on Chris Cardona, the economy minister.

Cardona was an easy target. He had acted as Koħħu's lawyer in the past, and he also knew one of the bomb makers. He had a motive. In the libel suits he had filed against my mother, after she reported on his alleged German brothel visit, he had trapped himself in a situation where he could lose his warrant to practise law and his parliamentary seat.

The police interrogated Cardona who, under pressure, 'suspended' himself from the cabinet. They found that Fenech's claims about Cardona's role in the murder did not add up and began investigating other crimes that Schembri's note revealed – a smuggling operation run out of the Malta freeport, for instance, which was under Cardona's control. They released him from custody. He was the first of Muscat's officials to be summoned by the police.

As Muscat's government crumbled and the murder investigation threw light on its corruption, the police force's honest officers were emboldened.

The next official they summoned was Schembri himself. When Fenech cracked, he told the police about the note that Schembri had given him. He then tried an elaborate defence of his own: he told the police Schembri sent the note because he was the true mastermind of the murder. Like Theuma, Fenech wanted a pardon to testify against Schembri.

'Everything,' Fenech told the police, 'started from Mr Keith Schembri.'

The police arrested Schembri and held him in the lock-up at the police headquarters in Floriana, interrogating him and Fenech in separate rooms. Schembri could not attend the emergency cabinet meeting Muscat had just convened at Castille.

It was now 8 p.m., and it had already been nine days since Fenech's arrest. The country was still alive with protests.

Inside, Muscat had summoned the police and the attorney general to brief his cabinet on the murder investigation. The ministers in attendance claimed to have been horrified by what they heard, as if their four years of defending Muscat, Schembri and Mizzi could have ended any other way.

One minister broke down and started crying at the meeting. A junior minister, who had had a long-running affair with Fenech, remained silent. The former body-builder MP, present as Muscat's consultant, shouted at the prime minister, 'That cuckold' – still an important man-to-man insult in Malta – 'fucked you!' He was referring to Schembri.

Muscat left the room so that the cabinet could discuss Fenech's request for a pardon in a free atmosphere. Schembri and Cardona were missing. Mizzi was missing: he had resigned a few days earlier outside the court building, after testifying in a corruption case involving his privatisation of Malta's hospitals. The cabinet denied Fenech a pardon on the police's advice.

Fenech had tried to persuade the police that Theuma was blackmailing him and sharing his money with the Bean and the Chinese. It was Fenech, in his police interview with Zahra, who described the hit men as 'the worst people in Malta'. Zahra then asked Fenech to explain the recordings.

Fenech said Theuma would sometimes point a gun at him to make him talk into a recorder. But the recordings showed their talk was relaxed, and that Fenech would voluntarily bring his young children along to some meetings. And it was Fenech who sounded threatening in the recordings.

It seemed strange to Zahra. Fenech, unable to explain, just shrugged. He said Schembri paid for the assassination. But there was no trace of the money he said Schembri had used. And Zahra knew that, on one of Theuma's secret recordings, Fenech said that when he told Schembri about the murder, Schembri 'went cold' and said: 'You should have come to me before you did what you did.' The timings Fenech gave did not work, the motives he suggested were confused, nothing made sense.

Only one thing did. Fenech, about to be charged with murder, showed no remorse. He was indignant. He sat opposite Zahra in the interrogation room, his arms sometimes crossed, his fists sometimes thumping on the table. 'It is something shameful,' he said, raising his voice, 'that I am here today and not Keith Schembri.'

Fenech did not deny his involvement outright, and he even admitted to funding the murder. But he kept saying the murder was Schembri's idea. Zahra pressed him on it to no real effect. And then, out of nowhere, Fenech said, 'There is another person who knows that Keith Schembri ordered the murder.'

'And who is this other person?' Zahra asked.

'The prime minister, Joseph Muscat, sir.'

'The prime minister.'

'I do not know whether he knew before but after he knew for sure. The prime minister, Joseph Muscat, in January this year called me to his office in Castille.'

Fenech said they spoke about the murder there. He said Schembri was present. But when the police checked the geolocation data on Fenech's phone, they found he was nowhere near Castille over that period.

The police had no choice but to release Schembri without charge at about 9.30 p.m. The emergency cabinet meeting was still running. Schembri called the wife of the bodybuilder MP who had sworn at Muscat to tell her, 'I know what your husband said about me,' and then retreated to his villa in Mellieħa.

The crowd outside Castille had no way of knowing what was being said at the police headquarters. So when the police published a statement saying they had released Schembri without charge, omitting any mention that he was still under investigation for homicide, the protesters erupted.

Matthew, back from Dubai, was among them. A Deutsche Welle television crew spotted him and asked for a comment.

'They're probably discussing how they're going to work things out,' Matthew said, 'either to give him his job back or get him to a country he can't be extradited from.'

As I watched the live broadcast at home in Bidnija, I heard the hundreds of people behind my brother chant, 'Mafia, Mafia.' They were held back from Castille by steel barricades and police officers. At one point, the police lifted the barricades in unison to push the protesters back. It looked lively.

My father was asleep. I took his car and drove to Castille. I got there at about midnight. Some two hours later, a government official emerged from a side entrance of the building on St Paul's Street to say Muscat would be holding a press conference. People rushed to the entrance. When the officials barring the way spotted Matthew, they announced that attendees needed a press card.

'Do you have one?' Matthew asked me. 'Then go!'

So in I went. I had an egg in my left jacket pocket, ready to throw at ministers as they left Castille. The man who checked my pockets, a member of Muscat's security detail, missed it. Another man, the Labour Party's head of communications, examined my press card, examined it some more, and grudgingly let me through. I walked down the hall with a BBC television crew.

No one knew where to go. It was chaos. We heard noise upstairs, so we headed towards it. In the room, an incomplete cabinet of ministers was lined up behind an empty podium. Owen Bonnici saw me and smiled. I resisted the urge to throw the egg at his face.

Muscat walked in rigidly and took the podium. He spoke a bit, took four questions, and left. His ministers filed out behind him. The idea was to appear united. They looked like prisoners. The thirty or so journalists present, myself included, got up to leave after them.

A group of unidentified thugs rushed in and blocked the two main doors so that we could not leave. Some crossed their arms, some held on to the door handles. 'Wow,' Stephen Grey said. 'Why are you locking the media in a room?'

No answer. No answer either when I asked who they were. I kept asking, and eventually one of them said, 'Security.'

'Whose security? Who the fuck are you?'

Tension built, I swore, until Muscat's head of communications popped his head through one door and gave an order to let us out. Outside the room, I saw there were thugs everywhere. More thugs than government officials. They had the run of Castille. I walked down, swearing, and left through Castille's front door. I remembered the egg in my jacket pocket.

'As one minister was driven away,' Reuters reported, 'one of Caruana Galizia's sons hurled fruit at his car and shouted obscenities.'

'Paul,' said my father when he woke and found me at my desk, 'a lot of "fucking" last night.'

He made coffee and went to the airport to collect Andrew. By the time they got home, we had received news that Fenech was to be charged at 8 p.m. I did not sleep before we headed to court to watch the charges being read out to him.

It was the typical magistrate's courtroom: the three rows of wooden benches, the bar and then the magistrate's seat. On either side of the room, the seats for journalists.

The seats were full, so some journalists occupied the

middle bench. My grandparents, aunts and cousins were on the bench against the back wall. My father sat at the bar with our lawyers, and Arnaud and Zahra. Two of Fenech's lawyers were there.

The journalists on the middle bench made way for my brothers and me. We sat in the centre of the bench, the empty front bench a few centimetres away. It was reserved for the accused. He was on his way.

A police officer received a message, got up and walked towards the courtroom doors. As he swung them open, for a moment I could see Fenech, in handcuffs. The plain-clothes officers around him removed his handcuffs and brought him in.

He sat at the end of the front bench, as far as possible from the three of us. The officers told him that he had to sit in the middle, directly opposite the magistrate. He shuffled along the bench, his eyes fixed on the floor. He kept his hands crossed over each other, as though they were still in handcuffs. Our view was of the back of his big shaved head, his pinstriped suit and his black leather basket-weave loafers.

Vanity of vanities. All that money, all that power, and here he was: alone in a magistrate's courtroom on a Saturday night, about to be charged with participating in a criminal organisation, with complicity in causing an explosion, and with complicity in the murder of my mother.

As Arnaud read out the charges, the magistrate ordered Fenech to stand.

'How do you plead?' she asked him.

'Not guilty.'

*

The following morning, Muscat resigned in a pre-recorded televised address.

We knew the announcement was coming because a film crew had been seen going into Girgenti Palace, an official residence of the prime minister in the south of Malta where he was hiding. It was here that, for the Poodle's birthday party held in February, Fenech had given him three bottles of Château Pétrus, one from his birth year and two from that of his twin daughters. In return, Fenech claimed, Muscat had told him that Theuma was unravelling.

Now Muscat was being filmed in his Girgenti office, claiming credit for solving the murder case without mentioning my mother. It was another one of his policy innovations: a murder without a victim.

In his place as prime minister, Muscat anointed the former bodybuilder. The Labour Party celebrated the replacement as the 'continuity' candidate. This was the man who had said of our campaign for justice that it was 'the mission of Caruana Galizia's children to derail the investigation'. It was, at least, the end of Muscat.

The scales were falling from the world's eyes: the Organized Crime and Corruption Reporting Project would soon vote Muscat 'Person of the Year in Organised Crime and Corruption'. His citation would read: 'A murdered journalist. Shady offshore deals. A tiny nation in the grip of large-scale criminal interests.'

I flew to London the day after Fenech was charged. The audio producer had made it back earlier. We did some more recording, and some more reporting. It was tiring work.

At home, I collapsed on the sofa near my pregnant wife. I said we should travel home for Christmas and then both take time off work. I would go ahead to Malta. There was only one more thing to do in London.

My colleagues had nominated me for a British Journalism Award. It was for best new journalist. At the evening reception in December, I drank too much, won the award, and then missed my flight to Malta. I booked myself onto another later that day.

I landed in Malta in time for my father to pick me up from the airport, ready with a tie and jacket, and drive us straight to court for me to hear Theuma testify for the first time.

I felt a weight lift off me like I had during the November protests. The court proceedings laid bare, publicly, what my family had been fighting for years. It was all there, exposed in evidence given under oath, with dates, times, names and faces.

It was no longer three pitiable brothers, their tired family filled with anger. Poor them, poor them. Now strangers walked up to us and shook our hands. Some congratulated us and called our mother a martyr. Malta was a country mad for them. We killed people and then we called them martyrs. They said my mother paid the 'ultimate price' for her work. But she wanted to live. They said she 'sacrificed' everything. She was not given the choice.

My mother, with all her being, was for life. She was against the cynicism represented by Muscat, a cynicism without limits. She said it was what made his rule dangerous. That the people in power had no limits.

'Do your worst, you bastards,' she had written when the

plan to assassinate her was already in motion, 'until the only option left to you is to take a contract out on my life.'

And as the details emerged in open court people again told us she was a martyr, and they gave us an old idiom, *iż-żejt dejjem jitla f'wiċċ l-ilma* – oil always rises to the water's surface; justice is inevitable. They said it to be kind and give us hope, so I just said, 'Yes, of course.'

But I thought about what my brothers and I had been through, were still going through, about how close Fenech was to getting away, and I told myself: 'We're only at the beginning.'

The public inquiry opened just before Christmas 2019. The three judges summoned Matthew first.

He spoke about the deep-rooted corruption my mother exposed. He spoke about how we had had to fight for the public inquiry. He said the inquiry could not provide a 'complete reckoning', but it was a chance to push Malta forward.

'We have to decide whether the statehood that landed in our laps should be used to improve the lives of citizens,' he said, 'or whether it exists only to continue providing a civilian front for the criminal organisation that killed my mother.'

Andrew and I gave testimony to the judges after Matthew. I talked about events as they were unfolding; how the evidence began to show that the Office of the Prime Minister of Malta was involved in the cover-up of my mother's murder.

'This is of concern in itself,' I told the board, 'but of

particular concern to the board because cover-up activity suggests involvement in the assassination.'

I spoke about Schembri, about the leaks and the note he had given to Fenech. And I spoke about how Schembri had mobilised the state to cover up the car bombing of a journalist. I talked about how Muscat had inverted the purpose of a state, so that its machinery fought against the common good. Instead of protecting its citizens, it killed them. Instead of providing, it stole from them.

'Crucially,' I concluded, 'the board must consider whether the prime minister knew or ought to have known' about the assassination and cover-up when his right-hand man did.

The three of us were now in Valletta: Jessica, me and our infant son. The first time we woke there we walked down to the sea at the tip of the peninsula for a swim. The sea's pulse moved the water, and my heart swelled with it. By the time I stepped back onto land, I felt I had reclaimed some lost part of myself.

The rocky coast where we sat and dried under the sun had been a sally port for free Jews, the only point through which they could enter the country. It was probably where the first Galizia, a Sephardi, entered and then received the same treatment as Christopher Marlowe's Jew of Malta. The play was written in the sixteenth century, just after Valletta was built.

It is a story of social division and violence, of sectarian loyalties and twisted motives, played out against the backdrop of a cynical society unified only by greed.

Barabas, the Jewish protagonist, shows how these 'men of Malta' use the cloak of their Christianity and the power it confers to steal money from Jews and accumulate wealth: 'From little unto more, from more to most.'

After enough time in Malta, the country's logic of power wins Barabas over. Having schemed his way to its governorship he proclaims:

For he that liveth in authority, / And neither gets him friends nor fills his bags, / Lives like the ass that Aesop speaketh of, /

That labours with a load of bread and wine, / And leaves it off
to snap on thistle tops.

I first read Marlowe's play when I was about seventeen
and researching my mother's Valletta magazine issue. I
remember sending her that passage because her favourite
book as a girl was a collection of Aesop's fables, now
passed on to my son.

But when I reread the play now in Valletta, I was more
struck by its closeness to the present. It was a fine sum-
mary of the culture of Maltese government, as though
more than four centuries hadn't passed. Barabas's rise to
power involves murder, and there is a point when his assistant, Ithamore, turns to the audience to ask: *Why, was there*
ever seen such villainy, / So neatly plotted, and so well performed?

At the end of the play, Barabas is killed while trying to
murder again, and the previous governor resumes power;
the cycle of greed and death repeats. Ithamore's question turns out to have been a passing moment when the
public is confronted with the truth and asked if they
want to stay the course or change it. At least, that's how
I read it now.

People had been urged to move on from and forget my
mother's murder. But the risks some of them took, the
work they did, and the sacrifices they made to get the truth
out meant that her murder was what might finally break
Malta free from its corruption.

My mother had resisted Valletta for a long time before
making it the focus for an issue of her magazine. She used
to say it was full of lawyer-men, strutting up and down

Republic Street, slapping one another's backs and gossiping about their clients. Or that it was full of priests, nuns and monks; or, more simply, that the city had died long ago.

Looking back, I suspect that her dislike of the city had a lot to do with how many times she was summoned to court there. After one libel hearing, where I gave evidence, we went to the Church of Our Lady of Damascus.

The building had been destroyed in the Second World War and rebuilt after. The knights had originally built it to house an icon of the Madonna they had brought from Rhodes. It was said that the melancholy Jean de la Valette, the French knight who founded Valletta, would visit the icon, and it was the icon my mother wanted me to see.

An elderly priest opened the church's carved door and guided us to it. It had survived the bombing that destroyed the original church. It was ancient, from the twelfth century, on a background of gold leaf, a symbol of incorruptibility. More gold leaf decorated the sleeves of the Madonna's tunic. Her son's arms were wrapped around her and his cheek was pressed to hers. She looked directly at the viewer, her eyes wide and brown and sad.

I stood by the priest, both of us transfixed. My mother watched us as we looked at this ancient depiction of a mother and her son.

The icon of Our Lady of Damascus would make it into my mother's magazine, but I suspected the point of the excursion had simply been for me to see it. Most Catholic iconography seemed like drama for the sake of drama to our irreligious family, but this particular image came to mean more and more to my mother. She would talk about it afterwards, and as her death approached, she decorated an entire wall at Dar Riħana with pictures of the Madonna and Child. She even became involved in the restoration of one of the city's first churches, and once its main parish church.

When I visited the Basilica of Our Lady of Safe Haven and St Dominic with her, a priest showed us how rainwater had seeped through the church's damaged stone, ruining its painted ceilings. The priest in charge of the restoration, the one who would say the final prayer for my mother before her burial, showed us a painting of Dominic's confrontation of heretics.

Dominic, the story goes, came across a sect preaching a strange and extreme doctrine. It was becoming popular. Dominic committed himself to winning them over with reason. He was unsuccessful, but he still created a large following of his own.

After the tour of the church, the priest invited us to the Dominican priory nearby. He said we would have to be careful as no women were allowed in.

We snuck in with the help of the prior, a plump man with a shiny head. He hurried us to a room with a large mahogany table and a sideboard made of olive wood inlaid with some kind of citrus, containing many bottles of whisky. Unprompted, he brought one out and poured us each a generous measure, and we sat there drinking and talking.

The priest talked about his childhood and his work. We talked about the Church and Maltese politics. I was surprised by how candid the two clerics were with us. They told my mother everything, and she just sat there, the reporter, listening and sipping her whisky.

When two monks heard our voices, they came to the door. The prior shot up and, blocking their view of my mother, turned them away. We returned to the whisky and the conversation, which turned to another painting hanging above us.

It was by Mattia Preti, a follower of Caravaggio. The knights had given Caravaggio himself refuge in Malta in return for paintings after he had beaten a man to death in Rome. Preti was a lesser artist, but his painting of Christ coming down from his cross really was something. I remember that the green tinge of Christ's body made me queasy.

We stumbled out into the early-afternoon sun and walked to meet my father for lunch at a restaurant on St Christopher's Street, one of my mother's favourites. I could not get through my pork medallions and roast potatoes. My mother explained that we had had a bit to drink. My father laughed at the thought of his wife in the priory. He said that Valletta was not so bad after all. We talked about what it would be like to live there. It felt real and possible.

I now walk past the restaurant where we had that lunch whenever I am nearby, to remind myself of the perfect moment it contains. I have not been inside since.

After my mother's death, when I was in Malta, my father and I began meeting for lunch in Valletta at his club, the Casino Maltese, which serves ravioli on Fridays. The pasta is filled with ricotta and served with a plain tomato sauce. My father used to eat there with his own father, and he sees our lunches as at least one tradition that continues.

When my brothers and I were boys, we used to meet him there with our mother. We liked the place. She liked the food. She would order a half-dozen more than the standard dozen ravioli, one of her favourite dishes. My father would pretend to be embarrassed by her order, but I saw that he liked her impatience with the place – with its regulating what people had to wear, how people ate and when they ate, and its rule that women couldn't use the reading room.

I wondered, as I ate with him now, what it was like to argue cases in front of judges whom your wife had criticised, to represent clients whom she wrote about, or sit down together for ravioli at the Casino Maltese among them all.

I can see why, when I first asked him to look back on it, he described his life with her as 'very helter-skelter. But fun.'

The court buildings are only a two-minute walk from my father's club, so your mind is still in one place when you get to the other.

In court, we saw more depravity, heard more arguments. Some sittings went on all day. Even if they ended early, there could be no day afterwards.

At the criminal proceedings, we sat in a small courtroom with Fenech's family. They tried to pack the room, just as they used to pack planning authority meetings when a decision on one of their developments was up for a public vote. Before Fenech's arrest, they tried everything to stop the investigation.

Now Fenech was trying to trip Theuma up in court

where we heard he had ordered enough cyanide from the dark web to kill a man of Theuma's weight. It was to be delivered to his Portomaso office, in his dead father's name, but it had been intercepted by the FBI. He then tried ordering a gun with a silencer. It was again intercepted.

Sitting in court, watching Theuma testify, Fenech smirked and gestured from behind his lawyers. His lawyers mocked Theuma. It was an ugly business. It became too much for Theuma to bear.

One night, away from his police guard for a few minutes, Theuma went into the kitchen of his safe house, grabbed a knife, and stabbed himself repeatedly in the throat and abdomen. His lawyer always called him at an agreed time, and when she could not get through, she called Arnaud and emergency services. They found Theuma in a pool of his own blood on the bathroom floor.

'Who did this?' Arnaud asked.

'Me,' said Theuma.

While Theuma was in hospital, I found myself praying for the survival of a man who had contracted my mother's murder. He was saved. A magistrate was sent to the hospital to ask Theuma why he had tried killing himself. Unable to talk because of the stab wounds to his neck, Theuma grabbed a pen and paper, and wrote: 'They are laughing at me.'

On another sheet of paper: 'Yorgen disappointed me', and then: 'I wish that the children of Daphne forgive me.'

In court, the criminal proceedings moved on while Theuma recovered. The corruption my mother had exposed, and which we continued to fight, was now used against her.

The defence argued that the police could not be trusted.

But it was not Silvio Valletta whom they cited as an example of a corrupt police officer. It was Arnaud, the man who caught Fenech. So what was a double injustice – a murder and a cover-up – became a triple injustice. The criminals claimed they were victims of the corruption they forced on us.

And as I sat in court, hearing these odious arguments, I thought about the column my mother once wrote about Karin Grech, the teenage girl killed by the letter bomb intended for her father in 1977.

'It is not easy to accept that among the rats who scurry on the peripheries of politics (and who sometimes make it to the inside) there are those who are capable of executing a plan to blow up another human being,' she wrote. 'If the murderers are traced eventually – a really small probability – the parents of Karin Grech may find that they are in for yet more suffering, if that is possible. They will have to sit through a trial in which the accused is let off because of insufficient proof, or is given a jail sentence which does not measure up to the destruction, in ghastly agony, of a 15-year-old girl.'

I thought of what my mother's thoughts might be now, and what her last thought was. In that moment of inconsolable aloneness, when she pulled up the handbrake, when she realised what had been done to her, what did my mother want us to know?

But still, the three of us were in Malta. We woke at 6.30 a.m. and made our way down to the coast at Valletta's sally port. The heat had not yet arrived. Nor had the people. In an hour, the city would be loud.

At the coast, there was one man setting up for the day. He offered us his patch, with chairs and a canopy, before his family arrived. He asked us where we were from.

Jessica got in the sea, which was still and glazed, while I sat with our son on my lap. We switched. She took our son and I headed for the water. I dived into the sea, over the limestone foreshore that had once been full of sea urchins. I swam underwater for as long as I could hold my breath, as though I was trying to swim outside myself. I was breath and movement. When my lungs tightened, I did a somer-sault and forced myself above the surface.

I turned and looked back. I followed the line of the city's walls, tall and mighty, behind a mother and her son.

Epilogue

The public inquiry continued with its hearings, despite Fenech's lawyers' attempts to stop it. It continued even though the government pushed the line that the public inquiry was a waste of time and money, and should be wrapped up.

The judges heard from 120 witnesses over ninety-three hearings. One of the last witnesses they called was the Poodle who, no longer in Parliament, rebranded himself as 'The Office of Dr Joseph Muscat' to do market research on his father's computer at their family compound near Bidnija. There was no space in the packed courtroom for the former prime minister's seven or so bodyguards, so they took turns squashing their faces against the square windows of the courtroom's door. As his two lawyers hurried him to the witness stand, I heard one whisper to the other, 'He's uncomfortable, he's uncomfortable.'

Muscat's hands trembled as he opened the ring binder containing the long statement he had brought with him. His spin doctor, who had made it into the courtroom, got ahead of himself and uploaded the whole statement to Facebook as Muscat was just starting up.

'Before answering to the board's questions,' the Poodle read aloud and sternly, 'I would like to put forward a number of points which are pertinent to the creation and existence of this inquiry.' The points: the judges had failed 'miserably' because they were controlled by my family and the opposition party; he had done nothing wrong in his career; and 'history' – and here he quoted Napoleon that 'history is simply a set of lies agreed upon' – not the board would judge him.

He then told the judges which questions he would answer. He didn't like their first one, about his former adviser Glenn Bedingfield singling out my mother for harassment in the run-up to her assassination. 'The question is not relevant,' Muscat declared, 'but I will reply.' His answer was that his government was entitled to harass my mother because she was influential and critical of his administration. When the judges asked Muscat why he took Keith Schembri along to official briefings about the murder investigation, he said that no one had told him not to.

The judges, expressionless, moved on to my mother's biggest story: Schembri's and Konrad Mizzi's Panama companies. 'When I asked Keith Schembri about the structures, he said that Bank of Valletta wouldn't be offering the services he required abroad,' Muscat said. 'Konrad Mizzi had said he needed it for his family. I believed them.'

A couple of days later, the judges called their final witness: Schembri. 'I never did anything without informing my prime minister,' he told them. 'I never did anything behind his back.'

The judges heard that an attempt to buy out the *Malta Independent*, which distributed my mother's magazines and carried her columns, had been organised by Schembri and backed by Fenech. And journalists claimed it was Schembri who gave them the false narrative that fuel smugglers had orchestrated my mother's murder, a claim he never responded to. The judges saw WhatsApp chats between Muscat, Schembri and Fenech in which the three men exchanged photographs of whiskies, wine, food and women. One witness told the judges that the material on Fenech's devices, which allowed the police to open eleven separate criminal investigations, would 'bring Malta to its knees'.

When the judges completed their 437-page report, in July 2021, their chair presented a copy to Andrew and my father at the Casino Maltese. 'His eyes were teary,' Andrew said. 'It was very emotional.' We had the report translated into English so that it could reach a much wider audience.

The judges found that the state 'failed to recognise the real and immediate risks' to my mother's life, 'failed to take reasonable steps to avoid them', and so was responsible for her death.

Their report cited an 'excessive closeness' between big business and government and found that Muscat, in collaboration with Schembri, had taken a political decision to retain control of all major economic projects. It said, 'If this style of leadership was one that gave them the expectation to profit unjustly from large government projects, they would have felt threatened by Daphne Caruana Galizia's investigative journalism. Journalism that could have harmed their profits and exposed their malice, as in fact happened.'

Under the heading 'Project ElectroGas', the report refers to the 'large quantity of information' that my mother had received about the power station deal between Muscat's government and a consortium of businessmen led by Fenech. 'She knew about the existence of 17 Black,' the report said. 'She knew ElectroGas was on the verge of failure and in September 2017 she wrote about this fact and soon after the government issued a guarantee through which the company achieved "financial closure" in November 2017, that is, one month after her assassination.'

The judges wrote that the state had 'created an atmosphere of impunity, generated by the highest echelons at the heart of Castille and which, like an octopus, spread its tentacles to other entities and regulators and the police, leading to the collapse of rule of law'. According to them, 'the country was moving towards a situation which could be qualified as a mafia state. It was the journalist's assassination that put a brake on this predicted disaster.'

There is much yet to be known.

While the Egrant inquiry did not establish the ultimate ownership of the Panama company that was set up along with Schembri's and Mizzi's companies, it uncovered a significant amount of documentation on 'suspicious transactions, concealed corporate relationships, and other indicators of probable money laundering and sanction evading activities' facilitated by the accountants who set up the companies and Pilatus Bank. Inroads were being made into Schembri's suspected money laundering network, and the accountants who industrialised so much of the Muscat-era corruption. They stand charged with corruption, fraud and money laundering. Schembri, who for years accused my mother of using forged documents to implicate him in corruption cases, was also charged with forgery and false testimony. As a correctional services van drove him into prison, where he was briefly held on remand, a woman shouted: 'How I wish Daphne could see you now!' Schembri has pleaded not guilty to all charges and denied any wrongdoing.

Pilatus Bank, the Azerbaijani laundromat protected by Schembri, had collapsed under the weight of my mother's reporting, which my brothers and I discussed with the FBI agents who prosecuted the bank's owner. We have continued to help other authorities looking to pick apart the bank's criminal asset base.

We have continued to file criminal complaints in Malta and wherever possible outside the country. France's national financial prosecutor has begun to investigate Fenech's property holdings there. We also asked the prosecutor to investigate the French banks supporting ElectroGas. We asked the Organisation for Economic Cooperation and Development to investigate an international shareholder in ElectroGas, a process that ended when the shareholder committed itself to funding anti-corruption projects. We pressed the European Commission to investigate the Electro-Gas deal. We helped journalists investigate the similarities between the ship that dropped its anchor on the Malta–Sicily underwater cables and a ship that had done the same to an underwater gas pipeline from Nigeria to Benin, which had then agreed to buy its replacement gas from Azerbaijan's SOCAR.

ElectroGas still has a monopoly on our electricity market. As Matthew told journalists, we send money to the Fenechs and their associates every time we switch on a light. We filed civil lawsuits in Malta to freeze Fenech's assets, and those of the hit men and Theuma. We filed and supported constitutional cases to bolster free speech and peaceful protest. We work to promote civic society in Malta. We campaign to have the public inquiry's recommendations implemented in full, so that nothing like my mother's murder can ever happen again.

We realised that our campaign for justice was far from over after Fenech was charged. It is a life sentence: there is no going back to normal, because our mother is never coming back. We have years of fighting ahead.

Vincent 'Koħħu' Muscat, one of the three hit men, received a fifteen-year sentence in exchange for his cooperation with prosecutors. His evidence led to charges against Robert and Adrian Agius, the 'Maksar' brothers, and another Maltese man called Jamie Vella for supplying the bomb that was planted under my mother's car seat. They all pleaded not guilty to the charges and denied any wrongdoing. A magistrate will rule on whether the case can go before a jury. If it does, it would be one of three jury trials over my mother's murder. Fenech's trial is expected to begin in the middle of 2024.

The trial of the two other hit men, George 'the Chinese' Degiorgio and his brother Alfred 'the Bean' Degiorgio, nearly didn't happen.

It was scheduled to begin in the summer of 2022. I travelled between London and Malta a number of times – once for just a day – in expectation of the trial starting. A few days before the first scheduled date, the brothers' lawyer quit. The court gave them ample time to find a new lawyer. They failed; the court appointed lawyers. The brothers filed a constitutional case, claiming they didn't have adequate legal representation. It was dismissed. Then the

Bean went on a hunger strike in protest against the decision. He was hospitalised, delaying the trial again. For a number of days, we were at an impasse. Then the Bean began drinking and eating again. A new trial date was set, the brothers filed another constitutional claim to stay the trial, and I flew back to Malta.

The night before the trial, the Bean overdosed on pills he had collected from other prisoners. He was hospitalised again, but experts there deemed him well enough to be brought to court. On hearing this news, my brothers, my father and I made our way to court a little after nine the next morning.

We walked through a crowd of potential jurors waiting outside the courtroom, gave the police officers guarding the door our names, and went inside. The room was still and full: our extended family members, police officers, journalists and marshals of the court were all there, in addition to the two defendants.

The Bean was in a wheelchair, wrapped in a blanket, with two nurses by his side. His eyes were closed, and he rolled his head back and forth to give the impression of illness. The Chinese sat silently behind the two court-appointed lawyers. Heavily armed prison officers stood around them.

We took our seats behind the defendants and watched jurors being selected one by one. I thought how strange it must have felt to be yanked out of normal life into a murder trial. It made me anxious to realise that, at the end of a five-year struggle, this group of people – among them a musician, a trader, and an accountant – would determine what kind of justice my mother would receive.

Once the jury was empanelled, the marshals dismissed the rest of the jury pool. They burst into loud cheers and left the courthouse. The judge briefed the jury on its responsibilities and gave jurors some time to notify their relatives that they had been selected and would be sequestered for the duration of the trial. Then she asked her registrar to read out the bill of indictment. Next the judge turned to the prosecution to outline its case. The deputy attorney general, who was leading the prosecution in court, asked the jurors not to think of my mother as belonging to one tribe or another, not to think of her as a 'witch', but to think of her as a person; as a daughter, mother, wife, sister. There was pin-drop silence as he spoke, and I tried to read each juror's face for signs of hate or sympathy.

The Bean's blanket occasionally fell off his body, and he made a show of being unable to get it back on. The Chinese looked ahead intently.

Sitting on the bare wooden bench, I wondered how I would make it through all-day hearings scheduled for Monday to Saturday for six weeks. The judge ordered a two-hour break for lunch, and I went with my father and Andrew to the Casino Maltese while Matthew went to the data protection commissioner's office in Sliema about a freedom of information request he had filed for more documents on the energy privatisation deal. I immediately felt I should have gone with Matthew: it was October, warm and busy inside the club, and I had no real appetite for the couscous and salad my father ordered for us. I had no interest in the newspapers and magazines lying around and no energy to make conversation. We headed back to the courtroom early.

When we got there, our lawyers approached us. During the lunch break, the Chinese had told the prosecution that they'd accept a 37-year sentence, Jason told us. They were locked in a holding room with the prosecution, awaiting a response.

The brothers had been campaigning for a plea deal for several years now, first asking for a complete pardon in exchange for evidence on other, separate crimes; then for fifteen years, because that was what Koħħu got; and then for twenty-something years.

The minimum sentence the brothers could receive if a jury convicted them, but not unanimously, was forty years. If the jury was unanimous in its conviction, the judge would be bound to sentence them to life. Our lawyers asked the prosecution to push the brothers' request up to forty years.

People began filling the courtroom again, but they wondered why the jury wasn't called back in and why the judge wasn't in her seat. I could hear them whispering to one another, asking what was happening and why the trial hadn't recommenced.

Our lawyers came back to tell us that the brothers had agreed to forty years. It was now up to the judge to agree with the deal or not. The thought of them getting out of prison alive was, to me, unbearably unjust. With a forty-year sentence, even after deductions for good behaviour, I thought that these men, in their late fifties, would likely die in prison. Part of me felt relieved: relieved that the decision had been taken out of our hands.

But the judge told the prosecution that she would agree to the sentence only if my family did. Her reasoning was that our lawyers, as a civil party to the prosecution, would have been allowed to make submissions in court ahead of her decision on sentencing at the end of the trial. I felt an enormous weight return to me. I wondered what my mother would have thought. I wondered, absurdly, whether she would have wanted a jury trial for her own murder.

Matthew had made it back from Sliema. We stood outside the courtroom, in a corner at the end of a hall with our lawyers. They found it impossible to advise us on this specific point.

Forty years. We decided it was enough.

The judge ordered that the brothers be examined by a medical doctor and a psychiatrist to ensure they were both in a fit state to make the deal. She came back into court, took her seat, and called the medical professionals to deliver their assessment. The brothers were fit to go ahead. The judge asked them if their position had changed.

The Chinese stood and said: 'Yes. Guilty.'

The Bean, still maintaining his inability to stand, entered the same plea through his lawyers.

The whispers in the public gallery above us and around the rest of the courtroom grew louder.

The judge asked the brothers repeatedly if they understood the implications of their decision. They said that they did. It was early evening by the time the judge sentenced the men to the agreed prison term and ordered them to pay €42,930 each in legal costs and to forfeit their €50,000 in criminal proceeds.

Before the guards carried the men back to prison, the Chinese turned to me and my family and said, 'Can I please address you?'

My aunts shouted 'No!' back at him and said that he could talk to the police. They began to cry. My brothers and I asked the guards to turn him away from us. They told us to calm down.

The Bean got up from his wheelchair, without any help, and turned to my father, who was sitting at the bar with our lawyers. Suddenly having regained the ability to talk as well as to stand, he told my father, 'One day soon, you will know exactly what happened.' My father stood up, remained perfectly still and looked right back at him.

At last the guards took both men out of the courtroom. The marshals began to clear the room, complaining loudly about what a long day it had been and urging us all to leave.

My father, my brothers and I walked slowly down the main staircase of the courthouse and out onto Republic Street. The memorial to my mother was directly in front of us. It would be the fifth anniversary of her death in two days, and people had begun laying flowers and lighting candles that flickered in the darkness.

Notes on Sources

As this book stretches wider than my own immediate experience, I drew on a range of sources for it.

I conducted multiple interviews with dozens of individuals located thousands of miles apart, from a small Caribbean island to a Maltese retirement home. The interviews covered all aspects of my mother's life, from her infancy on through her school years, her relationships with university colleagues, her first editors and colleagues, and beyond. Some sources had been my mother's own, and they helped me piece together parts of her reporting.

Some people proved difficult to access, and memories fade, so I did archival research to supplement the interviews. The *Times of Malta* archive proved invaluable, as did the National Library of Malta's collection of out-of-print publications, including the *Democrat*, which in 1986 carried a front-page investigation into the drug trafficker and his brigadier father. The CIA's declassified memo on US policy towards Malta, published on 31 July 1985, was useful. The *New York Times* archive provided good material on Malta around independence, as did old issues of *Foreign Affairs* and *Time* magazine. The internal memos from the British Colonial Office and the Ministry of Overseas Development that Simon C. Smith compiled in *British Documents on the End of Empire: Malta* were essential.

Judge Albert Magri's ruling on the libel case my mother

filed in 1998 was helpful, as was Magistrate David Scicluna's judgment on her 1984 criminal case. Ramona Depares's 2002 interview with Joseph Muscat for *Malta Today* offers timeless insight into the man. Jennifer Mifsud's 2008 interview with Michelle Muscat for the *Times* of Malta provided the same kind of insight into her. I drew on the history of press freedom in Malta that Joseph F. Grima wrote for the *Sunday Times* of Malta, and Adrian Busietta's pieces on the National Bank of Malta from the same newspaper. The reporting that *Malta Today* did on the National Bank of Malta story provided some additional details.

Unpublished material was also helpful. The interview my mother gave, ten days before her murder, to Marilyn Clark for a Council of Europe research project called 'A Mission to Inform: Journalists at Risk Speak Out' is an extraordinary thing. Michael Briguglio's undergraduate dissertation, 'State/Power: Hiltonopoly', on the development of Portomaso, which he campaigned against as a young activist, remains the best source on the subject. Anne Parnis's *My Life*, edited by her daughter Clara Tait, provided background on my father's family. Raphael Camilleri Parlato's research into the Vellas provided background on my mother's family. Roberta Grima's scrapbook from 1984 contained clippings of all the news coverage of my mother's criminal case and the protest in that year. I spoke to others involved in the process and drew on Portomaso's various underlying lease agreements that go back to 1964. Joseph Muscat's undergraduate and doctoral dissertations were useful. Some unpublished material came in the form of emails and letters, and some in the form of scrapbooks. My mother's unpublished notebooks were a gift.

Her published writing – from first magazine pieces and newspaper interviews in the late 1980s to her weekly and then twice-weekly columns from 1990 to 2017, and all her blog posts at daphnecaruanagalizia.com – was also essential, not just for her own views and how they changed, but as a chronicle of Maltese life over three decades. Joseph Debono and Caroline Muscat's *Invicta: The Life and Work of Daphne Caruana Galizia*, published a few weeks after my mother's death, contains moving chapters by her friends and colleagues. Its chapters by Ranier Fsadni and Paul Sant Cassia are rich with insights into how Maltese society shaped her writing.

Other chronicles were useful. Former prime minister and president Eddie Fenech Adami's autobiography, *Eddie: My Journey*, which includes a chapter by the nickname my mother gave him, 'The Village Lawyer', provided good detail. Former *Times* of Malta editor Victor Aquilina's *Black Monday: A Night of Mob Violence* is informative and enjoyable. Television Malta's Bijografiji documentary on Tumas Fenech provides a good view not just of the man but of his immediate family. Dominic Mintoff's memoir, *Mintoff, Malta, Mediterra: My Youth*, taught me a great deal about him, what he wanted, and where he came from. His attorney general Edgar Mizzi's memoir, *Malta in the Making 1962–1987: An Eyewitness Account*, is an interesting, if partial, account of Maltese history.

History books were my starting point. All wonderful: Robert Holland's *Blue-Water Empire*, Dennis Castillo's *The Maltese Cross*, Carmel Testa's *The French in Malta*, William Hardman's *History of Malta During the French and British Occupations*, Thomas Pettigrew's *Memoirs of the Life of*

Vice-Admiral Lord Viscount Nelson, Vertot de Abbe's *The History of the Knights of Malta*, Ernle Bradford's *The Great Siege – Malta, 1565*, Giovanni Agius de Soldanis's *Gozo: Ancient and Modern, Religious and Profane*, Walter Lord's *Sir Thomas Maitland: The Mastery of the Mediterranean*, Charles Price's *Malta and the Maltese: A Study in Nineteenth Century Migration*, Henry Frendo and Oliver Friggieri's *Malta: Culture and Identity*, especially Patrick Schembri's chapter, and Victor Mallia-Milanes's volume *Hospitaller Malta, 1530–1798*, particularly the chapters by Carmel Cassar, Stanley Fiorini, Alexander Bonnici, Alison Hoppen, and Frans Ciappara. Giovanni Bonello, Godfrey Baldacchino, and Anthony Bonanno's countless articles for the press and in academic journals throw light on Malta's development from the earliest times to the present. Godfrey Wettinger and Joseph Brincat's work on Malta's Arab period is fascinating, as is Charles Savona-Ventura's article 'The Medical Aspects of the 1565 Great Siege'. In a previous life, I wrote two history books – *The Economy of Modern Malta* and *Mediterranean Labor Markets in the First Age of Globalization* – that allowed me to move faster through piles of historical material.

Moving closer to the present, I relied on official reports. Some came from Malta's Office of the Ombudsman and National Audit Office, particularly the 596-page report on ElectroGas it published in 2018, but most were a product of the campaigning my family has done since 2017. Reports from the Council of Europe and its associated bodies, from the European Parliament, and from the countless non-governmental organisations that have supported us were important here. Similarly, I relied on the journalism by the Daphne Project and *The Shift News* for the more recent period, and for developments in my mother's case.

The really important sources on her case came from the various proceedings, heard in Maltese in open court, surrounding her murder. The Independent Public Inquiry into the Assassination of Daphne Caruana Galizia heard or collected volumes of public testimony, all under oath, on the wider circumstances surrounding her murder. Three sets of criminal proceedings – the first against the three men charged with executing her, the second against the man charged with financing them, and the third against the bomb suppliers – have also heard or collected volumes of witness testimony taken under oath in open court, as did the various related constitutional cases. I attended court hearings across all the proceedings, as well as interviewed people involved in the hearings. Court proceedings are ongoing and will keep going for some time.

This story is still being written. Here it is told in my voice, as my account, and so may upset some people. They will feel undue attention has been given to some areas while other areas have been neglected. They will have different views of Maltese politics and history, and of my mother and her work. And that variety is healthy. But ultimately this is my own work, the product of my own seeing and writing.

Acknowledgements

Over the writing of this book, I have worked with extraordinary people. Some have helped a great deal throughout the four years, others in more specific and important ways. I thank them all. Many wanted to remain anonymous, others didn't.

My wonderful grandparents, Michael and Rose Vella, talked to me extensively about my mother and their own lives. Their daughters, my aunts Cora, Mandy and Helene, have been a constant source of information and support. Matthew and Andrew, my brothers, have answered my questions with patience and care. They have read through various drafts and provided detailed feedback. My father Peter did the same and gathered court filings and judgments for me in between one hearing and another.

Tortoise is where I became a journalist. Its founders James Harding and Katie Vanneck have allowed me the time to work on this project. Keith Blackmore edited the first piece I ever wrote about my mother and helped me with the first draft of this book. Gary Marshall produced the podcast I reported about her. My compatriot Matt d'Ancona has been an important source of advice.

By speaking to my mother's friends, I learnt about her as a girl, a teenager and a young woman: Roberta Grima, Loredana Gatt, Sarah Sammut, Aloisia de Trafford, Clare Vassallo, Clare Zammit Montebello, Peter Fleri Soler, Karen

Bonello, Kristina Chetcuti, Petra Caruana Dingli, and Steve. The late Joe Micallef Stafrace told me about my mother as a journalism student. Her colleagues helped me piece together the rest of her development as a journalist: Ray Bugeja, Laurence Grech, Ramon Micallef, Noel Grima, John Formosa, the late Godfrey Grima, and Martin Galea, who now works for Ray Fenech.

I learnt a great deal from conversations with: Ranier Fsadni, who read a draft of this book and taught me anthropology; Paul Sant Cassia, who taught my mother anthropology; and Giovanni Bonello. Michael Briguglio, Iggy Fenech, the older Nicholas Diacono, Kenneth Delia, and staff at Malta's National Archives and National Library helped me find material. Justin Borg Barthet, David Grech and Chris Stratford helped me with particular areas of reporting.

Patrick Walsh, my literary agent, first asked me to write about my mother and didn't lose hope over many years and drafts. His team – John Ash, Margaret Halton and Rebecca Sandell – provided advice over the writing. It is thanks to Patrick that I got to work with the finest editors in the business, Helen Conford at Hutchinson Heinemann and Becky Saletan at Riverhead. I thank my managing editor, Laurie Ip Fung Chun, and my production editor, Katie Hurley. Thanks also to the copy editors, Katherine Fry and Andrea Monagle, and the proofreaders, Sarah-Jane Forder, Lavina Lee and Tory Klose.

From the start, our lawyers have been with us through thick and thin: Jason Azzopardi, Caoilfhionn Gallagher, Jonathan Price, Tony Murphy and Jennifer Robinson. Therese Comodini Cachia and Eve Borg Costanzi have also read a draft of this book. I want to thank ARTICLE 19, the Committee to Protect Journalists, the European Centre for Press and Media Freedom, the European Federation of Journalists, the International Press Institute, Index on Censorship, Reporters Without Borders, particularly Rebecca Vincent, Occupy Justice and Repubblika for all their support over the past six years.

My father, my brothers and I set up the Daphne Caruana Galizia Foundation, which will receive the proceeds from this book and any other projects that grow out of it. I thank Tina Urso and all the Foundation's other employees who fight for justice for my mother, for press freedom, and against corruption.

To Jessica, I offer my deepest thanks for everything and ask for forgiveness for the tumult. And to our boy, our son; my joy and my sorrows' cure: one day, you will find your grandmother in these pages.